AND THE WINNER IS

AND THE WINNER IS

70 Years of the BBC Sports Personality of the Year

Peter Donaldson

pitch

First published by Pitch Publishing, 2024

Pitch Publishing
9 Donnington Park,
85 Birdham Road,
Chichester,
West Sussex,
PO20 7AJ
www.pitchpublishing.co.uk
info@pitchpublishing.co.uk

A CIP catalogue record is available for this book from the British Library.

ISBN 978 1 80150 767 7

MIX
Paper | Supporting responsible forestry
FSC® C013056
FSC www.fsc.org

Printed and bound in the UK on FSC® certified paper in line with our continuing commitment to ethical business practices, sustainability and the environment.

Typesetting and origination by Pitch Publishing

Printed and bound in Great Britain by TJ Books, Padstow

Contents

Introduction

IN DECEMBER 2021 the BBC found itself embroiled in a curious spat with the heavyweight boxing champion of the world. Tyson Fury, who two months earlier had knocked out Deontay Wilder in a pulsating fight in Paradise, Nevada to retain his WBC belt, threatened legal action unless his name was removed from the list of contenders for the Corporation's Sports Personality of the Year (SPOTY) award. Bizarre though the threat was, it did not come entirely out of the blue. The Beeb and Fury had previous. Six years earlier, a surprise victory over then reigning heavyweight champion Wladimir Klitschko had propelled the self-styled Gypsy King out of (relative) obscurity on to the SPOTY shortlist and into an unsavoury media storm. In a series of post-fight interviews, the voluble but indiscreet Fury had made a catalogue of homophobic and sexist remarks. Although he had subsequently insisted that he was 'not a bigot', his unsolicited observation that his fellow SPOTY nominee Jessica Ennis-Hill 'slaps up good' had done little to placate the 140,000 people who had petitioned to have his name removed from the competition shortlist. The whole hullabaloo had ended relatively amicably with Fury, who, to the BBC's enormous relief, had finished outside the top three, compliantly attending the award ceremony and furnishing the watching millions with the sort of conditional apology the nation had come to expect from transgressive public figures: 'If I offended anyone …'

But the Gypsy King was not, by inclination, a man to forgive and forget. When he was nominated for SPOTY a second time, after reclaiming his heavyweight crown in 2020, he once more demanded the removal of his name from the shortlist and instructed people not to vote for him. Although Broadcasting House loftily refused his request, his fans were more accommodating and he duly finished in sixth and last place. By 2021, then, Fury was hardly in the mood to hold back when the BBC's 'independent panel of experts' yet again put his name forward. 'I don't need a shit award from a TV company to say well done for what I've done this year,' he told the editor of *The Sun* and anybody else who would listen. 'I am already,' he bragged, 'the people's champion.' But was he? By what measure? Surely no one, argued James Moore of *The Independent*, not even the Gypsy King, could claim to be 'the *de facto* BBC Sports Personality of the Year before there's even been a vote'.

And, of course, no one could. Fury could shout as loudly as he liked that the award 'means nothing', but the public who voted in their hundreds of thousands clearly felt otherwise. Undoubtedly, SPOTY is, as the late TV critic A.A. Gill damningly noted, full of the 'sort of end-of-term tomfoolery that makes *Blue Peter* seem raffishly post-modern', but it is still the best way we have of measuring how the wider public feels about the country's sporting heroes. So maybe Fury was right to proclaim himself the nation's favourite, but the beauty of SPOTY is that such a boast can be tested. Actually, as it turned out, he was wrong;

the real people's champion was an 18-year-old schoolgirl from Bromley.[1]

Compared with the bloated Christmas extravaganza that modern audiences are forced to endure, the early editions of SPOTY were very modest affairs indeed. First introduced in 1954 as a small segment in the BBC's new sports magazine show, *Sportsview*, the actual award was merely an adjunct to the much more prestigious *Sporting Record*'s Sports Man and Woman of the Year Awards. But from the outset SPOTY was innovative. 'For the first time,' Carl Doran, a future editor of the show, explained, 'you were seeing people you knew from the world of sport away from a sporting environment, in what was roughly an entertainment setting. It is all about giving the public just a little glimpse of the person behind the sports star – and *Sportsview* undoubtedly started all that.'

Personality was being judged as much as prowess. And although the BBC never defined what 'personality' actually meant – which the editor of *The Guardian* rather unkindly thought was 'just as well given that Nigel Mansell, Greg Rusedski, and Princess Anne are among the past winners' – the concept proved to be enormously popular. Hosted by suave former RAF pilot Peter Dimmock, the first show was watched by 20 per cent of the adult population and achieved an audience satisfaction rating of 85 per cent, a score usually reserved for FA Cup finals and Morecambe and Wise Christmas Specials. Viewer engagement quickly grew, with voting numbers (*Radio Times* coupons only please!) increasing tenfold in just five years, and then reaching into the hundreds of thousands when telephone polling was introduced in 1998.

Indeed, a clear indication of the show's growing importance in the cultural landscape was the increasing frequency with which allegations of vote rigging were aired. Speculation that all was not always as it might be was not helped by the BBC's insistence on guarding polling numbers as if they were state secrets.[1] Giles Smith of *The Telegraph* no doubt spoke for many (except, perhaps, ex-pat Venezuelans) when he suggested the 'electoral process' used in SPOTY 'would seem shady even by the standards of destabilised countries in South America'.

Although the BBC insisted it withheld the final counts simply to preserve the dignity of the runners-up, conspiracy theories still abounded. The most persistent concerned Essex angler Bob Nudd. In 1991, Nudd, who had just won the World Freshwater Angling Championship for the second time, received well over 100,000 votes to easily top the poll ahead of the Scottish distance runner Liz McColgan. However, the BBC deemed that the *Angling Times*' front page, 'Vote Nudd!', had breached its rules on canvassing and Bob was duly disqualified – although two subsequent world titles, a chart hit with 'Maggots in Ya Catapult', and an appearance alongside Irish puppet duo Zig and Zag on *The Big Breakfast* no doubt helped to soften the blow.[2]

For the more cynical, however, Nudd's exclusion from the SPOTY hall of fame had more to do with angling's failure to conform to the prerequisites of small-screen sport than it did with any notional violation of arcane competition rules. Television executives presumed, probably correctly, that there was a limited

1 It was not until the 21st century that voting figures were released to the public.

market for watching middle-aged men sitting motionless on riverbanks, and the TV schedules reflected their reservations. Fishing, of course, was exceptional in that participants far outnumbered spectators. But, for most people, sport was experienced passively, occasionally live, although more often than not mediated through television screens. From the 1950s onwards, British culture, including its sporting culture, became centred on television. The Queen's coronation in 1953, with an estimated television audience of 20 million, saw an enormous surge in demand for TV licences. For almost the next 50 years the vast majority of the population, including sports fans, experienced the same programming, the same sporting highs and lows through the duopoly of the BBC and ITV.[2]

Television not only shaped the nation's collective sporting memory but also redefined its understanding of what constituted a sport. Let two examples suffice. In July 1969 the BBC unleashed *Pot Black* on an unsuspecting British public to encourage viewers to invest in colour television sets, and in the process it transformed the shadowy habitués of snooker halls into sporting celebrities. When, a decade later, daily live coverage of the World Snooker Championship was introduced, a sport that had not previously troubled the SPOTY record keepers provided a top-three finisher in seven of the next ten years.

Maybe even more controversial for the sporting purist was the rise of darts. Certainly, the arthritic, chain-smoking 'Jocky' Wilson, World Professional Darts champion in 1982 and

2 Although BBC Two first aired in 1964 and Channel 4 started broadcasting in 1982, BBC One and ITV still enjoyed an audience share of over 80 per cent well into the 1990s.

1989, was few people's idea of a high-performance sportsman – although his self-proclaimed pre-match ritual of downing eight vodkas recalled, for some, George Best in his Fulham days. *The Guardian*'s Barney Ronay was one of those troubled by darts players' physical make-up. 'Anything,' he maintained, 'in which you don't sweat – not including sweating because you're very fat and dressed in a satin shirt – isn't sport.' But, of course, public perception was key. In the new millennium the growing presence of darts on terrestrial as well as satellite television introduced a new set of sporting warriors to the viewing masses. Leading the way was Phil 'The Power' Taylor. A 16-time winner of the Professional Darts Corporation World Darts Championship, he managed to gain enough traction with sofa-bound sports fans to secure second place in SPOTY 2010. Even this was not enough for some. The fact that 'The Power' had never won SPOTY was a 'disgrace', felt the former Crystal Place chairman and talkSPORT pundit Simon Jordan, and proved 'the game is still not being taken seriously'.[3]

Paula Radcliffe was, then, not too wide of the mark when she suggested, in the foreword to the BBC's glossy coffee-table book celebrating 50 years of SPOTY, that the show 'offers a fascinating insight into how British sport has evolved'. Critically, though, this evolutionary process has been funnelled and moulded through the back pages of the newspapers and, more significantly, through the sports programming of the TV channels. Publicity and visibility

3 The golfer Ian Poulter was less convinced by darts' sporting credentials. 'Darts comes second in the BBC SPOTY vote, get a grip,' he tweeted in 2010. 'I can't believe I didn't get a vote for winning the world tiddlywinks championship, I'm gutted.'

are all that counts in brand recognition. Why have more figure skaters won SPOTY than rugby players (of both codes)? Because the Winter Olympics receives blanket coverage on terrestrial television while league and union matches are largely hidden away on pay-per-view satellite shows. Popular opinion is filtered through the cathode ray tube (or whatever the technological equivalent is in the Samsung surround sound 60 inch QLED Smart TV). Not for nothing is the SPOTY trophy a replica of an old-fashioned, four-turret, outside broadcast camera rather than some allegorical representation of athletic excellence.[3]

Yet, as Jennie Price, Sport England's chief executive, reminded readers of *The Guardian*, television is not a neutral observer. 'Sport is seen through a male lens,' she noted, 'and coverage is given to mainstream male sports like football. But these aren't always the ones that women are interested in.' The statistical evidence would appear to support Price. According to the Sports Journalists' Association, only 10 per cent of sports correspondents are women, and less than half a per cent of all UK sponsorship goes to female sport. SPOTY reflects this bias. Of the 70 winners since 1954, only 15½ (if you count Jayne Torvill and Christopher Dean as one, which no doubt both of them are getting sick of) have been women. This gender imbalance was brought home most forcefully in 2011, when an 'expert' panel of 27 sports editors contrived to come up with an all-male shortlist. It was hard to fathom precisely how this could have happened. Incredibly, there was room on the shortlist for Andy Murray, who had singularly failed to win a Grand Slam or break the 'big three's' dominance in the rankings, but not for Rebecca Adlington and Keri-anne Payne, who had both taken world swimming crowns. Perhaps Clare Balding had the best explanation. 'Should I be surprised,' she tweeted, 'that *Zoo*, *Nuts* and the *Star on Sunday* didn't nominate any women for SPOTY?' The BBC's cause wasn't helped when it was later revealed that Tian Tian, a giant panda given to Edinburgh Zoo by the Chinese government, had been included on its list of women of the year. Naturally, Yang Guang, Tian Tian's mate, didn't make the cut for the equivalent men's award.

SPOTY's inequity does not stop with gender. Ethnicity and class get a look-in as well. For example, 22 of the 23 footballers who have occupied a top-three spot come from white British backgrounds, despite black players making up about a fifth of the labour pool in the English professional game since the mid-1990s. And *The Observer*'s chief sportswriter, Kevin Mitchell, is probably right to complain that the 'working-class heroes of fishing and darts … are never likely to win'.[4] But, then again, maybe they don't often win in life either. Of the country's 57 prime ministers, only 11 have been educated at non-fee-paying schools, while 20 have come from Eton College alone. And they all topped an even more significant poll than SPOTY – albeit one that until 1928 was less democratic.

For all its shortcomings, or maybe even because of them, SPOTY is, therefore, an important cultural signifier. It serves as a mirror on society, reflecting the attitudes towards sport of ordinary men and women. *The Guardian* may sniff that the show 'is as much of a national treasure as Eamonn Holmes' but, like it or not, Holmes's lightweight mass appeal kept him on the early

4 The sports historian Richard Holt agrees with Mitchell. Angling, he argues, is generally ignored by television because it seems steeped in 'a world of cap-shifting, head-scratching and the odd involuntary click of false teeth'.

morning news sofas for well over two decades (and still keeps him there if you consider GB News's *Breakfast with Eamonn and Isabel* to be a current affairs programme, which inexplicably about 50,000 people a day apparently do).

A more pertinent criticism of SPOTY came from the 1974 winner, Brendan Foster. 'How could,' the Geordie distance runner wondered, 'I be judged alongside the world light-heavyweight boxing champion, John Conteh, who was second?' But, of course, it is the very outrageousness of that sort of comparison that provides the show with its raison d'être. As one reviewer astutely notes, SPOTY's main function is to generate debate and 'make people angry'. Is, for example, *The Times* right to complain that first place 'almost always goes to the wrong person, or the right person in the wrong year'? Or does the public's choice in 1994 of Damon Hill, runner-up in the F1 Drivers' Championship, instead of Colin Jackson, Commonwealth, European outdoor and indoor hurdles champion (the latter in a world-record time no less), reveal a national soft spot for plucky losers? And what does the fact that the same number of royals have won as golfers tell us about the country's sporting priorities (and, indeed, its constitutional priorities)? Or even (whisper it gently), is figure skating really a sport? These are the sort of nagging questions that an obsessive study of SPOTY can throw up, and this book will look to exorcise.[4]

Chapter Notes

1 *Guardian*, 14 December 2020; 7 December 2015; *Independent*, 3 December 2020; *Daily Mirror*, 16 December 2021; *Sun*, 19 December 2021; *Sunday Times*, 21 December 1997; 17 December 1995.

2 Martin Kelner, *Sit Down and Cheer: A History of Sport on TV* (2012), p.72; *Guardian*, 16 December 2012; Steve Rider and Martyn Smith, *BBC Sports Personality of the Year: 50th Anniversary* (2003), pp.236–237; *Independent*, 12 February 1995.

3 Kelner, *Sit Down and Cheer*, p.43; p.120; Alwyn Turner, *All in it Together: England in the Early Twentieth Century* (2021), p.132; *Guardian*, 18 December 2010; *Daily Star*, 4 May 2022; *Daily Mirror*, 21 December 2010; Smith and Rider, *BBC Sports Personality of the Year*, p.6.

4 *Guardian*, 14 December 2011; 30 November 2011; 29 November 2011; 18 December 2010; *Manchester Evening News*, 29 November 2011; *Times*, 29 December 2011; *Observer*, 16 July 2006; Richard Holt, *Sport and the British: A Modern History* (1990), p.193; David Goldblatt, *The Game of Our Lives: The Meaning and Making of English Football* (2014), p.165; *Press Gazette*, 23 December 2022; Brendan Foster and Cliff Temple, *Brendan Foster* (1978), p.128; Rider, *BBC Sports Personality of the Year*, p.276; *Sunday Times*, 18 December 1994.

Chapter 1

Athletics: The Amateurs?

Chris Chataway (1954) – Gordon Pirie (1955) –
Dorothy Hyman (1963) –
Mary Rand (1964) – David Hemery (1968) –
Mary Peters (1972) –
Brendan Foster (1974) – Steve Ovett (1978) –
Sebastian Coe (1979)

AT THE 2010 SPOTY ceremony, held in Birmingham's cavernous LG Arena, there was an unexpected recipient of the Coach of the Year award. As Clive Woodward and Fabio Capello looked on, a self-employed builder from Billericay, resplendent in jeans and a Sergio Tacchini retro tracksuit top, strode on to the stage to receive his award from a fawning Sir Steve Redgrave. It was, by any calculation, a remarkable choice and the acceptance speech that followed was no less astonishing. Having first checked with Paula Radcliffe that she knew where the toilets were and commiserated with 'Giggsy' for his failure to break into the England squad, Smithy launched into an excoriating attack on the lack of drive and ambition in British sport. 'I don't see a room full of sporting legends,' he scolded his audience of superstars, 'I see a room full of people looking for their next sponsorship deal, book deal, TV series. You wouldn't see W. G. Grace demean himself on *Ready Steady Cook*; Roger Bannister wouldn't have a Twitter account.' To the strains of Hubert Parry's 'Jerusalem', the address came to a stirring conclusion. 'Can we win the World Cup? Yes we can! Can we win at Wimbledon? Yes we can! Can we win at the Olympics? And I'm talking proper medals, not just swimming and cycling, ones that actually count – basically running. Yes we can!'

As with all good comedy, James Corden's cameo as Smithy that evening at the LG Arena feeds off deeply embedded popular attitudes. Over the last century and a quarter, the Olympics may have burgeoned into a multi-sport extravaganza, but for most of the viewing public the core has remained the track and field programme. This belief can certainly be seen in the public's choice of Sports Personality of the Year. Athletics is way out on its own in the SPOTY league table, with more winners than the next two sports (Formula One and tennis) combined. Indeed, if SPOTY is anything to go by, Smithy could have gone even further when refining his definition of 'proper medals'. Of the 18 athletes who have received the SPOTY trophy, not only have 13 been runners but ten have specialised in middle- and long-distance events.

This British love affair with endurance running was reflected by the popular vote in the first two years of the BBC award. Chris Chataway and Gordon Pirie, the winners in 1954 and 1955 respectively, were both world-record holders over 5,000m, and between them ensured meetings at the White City were sold out for much of the first half of the 1950s. They could, said one of their contemporaries, 'have drawn a crowd for a wheelbarrow race'. Yet, while their remarkable talent helped to popularise track and field, their contrasting backgrounds and divergent approaches to training and racing also ensured that the tensions that surrounded post-war British athletics were exposed to the harsh glare of public scrutiny.

Athletics, along with many other sports, experienced a huge surge in spectators in the decade following the end of the Second World War. Boosted by the success of the 1948 London Olympics, domestic competitions regularly drew crowds that only a few elite football clubs could hope to emulate. In 1952, over 50,000 turned out to watch the Amateur Athletic Association (AAA) championships at the White City Stadium. Even a meeting as modest as the Blackheath Harriers annual championship was enough to persuade 7,000 people that standing on the terraces of a blustery Motspur Park, watching enthusiastic club athletes battle the elements, was a productive way of spending a Saturday afternoon. However, for the blazered gentlemen who ran British athletics, although such interest was more than they could ever really have hoped for, there was a price to pay. A new demographic was drawn to the sport. Emboldened by welfarist educational policies, men and (to a lesser extent) women from lower-middle and working-class backgrounds flocked to local athletics clubs, harbouring expectations and aspirations very different from those of the administrators and committee members who ran things. In particular, the battle lines were drawn around the issue of amateurism.

Founded in 1880 by three Oxford graduates, the AAA enshrined the Victorian cult of the amateur gentleman. The

Association's primary function was to ensure that the army officers, civil servants, university men and business owners who made up its membership could compete without having to mix with the professional branch of the sport, pedestrianism, where runners vied for prize money. Strict and lengthy directives outlined the precise parameters of amateurism. In essence, though, the rule was if you were not a gentleman, then you could be pretty certain you were not an amateur either. As the sports historians Richard Holt and Tony Mason succinctly noted, amateurism was essentially a moral code, a deft way of ensuring that the social classes were carefully and permanently separated. Although societal changes meant the barriers between the classes gradually became more porous as the 20th century progressed, the definition of amateur remained as rigid as ever. On the eve of the 1948 Olympics, the International Amateur Athletic Federation (IAAF) saw fit to remind would-be competitors that to be deemed an amateur one must 'practise and compete only for the love of sport'. Although the federation did allow some relaxation around athletes' rights to compensation for lost earnings – what were called broken-time payments – even this minor concession was a step too far for the delicate sensibilities of British officialdom.

For the most part, Britain's insistence on holding the line on amateurism was down to the mulishness of three leading post-war athletics administrators – Jack Crump (the secretary of the British Amateur Athletic Board (BAAB)), Harold Abrahams (the secretary of the AAA) and Lord Burghley (the president of the AAA and chairman of the British Olympic Committee). Predictably, all three enjoyed privileged lifestyles borne of inherited wealth. And, even more predictably, all three were given to offering up lengthy homilies about the corrupting influence of money. Abrahams and Burghley, who had won Olympic golds in 1924 and 1928 respectively, both held firm to the belief that any form of financial reward would undermine the very purpose of sport. Participating solely for 'the thrill and good fellowship of competition', Burghley told a group of his peers at the AAA's annual general meeting in 1959, would help athletes become 'good citizens'. Crump, if possible, was even more unyielding. The International Olympic Committee's (IOC) decision to grant competitors at the 1956 Olympics in Australia a trifling daily allowance for incidentals was proof, he felt, that sport was going to hell in a handcart. Consequently, while he and his fellow administrators enjoyed an all-expenses-paid stay at one of Melbourne's finest hotels, British athletes were not even given the IOC's corrupting pocket money to spend on a soft drink and light snack in the Olympic village's communal cafeteria.

Inevitably, this refusal to countenance any change, no matter how negligible, to the boundaries of amateurism provoked opposition from athletes trying to balance work and training. Combined with other petty indignities (separate tables at mealtimes for Oxbridge athletes, first-class travel for officials while competitors slummed it in economy), intransigence over any form of financial compensation added to the impression of a sport stuck in the era of the Victorian gentleman amateur. Tensions were hardly eased by Crump's penchant for courting controversy in the press. 'In general,' he undiplomatically informed readers of the *Daily Mail*, 'the less fortunately educated tended to display a slight inferiority complex and were less ready to feel on equal terms with the university athletes.' This sort of talk did little to appease working-class runners from the industrial north, such as Walter Hesketh, the British six-mile record holder. Hesketh, who had started work shining shoes in Manchester's St Anne's Square aged 14, was sure his exclusion from the 1952 Helsinki Olympic squad was the result of institutional prejudice. The selectors, he complained to a Manchester AC club-mate, 'will always pick a Southerner [in preference to a northerner]. And they would always choose a university man over a non-university man, and of the university people Oxford and Cambridge over the rest.'[5]

Yet, if the first poll for the BBC's SPOTY was anything to go by, it was just possible that Crump and his cronies had been reading the public mood accurately after all. Born in Chelsea, educated at Sherborne and Magdalen College, Oxford, and a member of the exclusive Achilles Club, the public's choice for SPOTY 1954, Chris Chataway, could not have conformed more closely to the establishment's ideal of a true amateur even if Burghley himself had been given the casting vote. In fact, it just so happened that Chataway was part of a talented cohort of Oxbridge athletes (which included sub-four-minute miler Roger Bannister and Olympic steeplechase gold medallist Chris Brasher) who were coming to their peak in the mid-1950s. Both in approach and attitude, these men seemed to be throwbacks to a lost golden age. Bannister insisted that running was no more than a diversion. He trained for 45 minutes two or three times a week he revealed to the editor of *Athletics Weekly*, but 'couldn't give precise details on what he did because it all depended on how he felt'. Chataway followed an equally relaxed regimen. He was anxious, he later recalled, 'not to get too stale … by pounding out mile after mile'. Sport was, after all, 'a hobby', and he wasn't prepared to 'subjugate his life to it'.

Chataway's gentlemanly ethos and (the less charitable might argue) limited training were both in evidence at his first outing to the Olympics in 1952. Pushing himself to the very edge of exhaustion, he surged into the lead with just 300m to go in the 5,000m, before dramatically collapsing to the track as the imperious Czech Emil Zatopek swept past him round the final bend. Fifth place may have been bitterly disappointing after coming so close to victory but, as every English schoolboy raised on a diet of Rudyard Kipling knew, it was how you treated the imposter of disaster that defined character. And Chataway was the embodiment of magnanimity. 'I have no complaints,' he cheerily told the *Daily Mail*. 'Zatopek may have brushed past me causing me to lose my balance but I was at the end of my tether when I fell. The better man won.' Here was the true amateur spirit. No wonder, the *Mail* enthused, 'our man received an ovation as great as that of the winner'.

It was, though, in 1954 that Chataway really broke through into the popular consciousness. Having helped Bannister to his historic sub-four-minute mile in May, he then narrowly missed securing a world record for himself the following month when winning the two miles at the British Games. His time of 8min 41sec was less than a second shy of the mark set by the great Belgian Gaston Reiff. Once again, for the press, it was Chataway's nonchalant manner that was most noteworthy about the performance. 'The outlook of a man who celebrates the missing of a world record by about four yards in two miles by smoking a cigarette,' the *Sunday Times* wistfully suggested, 'is something worth keeping in the age of grim determination to run faster and ever faster.' Four months later, the Oxford man's athletic prowess and disarming insouciance combined to deliver the sporting moment of the year.

After lengthy negotiations, the AAA had managed to secure permission to invite, for the first time, the all-conquering Soviet team to Britain for a match between London and Moscow at the White City. In the Cold War era, such encounters were about much more than simply sport; they were seen as key battlegrounds in the struggle for prestige between East and West. For Britain, in particular, creaking under the weight of its industrial and imperial past and largely sidelined in the emergent superpower conflict, victory against Eastern Bloc athletes provided some form of reassurance that all was not entirely lost. Little wonder then that the BBC chose to broadcast the meeting live, and that 12 million viewers opted to tune in to watch the drama unfold. In a night full of intriguing clashes, the most eagerly anticipated was the duel over 5,000m between Chataway and the new Soviet star Vladimir Kuts, who had broken the world record for the event just two months earlier when taking the European crown in Bern.

And, for once, the action lived up to the hype. On a crisp October night, with spotlights sweeping round the track, the two favourites matched each other stride for stride until Chataway, head flung back, inched ahead in the final few yards to breast the tape in a new world record. For a nation steeped in the amateur tradition, here was proof that our best years could still be ahead of us. 'The gay blade from Oxford who will smoke a cigar and drink a glass of stout with the best of them,' the *Daily Mirror* raved, 'has shown that we've still got it in us to turn in with nonchalance a world-shattering performance, an epic with a grin.' A weakness for the occasional gasper was also used as shorthand for innate superiority by the *Mail.* Casually puffing away on a well-earned cigarette at the post-race press conference, Chataway, the paper admiringly noted, readily admitted to not having 'trained so hard in the past five weeks. I usually smoke ten cigarettes a day, but I cut those out in the last three days.' Such an easy-going attitude, it was assumed, would hardly have cut the mustard with the taskmasters who oversaw the merciless training schedules of the Soviet squad.

Having attracted front-page headlines and a mass television audience, it came as a surprise to no one (except apparently the BBC) that Chataway went on to be crowned the inaugural Sports Personality of the Year at the Savoy Hotel in December. Roger Bannister, whom the mandarins at Broadcasting House had assumed would win but whose epoch-defining feat had been played out, not at the White City on live TV, but in the rather more homely surroundings of Oxford's Iffley Road track in front of just one static camera, had to settle for second place on the night and the opportunity to present his erstwhile pacemaker with the trophy. The press was certain the right man had won. Pat Reckie of the *Mail* summed up the prevailing view. Not only had Chataway, by defeating Kuts, proven he was a world-class athlete in his own right, declared Reckie, but 'he had also found glory in helping others without ever attempting to attract to himself that glory which he earned for them'. Who said the days of the old Corinthian spirit were over?[6]

Well, perhaps Chataway's successor as Sports Personality of the Year didn't say it, but he almost certainly thought it. Determinedly confrontational in public and ruthlessly professional in private, the only quality that Gordon Pirie appeared to share with his Oxford-educated predecessor was a preternatural talent for distance running. The difference between the two stars was not lost on the press of the day. 'Never were there two such contrasting types!' a headline in *Picture Post* gleefully announced on the eve of the Melbourne Olympics. In the accompanying six-page spread, Pirie, 'the paint salesman', was presented as an austere automaton who spent his every waking hour grinding out his professional coach's punishing training sessions, while Chataway, the gifted amateur who had 'entered running almost by accident', was cast as a cheerful bon viveur who, when the fancy took him, went for the occasional jog.

The popular monthly magazine *World Sports* juxtaposed extracts from interviews with the two athletes to draw out equally stark distinctions. 'To achieve world's best performances,' Pirie rather ominously insisted, 'the athlete must concentrate on … time and distance devouring schedules, unimaginable a decade ago, which will produce a machine.' This brave new world of athletics was too much for Chataway. 'There remain,' he demurred, 'a number of athletes who cannot or will not train everyday throughout the year. A more limited programme, perhaps an hour four days a week during the training months may produce a fresher approach on the day of the big race.' Even the visuals were used to accentuate differences. A photograph of the two rivals training together, which appeared in another feature, this time in *Picture Post*, had a jaunty Chataway springing along dressed in his GB kit, while a grimly determined Pirie followed on wrapped up in a blue tracksuit emblazoned with the letters CCCP – a daring sartorial choice for the Cold War era.

Pirie's courting of controversy was not simply restricted to his choice of training gear. He was, his wife said, 'a kind of Angry Young Man'. And like John Osborne and Kingsley Amis, he railed against the attitudes and values of the Establishment. In particular, he had no time for the 'elderly dictators' who, through 'the old school tie and the old pals' act', upheld what he called the 'hypocrisy of British amateurism'. If athletics in Britain was to catch up with the rest of the world, he argued, it would need scientific training, state investment and permission for athletes to make 'a reasonable living free of humiliating patronage'.

Such views were hardly exceptional in the 1950s – even Chataway thought athletics should be made into an open sport as quickly as possible – but what did make Pirie stand out was the vigour with which he pursued his convictions. Both in the sports pages of the daily press and, more importantly, on the athletics tracks across the world, he made abundantly clear that he was committed to approaching his career in a scientifically professional manner. He freely admitted to giving up his job as a bank clerk to work as a sales rep for Wilkinson's paint so he could have more time to devote to training. And this was at a time when AAA regulations specifically stipulated that an athlete could be employed as a salesman 'only if it was his normal activity'. His training regime of two sessions a day and over 100 miles a week was revolutionary in its intensity, and left little doubt to even the most casual observer that running, far from being an amateur hobby, was to all intents and purpose his primary focus in life. Perhaps most controversial of all was his association with the professional coach Woldemar Gerschler. There were dark rumours that Gerschler used athletes as guinea pigs to test some of his more contentious techniques, and pictures of Pirie, oxygen mask clamped to his face being put through his paces at Gerschler's Institute of Physical Training in Freiburg, hardly helped to quell the disquiet.

But, of course, despite all the controversy and occasional negative publicity, Pirie's public standing chiefly depended on his performances on the track and over the country, and here he consistently delivered. In 1951, when only 20, he broke the British record for six miles. Two years later he set new British records at two miles, three miles, 5,000m and 10,000m. He won the National Cross Country Championship three years in a row between 1953 and 1955. And, in 1956, he broke the world records for both the 5,000m and 3,000m, the latter twice. The one blemish on what was an otherwise impeccable CV was an inability to translate record-breaking form into championship medals. His tally of one Olympic silver (for the 5,000m in Melbourne) and one European bronze (5,000m in Stockholm) did not really do justice to his enormous talent. Nonetheless, the combination of scandal and expectation that surrounded Pirie ensured that, from an early age, he was sporting box office. During the 1950s, his biographer claimed 'no man or woman in British sport made headlines more consistently'. And there is certainly plenty of evidence of his public appeal. A waxwork of Pirie featured in Madame Tussauds; he was interviewed on *Woman's Hour*; he made an appearance on *What's My Line?*; he was even nominated as one of *Picture Post*'s 'Britons who will make a mark in 1954', alongside Harold Macmillan and (who else?) Benny Hill.

Ironically, Pirie's SPOTY triumph came in what was for him a relatively lacklustre year. A series of world-record attempts over the summer of 1955 all ended in failure and his season appeared to be about to fizzle out in late autumn when, as had happened for Chataway a year earlier, a televised match against a team from behind the Iron Curtain captured the public's imagination. For the first time since 1948, the great Emil Zatopek, the reigning Olympic champion over 5,000m, 10,000m and (incredibly!) the marathon, was due to race in Britain as part of the 'Prague' team for a match against London. With the White City arc lights barely piercing the gloom of a foggy October evening, the key clash, Zatopek versus Pirie over 10,000m, unfolded in front of 40,000 exuberant spectators and a live television audience of nearly 11 million. Zatopek, elbows akimbo and head lolling like a man in the last throes of strangulation, repeatedly attempted to break the field before eventually succumbing to a last-lap surge by a triumphant Pirie. The tabloids were again quick to locate the victory in the wider context of Cold War geopolitics. Pirie's heroics, the front page of the *Daily Express* reassured middle England, had 'put the prestige back in Britain'. Four days later, a second defeat of Zatopek, this time in Manchester over 5,000m, helped to install Pirie as one of the front runners for the SPOTY trophy.

For most athletes, being crowned Sports Personality of the Year is a time for proud reflection, a chance to bask in some well-earned glory and to graciously thank family and friends for their support. Few would consider it the opportune moment to launch into a vitriolic assault on the sporting press. But Pirie, of course, never felt much bound by convention. With the *Sporting Record*'s 'Sportsman of the Year' award up for grabs as well as the BBC's SPOTY, it was, in retrospect, probably an unwise move to save until the night of the ceremony the news that journalists had not even included the nation's favourite athlete on their shortlist of likely winners for either honour. Comfortably topping the public polls for both awards did nothing to improve Pirie's mood. 'Fleet Street sportswriters,' he admonished his audience of Fleet Street sportswriters, 'do incredible damage to British sport. A few unkind words inflict more damage than they realise.' They must, he therefore concluded, try to 'be kinder in future'. It was hard to tell whether the single clap that broke the ensuing silence was ironic.

The response in the following morning's papers was as harsh as it was predictable. The *Daily Mirror*'s veteran sports editor, Peter Wilson, had been so affronted by Pirie's speech, he revealed to his readers, that it had made him 'storm out', although not apparently before he had heard enough to know that it was 'all mawkish rubbish'. Even *The Express*'s Desmond Hackett, who had been specifically exempted from the blanket criticism of the night before, was critical of what he felt was an 'ill-timed outburst'. One of the few more balanced assessments of the whole sorry episode came, perhaps unsurprisingly, from a journalist who had also experienced the pressures of top-class athletics. Pirie's resentment, Chris Brasher felt, was understandable given 'he has had, since he was 20, the publicity of a film star without any of the material benefits that compensate for the assumption by the public and press that they own part of anyone in the news'. Brasher's eulogy at Pirie's memorial service 35 years later was equally perceptive and served as a fitting summary of his great rival's career. 'Gordon was,' he told the gathered mourners, 'the first Briton to throw off the cloak of amateurism and put his whole being into the pursuit of excellence.'[7]

For three of the next four athletes to be voted in as Sports Personality of the Year, it was not only the challenges of amateurism that had to be confronted but also the injustices of sexism. In many ways, attitudes to female athletics in Britain had made little progress in the half-century since the pioneering medic, Dr Mary Scharlieb had claimed that 'excessive devotion to athletics and gymnastics tends to produce what may be called the neuter type of girl'. In 1951, the governing body of English Schools Athletics banned girls from competing in the long jump because the risk of 'displacing internal organs' was too great. Exactly why boys' livers and kidneys should remain reassuringly intact as they flung themselves into sandpits was never made clear. Such restrictions went right to the top of the sport. The 400m was not introduced for women until the 1964 Olympics, female metric milers had to wait until 1972 for their Olympic call-up, and if a young girl fancied herself as an aspiring Olympic steeplechaser, she had to hold on until well into the 21st century for the chance to fulfil her dream.

A warped understanding of female physiology was not, of course, the only reason for the limited Olympic schedule for women in this period. Good old-fashioned sexism played its part as well. Few in the male-dominated world of British athletics would have thought the *Daily Mirror*'s sports editor was speaking out of turn when he concluded a review of the North's match against Moscow in 1954 with the dismissive observation that 'women's races can never be anything but an out-of-focus and unfunny caricature in somewhat dubious taste of the men's events'. And if all this was not enough to dent the aspirations of sporty schoolgirls, then how about the mortifying prospect of obligatory sex tests? These may have varied in method, from gynaecological exams to parading naked in front of a panel of doctors, but never in brutishness. They were, the great Irish pentathlete and SPOTY winner for 1972, Mary Peters, recalled, 'the most crude and degrading experiences I have ever known in my life'.

Yet, despite these seemingly insurmountable hindrances, female athletics still emerged as a major force in the 1960s. One of the first women to break through as a new star of the track in this era was the sprinter Dorothy Hyman. Born into a mining family in Cudworth on the outskirts of Barnsley, Hyman's early career provides a startling glimpse into some of the challenges faced by athletes from working-class communities in the northern heartlands. Even as her career took off, she had no regular coach for guidance, no athletes' group for support, and no nearby cinder track for training. Worse still, the grass track on which she did most of her speed work sloped uphill and, as there were no changing facilities, she had to rely on the generosity of neighbours to have a wash, her own home having no bathroom.

As well as these practical disadvantages, Hyman also had to overcome entrenched class and regional prejudices. British teams, she recalled some years later, were made up of 'schoolteachers and university people from the South' who came from the same 'privileged backgrounds' as the selectors. The *Daily Mirror*, ever prepared to fight the cause of the downtrodden, was equally certain something was amiss. How, it questioned on the eve of the Rome Olympics, could anyone be 'proud to be British when it comes to a gutsy girl like Hyman having to face obstacles which make it impossible for her to compete on level terms?' Even the *Daily Mail*, hardly a champion of the revolutionary Left, felt moved to condemn the lack of athletics infrastructure in 'the South Yorkshire coalfields … when Russian girls have the finest training facilities'.

It was, therefore, testament to Hyman's precocious talent that her career developed as rapidly as it did. She made her international debut aged 16, won Commonwealth gold the following year, and became a double Olympic medallist before she was 20.[5] Although success continued in 1962, with gold in the 100m at the European Championships and the sprint double two months later at the Perth Commonwealth Games, it was, in fact, to be 1963, a non-championship year, that she was to have her *annus mirabilis*. She won all her races that year, including the 'Little Olympics' in Tokyo, and in the process set European and Commonwealth records at both 100m and 200m. Critically, for her public profile, the international matches against Hungary, USSR and USA were all covered by the BBC. Rounding off the year as the first female athlete to win SPOTY was, most felt, just reward for a season full of remarkable triumphs, although the sports editor of *The Mirror* still somehow managed to make political capital out of the moment. 'Our Dorothy' was the people's favourite, he claimed, because of the 'shameful difficulties she has had to overcome and her determination not to be lured away from her beloved home territory'.

Unfortunately, Hyman's difficulties continued the following season. Plagued by injuries, she was below her best at the Tokyo Olympics and then, worried about her family's 'occasional cash

5 She was part of the world-record-setting 4x110yds relay squad in Cardiff in 1958, and in the Rome Olympics two years later won silver in the 100m and bronze in the 200m.

problems', agreed to release an autobiography for which she unwisely accepted a one-off payment of £150. Although this sum amounted to less than two months' salary for the average factory worker, it was still deemed enough for the aristocratic Old Etonian who presided over the AAA to hand the miner's daughter from Cudworth a life ban.[6] She was only 23 years old. In later life, despite this shabby treatment, Hyman remained resolutely wedded to the principles of amateurism. Maybe there had been 'too many presents and not enough money', she reflected 30 years later, but the solution was not to reduce athletics meetings to the 'atmosphere of the dog-track' by offering 'appearance or prize money'. Instead, all that was needed was the sanctioning of 'earnings from the commercial spin-offs that sporting fame brought'.[8]

Of all the athletes to win SPOTY before the advent of the professional era in the 1980s, it was Hyman's successor who had the greatest potential for monetising celebrity status. Well before she became the nation's first female Olympic field event champion, with a world record in the long jump at Tokyo, Mary Rand had been universally acclaimed as the golden girl of British athletics. From a similar working-class background to Hyman and equally talented as a youngster, Rand's athletics career could easily have followed the same trajectory as that of the Cudworth sprinter had she not been offered a scholarship to Millfield, an exclusive public school renowned for its focus on sporting excellence. Although the scholarship did not furnish Rand with

6 In fact, Hyman made a comeback at the end of the decade, winning the AAA's 100m in 1969. However, she remained banned from competing in international competitions.

any academic qualifications, that, of course, was not its purpose. What it provided instead was much more valuable. It allowed her sporting gifts to be carefully nurtured, and it added to her natural wholesomeness an effortless poise that the expensively educated so often possess. There was, as well, a less positive upshot to this period of personal growth. Rand was now hot news for the tabloids.

Her sporting achievements on the international stage – silver at the 1958 Commonwealth Games, two bronzes at the 1962 European Championships, a British record in the long jump at the Rome Olympics – undoubtedly warranted the media's attention. But, in the unreconstructed 1960s, it was not always a sportswoman's athletic ability that piqued the interest of the almost exclusively male press corps. Rand, invariably described as 'shapely', was reimagined on the back pages (and not infrequently front pages) of the dailies as a curious amalgam of wholesome young mother and sensual femme fatale. The *Daily Express* was firmly in the glamour camp. Eager to dispel any misconceptions that women's athletics was solely populated by beefy Russian shot-putters and muscle-bound East German sprinters, the paper gushed that Rand was proof 'if proof were needed, that girl athletes, far from being unfeminine, can run rings round model girls and movie stars for sheer beauty'. And to underline the point, readers were treated to a photograph of a chic Rand astride a Vespa; the very epitome of the 'It' girl with a hectic social schedule to keep.

The *Daily Mail*, just as keen to promote Rand's femininity, was less certain that the image of a young mum gadding about town on a scooter as if she hadn't a care in the world would sit easily with its largely middle-class subscribers. Instead, a 1961 profile presented the nation's favourite athlete as a typical suburban housewife who passed her evenings 'in her flat dressmaking and polishing her trophies'. These two conflicting media representations of Rand were perhaps best captured in a wonderful vignette by Neil Allen of *The Times*. 'An Italian journalist,' Allen recounted in his regular 'Olympic Diary' column during the Tokyo Games, 'gave a melting look at the long legs and swinging hips as Mary Rand walked across the grass then surveyed again the world-record long jump on the indicator board and reluctantly handed me back my binoculars, misty by now. He shook his head in amazement and pronounced the accolade, "All that and a mother too!"'

Allen's Italian colleague had good reason to be astounded by Rand's performance at the Tokyo Olympics. She remains the only British female athlete to come away with three medals from the same Games, winning gold in the long jump with the first-ever leap over 22 feet, silver in the pentathlon with a new national record, and bronze as part of the 4x100m squad, again breaking the British record. Rand, along with Ann Packer, who had set a new world record when winning the 800m with an astonishing sprint finish, had markedly raised the profile of female athletics. So it was no surprise when the two finished first and third, respectively, in the voting for SPOTY at the end of the year.[7]

Neither was able, however, to capitalise on this resurgence of interest in women's track and field. Packer retired immediately after her victory in Tokyo, and Rand, beset by a series of niggling

7 Barry Briggs, the World Speedway champion, was runner-up.

injuries, never regained the same form. To add insult to (literally) injury, in the aftermath of her Olympic triumph Rand turned down a series of lucrative commercial opportunities, including the chance to star as a female 007, in order to retain her amateur status. Even the one offer the AAA's antediluvian rules did allow her to accept, a modestly paid role as a columnist for the *Sunday Mirror*, came with the strict condition that there must be no mention of athletics. What was the best female long-jumper in the world permitted to write about then? Housekeeping, of course. It was a rather sad end for a sportswoman that the *Sunday Times* had called 'one of the greatest natural athletes of all time'.[9]

The third and last female athlete to win SPOTY in the amateur era was in full agreement with the *Sunday Times*' assessment of her predecessor. Mary Rand was, fellow pentathlete Mary Peters stated with typical modesty, 'the greatest all-round sportswomen I have ever met'.[8] But, as the magnificent football journalist Brian Glanville acutely observed, if 'Mary Rand was the queen of naturals then Mary Peters was the queen of workers'. And Peters's dedication and perseverance were apparent from very early on in her career. How many other 15-year-old girls would ask for two tons of sand as a birthday present so they could build a long-jump pit in their back garden? How many other parents, for that matter, would accede to such a request? Actually, sacks of sand were not so odd a birthday wish because, predictably, the sporting facilities in 1960s Northern Ireland, where the English-born Peters had moved to when she was 11,

---

8 Mary Peters was well qualified to make this judgement, having come fourth behind Rand in the first-ever Olympic pentathlon in Tokyo.

were as poor as those Hyman had been forced to put up with in 1950s South Yorkshire. To reach the run-down grass track that served as Belfast's premier training venue, the future Olympic champion had to lug her starting blocks and shot put on to two buses for an hour-long journey across the city.[9]

As ever, the situation was hardly helped by the AAA's refusal to cover the expenses of athletes on international duty. Peters, just as Hyman and Rand before her, was compelled to change job so she could find an employer willing to cover the costs of her increasingly lengthy competitive absences. Yet, even in her new role as 'the dog's-body factotum' at Buster McShane's Belfast gym, she almost fell foul of the blazerati at the Olympic Committee's headquarters in Lausanne. By occasionally offering 'health instruction' to some of Buster's patrons, she was, technically, in breach of a regulation that prohibited amateurs from 'teaching or assisting in the pursuit of athletic exercise as a means of livelihood'. Her outraged response to the possibility of a ban was as good a commentary as any on the farcical rules that governed amateurism in the 1950s and 1960s. 'I was now,' the mild-mannered, law-abiding Peters angrily recalled, 'under the quite ludicrous edict laid down by the millionaires and noblemen of the IOC, a professional. Within their terms of reference, I was a cheat throughout the remainder of my career. I was investigated several times and on each occasion had no compunction at all about telling the first lie that came into my head.'

---

9 Her experience of struggling to find suitable facilities as a young athlete encouraged Peters, in later life, to establish a public fund to finance the building of an international stadium. The Mary Peters Track opened on Easter Monday 1976.

Peters's bloody-minded determination certainly helped to overcome the slew of obstacles she faced but so too did her willingness to experiment and innovate. She was, for example, one of the first female athletes to incorporate a punishing weightlifting programme into her training regime. At a time when any sort of strength work was considered distinctly unladylike, Peters could, an admiring Sean Ingle of *The Guardian* excitedly pointed out, 'quarter-squat 825lbs on her back'. And for those unable to visualise that sort of weight, Ingle was happy to help out. 'That is,' he explained, 'roughly the combined weight of four giant pandas!' The increased focus on strength and conditioning quickly paid dividends. After a disappointing ninth place in the pentathlon at the Mexico Olympics in 1968, Peters secured double gold at the Commonwealth Games in Edinburgh two years later, winning both the pentathlon and the shot put. Her sights were now set on 1972. At the age of 33, in what would be her third Olympic Games, she was aware that Munich would almost certainly be her last chance of becoming Olympic pentathlon champion.

Of the five disciplines that made up the pentathlon at the 1972 Olympics, Peters's strongest, the 100m hurdles, shot put and high jump, all came on the opening day of the two-day competition. In stark contrast, her main rival, West German favourite Heidi Rosenthal, was a specialist in the remaining two events, the long jump, for which she held the world record, and the 200m. It was entirely predictable, therefore, that Peters's overnight lead of 301 points had been whittled down to just 74 by the time the two athletes lined up for the final heat of the 200m. To take overall victory, Peters needed to finish no more than 1.2 seconds behind Rosenthal; Rosenthal's personal best was 1.1 seconds better than Peters's. The stage was set. As a sell-out 80,000-strong crowd in the Olympiastadion roared the athletes down the home straight, Rosenthal breasted the tape first to break the world pentathlon record with a total score of 4,791 points. Just over a second later Peters crossed the finish line to become Britain's only track and field champion of the Games. She had taken the gold and the world record by just ten points. It was enough to secure her the SPOTY title ahead of the England goalkeeper Gordon Banks, and the Olympic eventing individual champion Richard Meade.

Peters continued competing for a couple of years more after Munich, fittingly rounding off her career with pentathlon gold at the Commonwealth Games in Christchurch. Yet, despite all her success on the international stage, and the time and effort she devoted to training, she clung tenaciously to the belief that athletics should never be viewed as anything more than 'a hobby'. She may have been, for a brief time, a member of what was effectively a professional elite, she recalled in retirement, but the purpose of that elite was to act 'as a shop window' for what was 'basically an amateur sport'. This was a view that Rand and Hyman in the 1960s, and Chataway in the 1950s, would have been happy to endorse. A new generation of male athletes, however, was less enamoured with the sport's all-pervading amateur culture, and started to push for Peters's professional elite to be given the respect (and rewards) they felt it deserved.[10]

Throughout the 1960s, and for much of the 1970s, men's athletics was in a desperate state. In the 1960s, David Hemery was our only Olympic champion on the track, with gold in the 400m hurdles in Mexico in 1968.[10] The 1970s were, if possible, even worse. The best the British men could achieve was three bronzes: Hemery in the 400m hurdles and Ian Stewart in the 5,000m in Munich in 1972, and Brendan Foster in the 10,000m in Montreal four years later. It was hardly surprising, therefore, that in the two decades following Pirie's SPOTY triumph in 1955 only two male athletes lifted the BBC trophy: Hemery in 1968 and Foster in 1974. Perhaps equally predictable was the determination with which both these athletes attempted to reshape the sport they loved. They were fully aware that the harsh commercial realities of the new televisual age meant sports like athletics, where the amateur culture was all-pervading, were confronted with a stark choice of adapt or die.

Although Foster, as we will see, played a significant role in steering athletics towards the professional age, it was Hemery who was more conspicuous in demanding and embracing change. There was a certain irony to this, for the 1968 Olympic champion was regarded by many as the epitome of the Corinthian ideal. He was, the flyers for his autobiography claimed, 'the last of the true amateurs'. This may have been marketing hyperbole but there was still a good deal of truth in it. With his patrician manner and graceful fluidity over the hurdles, Hemery was uncannily reminiscent of the great Lord Burghley in his prime. And his values seemed to match his appearance. Throughout his career, he was a firm believer that the spirit as well as the letter of the laws governing amateurism must be observed, a stance he credited

10 Britain's other three track and field champions were Don Thompson (50km walk) in Rome, 1960, and Ken Matthews (20km walk) and Lynn Davies (long jump) both in Tokyo, 1964.

to his early upbringing in a Plymouth Brethren household.[11] (Happily, the Brethren's ambivalent position on competitive sports seems to have had a less enduring impact.) Some may have thought him naïve, he acknowledged in later life, to turn down Nike's offer of £1,000 to switch spikes on the eve of the Mexico Games, but 'staying clean' had allowed him to feel 'lifted and strengthened within his own mind'. Baron de Coubertin himself could not have expressed it better.

It was, then, fitting that Hemery's great triumph should occur at that last bastion of amateurism, the Olympic Games. As reigning Commonwealth high hurdles champion, and with training suggesting that his speed endurance was better than ever, he arrived in Mexico confident that he could better his 400m hurdles bronze from four years earlier. The only uncertainty was the impact Mexico City's altitude of 7,500ft would have as athletes entered oxygen debt towards the end of races. To ease any concerns and help with acclimatisation, the British team travelled out four weeks early and were even treated to an encouraging royal pep talk. Prince Philip's insistence, however, that he had been untroubled when playing polo at a similar altitude the previous year did not reassure everyone. 'How did the horse feel?' asked the Welsh long-jumper Lynn Davies. Happily, on the day, Hemery's rigorous preparations paid off and he destroyed a top-class field to win by nearly ten metres in a world-record time of 48.1 seconds. He was the first British male athlete in over 30 years to achieve gold with a world-best performance, and the first in over 50 years to collect a full set of Olympic medals.

11 The Hemerys withdrew from the Brethren when David was still young.

Already a moderately well-known sporting figure, those 48 seconds in Mexico turned Hemery into a huge national celebrity. The Games were the first to be shown live on television in Britain, and although the 400m hurdles final took place at 2am British time, the BBC was determined that no one should miss out on the nation's only golden moment in the athletics stadium. Over the next two weeks the race was replayed 27 times. Helped by an iconic piece of David Coleman commentary ('David Hemery wins for Great Britain, in second place it's Hennige, and who cares who's third? It doesn't matter!'), the coverage drew enormous viewing figures.[12] Suddenly, Hemery found himself inundated with demands to attend a never-ending carousel of media interviews, product endorsements and civic receptions. He was constantly being recognised 'even by people who were not sports fans', although he also remembered that his arrival at functions occasionally resulted in confused looks from disappointed fans of Dick Emery. But even the staunchest devotee of saucy slapstick could hardly have been surprised when, on 5 December at London's Television Theatre, Ron Clarke, the supreme Australian distance runner, stepped forward to present Britain's only Olympic champion with the SPOTY trophy.

Yet, as was true for so many great sports stars before him, Hemery found the realisation of a lifetime ambition a bitter-sweet moment. 'Where do you go,' the 24-year-old hurdler asked himself, 'after a world record and an Olympic gold medal?' The

---

12 Of course, it actually mattered a great deal. Unnoticed by an over-excited Coleman, Britain's John Sherwood had managed to squeak through into third place. His bronze, along with wife Sheila's silver in the long jump, accounted for half of the British athletics team's total medal haul at the Games. The final medal was Lillian Board's silver in the long jump.

answer, bizarrely, was the decathlon. A brief flirtation with the multi-discipline event resulted in an international cap but, inevitably, he soon returned to the barriers. Although he secured Commonwealth gold in 1970 and Olympic bronze two years later, this was still not enough to compensate for the lack of financial reward, so in 1973 'the last of the true amateurs' turned professional.

In reality, at least in terms of approach and attitude, Hemery had always been professional. Brought up in America, his formative years as an athlete had been spent on the extraordinarily competitive collegiate circuit. Funded through lavish university sports budgets, the slick professionalism of American race meets was a world away from the village fete atmosphere of most AAA competitions. The intensity of the US system suited Hemery's personality perfectly. Fiercely self-disciplined and keenly self-reflective, he approached any task with the all-consuming passion of the obsessive. Proof of this can be found in his autobiography. There can be few other sporting memoirs that cover so extensively the minutiae of training schedules or deconstruct so meticulously the finer details of competitive performances. And surely fewer still contain a whole section devoted to Abraham Maslow's theory of the five levels to self-actualisation?[13]

Experience and inclination, then, buttressed Hemery's belief that athletes should reap some financial benefit from their effort and talent. Everyone, he insisted, including sportsmen and women should be allowed to 'make a living from doing

13 Interestingly, Hemery's rigorously scientific approach to sport did not appear to extend to nutrition. His pre-race diet remained, throughout his career, 'Cadbury's chocolate and a Coke'.

something they both enjoy and do well'. But, as the athletics authorities, most notably the IOC, took a very different view on the matter, he was forced to find new sporting challenges if he was going to cash in on his fame. He had a brief flirtation with the International Track Association (ITA), a short-lived experiment in professional track and field, and a rather lengthier involvement with a new TV show, *Britain's Sporting Superstars*.[14] First broadcast by the BBC in December 1973, the sole aim of *Superstars* was, apparently, to conclusively prove what most of the viewing public already intuitively knew: that heavyweight boxers make very poor steeplechasers and First Division footballers should, at all costs, steer clear of cycle racing. Hemery, however, was particularly adept at the format and took the £4,000 first prize in the inaugural show, although his habit of tackling the water jump headfirst in the 600m steeplechase proved to be something of a drawback in later editions.

But it was away from the competitive arena that Hemery had the greatest bearing on the future direction of athletics. After the Munich Olympics he was one of a small group of leading athletes who wrote an open letter to the BAAB calling for the 'complete revision' of the administrative structure as the 'current, part-time, amateur establishment are no longer equal to the task'.[15] Although the dead hand of bureaucracy ensured reform would be some time

14 Formed in America after the Munich Olympics, the ITA failed to attract much interest from television companies and folded after just four years.

15 The other three athletes involved were long-jumper Lynn Davies, Scottish sprinter Les Piggot and Hemery's fellow hurdler Alan Pascoe. Pascoe recalled, as a result of the protest, the athletics authorities made him feel like 'a combination of Che Guevara, Arthur Scargill and Tariq Ali' – a heady brew indeed!

in coming, the letter was an important step in highlighting just how critical the situation was. And, paradoxically, it was Hemery's impeccable reputation as an amateur that mobilised the media to the cause of professionalism. 'If David Hemery, this almost unreal Corinthian, thinks something is wrong,' the *Daily Mirror*'s Frank McGhee reasoned, 'then I am prepared to believe it is wrong.' Just over quarter of a century later, having been elected president of UK Athletics, the sports newly reconstituted governing body, Hemery was finally in a position to guide British athletics into the modern commercial age.[11]

Although less involved in the high politics of athletics governance, Brendan Foster was no less important than Hemery when it came to identifying and exploiting the economic opportunities of open competition. At a time when British athletics was in the doldrums, Foster, our only track and field medallist in the 1976 Montreal Games, gave fans something to get excited about. Born in Hebburn, County Durham, it was not until his final year studying chemistry at Sussex University that he really broke through into the ranks of the elite with a win in the annual triangular match between British Universities, the English Cross-County Union and the Combined Services. From there his progress was rapid. He took 1,500m bronze at the Commonwealth Games in 1970 and the European Championships in 1971, before, in August 1973, breaking the world record for two miles in front of an excited home crowd at the Crystal Palace International.

But it was 1974, the year he won SPOTY, that proved to be Foster's best season. Having already broken the world record for 3,000m in the inaugural meeting of his home track in Gateshead, he travelled to Rome in August for the European Championships 5,000m and a showdown with the great Lasse Viren, Finland's reigning Olympic champion and world-record holder. Taking the lead from the gun, Foster, by 3,000m, with only Viren for company, had broken clear of the rest of the field. Then, glancing briefly behind to check on the Finn, the British favourite threw in his trademark 'hard lap' and quickly found himself away on his own. Unchallenged for the rest of the race, by the finish he was over 60 metres clear. At last British distance running seemed to have found a worthy successor to the golden generation of the 1950s. 'Not since Kuts in Berne twenty years ago,' *Athletics Weekly* enthused, 'had a European field been humiliated in this manner.' Foster's exploits made him a household name. An indication of just how famous he had become, and the greatest accolade he ever received, he claimed in his autobiography, was the chance to star in a specially arranged 3,000m at Wembley as part of the build-up to the FA Cup Final between Liverpool and Newcastle United. Decked out in the black and white of his home team, Foster, of course, comfortably won; and Newcastle, of course, comfortably lost.

Foster never quite rose to the heights of his SPOTY-winning year again. Yet, in many ways, his most significant contributions to British athletics still lay in the future. Although he turned down the chance to join the professional International Track Association circuit – 'I would have found it hard to muster the enthusiasm to train hard for a race against an electronically paced spotlight' – he was, nonetheless, fully aware of just how marketable top-flight athletics was. In helping to establish the Gateshead Games in the 1970s and the Great North Run in the 1980s, he was anticipating two of the staples of modern commercial running: the elite spectacle of the Diamond League and the grassroots enthusiasm of mass-participation road racing.

After his 3,000m world record in 1974, Foster had promised the *Daily Express*: 'That was just the start. Dave Bedford and I have big plans to put the sport back on top.' And, to an extent, he fulfilled this pledge. His own efforts organising events in the North East, and Bedford's marketing work with the London Marathon, did undoubtedly help to reshape and revitalise athletics. But, for performances on the track to reach the heights of Chataway and Pirie once again, the British public had to wait until the end of the decade when the rivalry between two new, precociously talented young athletes over the classic distance of one mile captured the attention of a worldwide audience.[16] ***12***

Steve Ovett and Sebastian Coe, SPOTY winners in 1978 and 1979 respectively, dominated middle-distance running in the late 1970s and early 1980s. Their rivalry not only helped to restore the reputation of British athletics but also hastened the demise of amateurism. And, of course, it divided a nation. The two were, according to the sportswriter Pat Butcher, 'as distinct as Apollo and Dionysus'. Although few outside the ranks of Nietzschean scholars would, perhaps, have quite expressed it in those terms, the contrast between Coe and Ovett was certainly stark. On the track, they could not have been more different. Ovett, physically dominating, supremely confident, was never happier than when

16 Pat Butcher, the veteran athletics correspondent, considers the mile to be 'the perfect distance', long enough to have a narrative arc without the 'tactical ennui' of long distance or the 'witless energy' of sprint races.

mixing it in the rough and tumble of a racing pack. While for the slightly built Coe, it was in fast-run races, where opponents quickly became strung out, that his gift for effortless high pace was best revealed.

But, as the historian Dominic Sandbrook has rightly noted, the difference between the two was about much more than physicality. In an increasingly polarised Britain, in which the post-war consensus between Labour and the Conservatives seemed to be breaking down, to support Coe or Ovett was to make a statement about your identity. Ovett was the brash, working-class maverick, who raced in a Soviet vest and was contemptuously dismissive of both the athletic authorities and the sporting press. He might not quite have been a real-life version of Smith, Alan Sillitoe's rebel in *The Loneliness of the Long Distance Runner*, but he was not far off it. By contrast, the smooth, well-mannered Coe, with the veneer of a public schoolboy, appeared the epitome of the smart, young Tory. The fear for many, as Simon Barnes of *The Times* put it, was what might happen to 'the lovely Sebastian' when he met 'the horrid bully' Ovett.

Of course, these characterisations were, to a large extent, press constructs. As the socialist barrister and author of an engagingly impressionistic account of the Coe/Ovett years, David Renton, has pointed out, there was much that connected the two athletes. Both were students, both served their sporting apprenticeships in the schools and county systems, and both had their early careers shaped by a dominant parent – for Coe, his father (and coach), Peter, and for Ovett, his mother, Gay. Even the much-hyped class difference between the market trader's boy and the company executive's son was overstated. It was Ovett who was the southern grammar schoolboy, while Coe went to a secondary modern in Sheffield, hardly an engine of privilege and exclusivity.

But, no matter how similar their backgrounds, there was no love lost between the two. To Coe, Ovett was a poor role model. 'I really cannot condone so much of Steve's behaviour on and off the track,' he rather priggishly stated in his 1981 autobiography. 'He is without question a wonderful athlete … but he does conduct himself in a way which has often left so much to be desired. He should not belittle inferior opponents in lesser races the way he sometimes has. That is sheer bad manners.' In return, Ovett felt Coe was simply unpleasant. He vividly recalled a brief exchange with the Sheffield athlete immediately after the 1,500m final at the Moscow Olympics. 'Oh good,' Coe, the now happy owner of a gold as well as a silver medal, had responded to the news that his arch-rival had won bronze to add to his 800m gold. 'I know those two words had a double meaning,' Ovett darkly observed, 'but I have the memory of the way he said it. They tell me more about the man than the race did.'

Although Coe went on to have the more successful championship record, it was Ovett who initially seemed to hold the greater promise. Born in Brighton to a tight-knit working-class family, he was a prodigiously talented youngster across a range of distances. He broke 50 seconds for 400m when he was only 15, ran a sub-four-minute mile at 17, and won the under-20 National Cross Country Championship by over half a minute as a 19-year-old. As a senior he continued in the same vein. In 1977 he sandwiched victories in the European and World Cup 1,500m finals with an impromptu visit to Dartford to defeat a (no doubt dumbfounded) field of international road racers at the inaugural 'Winlighters' half marathon. It was a feat that must have had distance coaches across the country tearing up their training manuals in bewilderment. By the end of 1978, at just 23, he had won 1,500m gold and 800m silver at the European Championships, broken Brendan Foster's world record over two miles, and not been defeated in the metric mile for over 18 months (a run that was to continue until the Moscow Olympics in 1980).

Possibly even more remarkable than the victories themselves was the manner in which they were achieved. Ovett seemed to be having fun. In the increasingly dour world of high-performance athletics, this was unusual indeed. Even in defeat (a rare occurrence during this period), the Brighton athlete's happy-go-lucky cheeriness remained undented. Edged into a surprise second place by the intriguingly muscled East German Olaf Beyer in the 1978 European Championships 800m, Ovett's instinctive response was a smile, a nonchalant shrug of the shoulders and a wave to his mum and dad in the stands.[17] But, of course, more enjoyable still was winning. Watching him again on YouTube, as he exuberantly gesticulates to an ecstatic Crystal Palace crowd while effortlessly accelerating away from Henry Rono to break the two-mile world record, it is hard not to be struck by the sheer pleasure he is obviously taking from the moment.

Not everyone, however, was won over by Ovett's brand of carefree nonconformism. Predictably, the athletics authorities found dealing with their fiercely independent star performer a challenge. In particular, the BAAB's insistence that it should

17 In the tunnel immediately after the race, Ovett is reported to have leaned towards Coe, who finished third, and conspiratorially whispered, 'Who the fuck was that?'

have the final say over an athlete's international racing schedule strained relations to near breaking point. More unexpected, maybe, was Ovett's spectacular falling-out with the press. Once again, overseas commitments were at the heart of the furore. Having just been crowned national champion over 800m in August 1975, he told journalists at the obligatory post-race press conference that he would have to miss the upcoming Europa Cup Final because it clashed with his then girlfriend's British debut in the European Junior Championships. This was too much for the *Daily Mail*'s man, former RAF pilot Terry O'Connor. Possibly confirming for some that he was indeed the inspiration for *Private Eye*'s archetypal drunken journalist, 'Lunchtime O'Booze', O'Connor let his professional veneer slip. 'You're not going to be competing for your country,' he disbelievingly spluttered, 'because you're going to be following some bird around Europe.' It was six years before Ovett attended another press conference. Even as late as 1998 he emphatically told one TV interviewer, who had asked if there was anyone in the media he trusted, 'No, no one.'

What was remarkable, then, about the BBC's traditional review of the sporting year in 1978 was not that Ovett won SPOTY, but that he was actually there to collect the trophy. His media boycott had forced the programme's producers to break protocol and tell him in advance that he had topped the public vote – and even then his mother refused to attend! For the publicity-shy winner there were other, admittedly more mundane, concerns praying on his mind. He didn't own a suit and he hated giving speeches. Both issues, however, were swiftly resolved by those two constants of life in late 1970s Britain: Marks and Spencer and wildcat strikes. Nattily turned out in one of M&S's

best, and clutching the trophy he had moments earlier received from Prince Charles, the newly crowned people's champion just had time to mutter thank you before floor technicians pulled the plug and walked off set in protest over pay. For the next SPOTY winner, though, the Winter of Discontent was about to turn into a summer of unparalleled record-breaking.***13***

Compared with Ovett, Sebastian Coe was a late developer. It was not until 1977, in his first year as an economics undergraduate at Loughborough University, that he really broke through at international level. In March he won the European Indoor 800m in a new British record and six months later claimed the outdoor record for the same event. His progress from then on was electric. In September 1978 he became the first British man to break 1:44 for 800m, and the following year, in the space of just 41 days, he took the world records for the 800m, 1,500m and mile, the first athlete to hold all three marks simultaneously.[18] The press was jubilant. In the clean-cut, well-spoken and, critically, media-friendly, young Loughborough student, it had at last found the antidote to the surly, non-communicative Ovett. Gleefully insisting that Coe must now be 'indisputably the world's greatest middle-distance runner', the *Daily Mirror*'s sports editor could not resist a brutal twist of the knife: 'How does that feel, Steve?' For BBC *Grandstand*'s veteran frontman, Frank Bough, the new track star's combination of telegenic good looks and polished articulacy was all nearly too much. Turning back to face the viewing public

18 In the mid-1960s, the great American runner Jim Ryun did hold the records for the half mile, 1,500m and mile at the same time, but his estimated time for 800m (1:44.3) during the half-mile race was never ratified as a world record.

after concluding an onscreen interview with Coe, Bough gazed longingly down the camera and gently purred, 'What a very attractive young man.'[19]

But not everyone was so besotted. He may be 'an inspiration on the track', thought one *Daily Mail* reader from Macclesfield, 'but he has all the personality of the speaking clock'. And although it was universally agreed that Coe in full flow, ethereally gliding over the track, was a beautiful sight, some found it difficult to fathom the nature of his relationship with his father and coach, Peter. An executive at a Sheffield steel firm, with no background in athletics, Peter Coe appeared to outsiders to approach coaching his gifted son with the same scientific detachment he might apply to one of his work's engineering projects. Their habit of addressing each other as 'Peter' and 'my athlete' did little to make the set-up seem any more conventional. In fact, as Seb noted in his autobiography, one of the key reasons the arrangement worked so well was the ability he and his father had to compartmentalise their professional relationship and their family life. Certainly, whatever reservations there may have been about the arrangement were not enough to prevent the public from comfortably placing the triple world-record holder ahead of Ian 'Beefy' Botham as BBC sports personality for 1979.

One of the great regrets for athletics fans at the end of the 70s was that the nation's two all-conquering track champions had only raced each other on two occasions, and one of those was over

19 Subsequent revelations about Bough's predilection for 'spank'n'wank' parties have not helped make this incident seem any less odd.

the country in a schoolboy race.[20] But, a year after Coe's SPOTY triumph, a showdown was finally on the cards. And this time it wasn't going to be over some muddy fields in Hillingdon but on the greatest stage of all, in the Luzhniki Stadium at the Moscow Olympics. At least that was the plan. The Soviet invasion of Afghanistan, and America's subsequent resolve to use sport as a lever in Cold War politics, placed Britain's participation in the Games in jeopardy. The Thatcher government tried everything it could to persuade athletes not to go. The Scottish sprinter Allan Wells recalled receiving six increasingly unnerving letters from No. 10, 'the last of which included a picture of a young girl sprawled dead on the ground with a doll lying six inches from her fingertips'. For once, however, the sport's authorities chose to exert their independence and a British team was sent to Moscow, albeit under the neutral flag of the Olympic Movement.[21]

Once the Games got underway, the action was all the waiting public could have hoped for. In a physical 800m final, Ovett unexpectedly triumphed against a tactically naïve Coe. The Loughborough man looked devasted. Clearly not comforted by his father's appraisal of the race – 'You ran like a cunt' – Coe found it difficult to mask his disappointment as he received his silver medal. Standing on the podium with the haunted look of a recent trauma victim, he accepted Ovett's handshake, the TV critic Clive James observed, 'as if he had been handed a cold turd'. Five days later,

---

20 In the 1972 English Schools Cross-Country Championships, Ovett finished second and Coe tenth.

21 The BBC also resisted pressure to have a Games blackout but did reduce its coverage from 180 to just 40 hours. The government did, however, get some measure of revenge, and no track and field Olympic champion appeared in the New Year Honours List.

though, he got his revenge in the 1,500m. Running, it seemed, on pure anger, he accelerated away to victory in the home straight while an off-the-boil Ovett had to settle for third. It was not just Coe who was relieved by the result. For the *Daily Mail*, decency had prevailed. Coe's run in the 1,500m had, it loftily asserted, 'lifted the soul, ennobled his art and dignified his country'.

Both athletes continued breaking records the year after their triumphs in Moscow, but then injuries and illnesses began to take their toll. Ovett never seemed to recover fully from a serious knee injury after running into some church railings in December 1981, and Coe had a lengthy lay-off when he was diagnosed with toxoplasmosis in 1983. Much to the disappointment of the viewing millions, the 1984 Los Angeles Olympics were not destined to be a repeat of the drama four years earlier. Although Coe was back to his best, winning silver in the 800m and retaining his 1,500m title, a bronchial infection, combined with the City of Angels' famous smog, landed a distraught Ovett, who had miraculously qualified for both middle-distance finals, in hospital. Like a couple of old boxers recalling their glory days, the two met for a final track showdown in the 1989 AAA 1,500m final. Incredibly, it was the first time they had raced each other on a British track. The result was largely immaterial (although possibly not to Coe, who won). If the race held any significance, it was as a reminder of what had been lost. Rather like the Cold War itself, the rivalry between these two supreme athletes had been played out as a proxy conflict, fought indirectly with world records and personal bests.

Of course, there was a very good reason why Coe and Ovett had only raced one another six times as seniors, each occasion being a championship final: money. With their careers coinciding with the sport's transition to professionalism, it made commercial sense to keep the public guessing about who was the better runner rather than race and provide a definitive answer. Or certainly, if they were going to race, the price had to be right. It irked Ovett, for example, that he and Coe could 'fill a stadium of their own' but had to race the Moscow Olympic 800m final 'for nothing'. And, with results in Moscow failing to settle the debate about who was top dog, both athletes were determined to cash in on the continuing fascination with their rivalry. In May 1982, Mark McCormack's International Management Group, the sports marketing firm that had just recently signed up Coe, negotiated a three-race head-to-head series, sponsored by Citizen Watches.[22] It would, said Ovett at a promotional press conference, be reminiscent of the clashes between Walter George and William Cummings, the two most famous professional athletes of the late Victorian age. It was a comparison that would have had the recently deceased Burghley and Abrahams spinning in their graves.

In the end, injury resulted in the cancellation of all three races, but the very fact that the series had been approved showed just how far along the road to outright professionalism athletics had already travelled. Even in the late 1970s, when cash payments were still outlawed, Coe occasionally pocketed appearance fees worth more than his termly student grant, while Ovett would happily race for '$200 and an air ticket or two'. It was 'a murky

22 The three races were to be a 3,000m at Crystal Place on 17 July, followed by an 800m in Nice on 14 August, and concluding with the mile in Eugene at the end of September.

world,' Seb recalled 40 years later, 'where honest men were forced to become dishonest'. The two great rivals might have agreed that amateurism had had its day but, inevitably perhaps, they came to their positions from very different starting points. For Ovett, ever the working-class hero, it was a matter of righting the social injustices of the past. The amateur code, he argued not without justification, was part of 'an outdated English way of life created to protect the gentleman from the artisan'. Coe, by contrast, was inspired by the opportunities of the present. 'I'm a great believer in personal liberty,' he told one interviewer, 'and I do believe in the interplay of market forces. If anybody is good enough and in demand in whatever field they are in, then you will find people are prepared to pay. And if somebody can make a living out of what they are good at, I don't really see what grounds anybody can say no.' It was pure Thatcher.

Paradoxically, then, Britain's last two great track champions of the amateur era looked both to the past and the future. By proving, as the *Daily Express* insisted, 'that we can still take on the world and win', Coe and Ovett seemed to be throwbacks to the triumphal days of Chataway, Pirie and Bannister – or even (surely *The Express* would not dare?) to the past glories of Clive, Rhodes and Livingstone. Yet, in their ruthless pursuit of individual excellence, they were also representatives of the new, highly competitive, socially atomised landscape of late-20th-century Britain. Their rivalry ushered in a sporting world, so far removed from the Corinthianism of the immediate post-war years that the next athlete to win SPOTY could unblushingly assert, 'Winning is the only prize anybody cares about.'[14]

Chapter Notes

5 BBC1, *Sports Personality of the Year*, broadcast 19 December 2010; Steve Rider, *BBC Sports Personality of the Year: 50th Anniversary* (2003), p.250–251; Dick Booth, *The Impossible Hero: A Biography of Gordon 'Puff Puff' Pirie* (1999), p.44, 85, 101, 120; Adrian Smith and Dilwyn Porter (eds), *Amateurs and Professionals in Post-War British Sport* (2000), pp.88, 95–96; Richard Holt and Tony Mason, *Sport in Britain, 1945–2000* (2000), p.43–46; Pat Butcher, *The Perfect Distance: Ovett and Coe, the Record-Breaking Rivalry* (2012), ch.17; Jack Crump, *Running Round the World* (1966), p.84, 117.

6 Andrew Boyd Hutchinson, *The Complete History of Cross-Country Running* (2018), p.3; Booth, *Impossible Hero*, pp.118–119; *Daily Mail*, 25 July 1952, 14 October 1954, 31 December 1954; *Sunday Times*, 13 June 1954; Dominic Sandbrook, *White Heat: A History of Britain in the Swinging Sixties* (2006), p.441; Holt, *Sport and the British*, pp.278–279; *Daily Mirror*, 14 October 1954; Rider, *BBC Sports Personality of the Year*, pp.10–11.

7 *Picture Post*, 10 December 1956, 26 November 1956, 2 January 1954, 7 November 1953; Booth, *Impossible Hero*, pp.95, 143, 223, 334; Dominic Sandbrook, *Never Had it So Good: A History of Britain from Suez to the Beatles* (2005), p.275; Gordon Pirie, *Running Wild* (1961), p.85; *Daily Express*, 10 May 1960, 29 December 1955, 13 October 1955; Smith and Porter, *Amateurs and Professionals*, pp.101–103; 'Pirie Beats Zatopek', Pathé News, 14 October 1955; *Daily Mirror*, 29 December 1955; *Observer*, 5 May 1957.

8 Lynne Duval, 'The Development of women's track and field in England', *Sports Historian* (2001), p.33; Mary Peters, *Mary P. Autobiography* (1974), p.55; Holt and Mason, *Sport in Britain*, p.46; Dorothy Hyman, *Sprint to Fame* (1964), pp.66, 117–122; *Daily Mirror*, 19 December 1963; 23 February 1960, 18 October 1954; *Daily Mail*, 4 March 1960; British Library Oral Archive, interview with Dorothy Hyman, August 1999.

9 Mary Rand, *Mary, Mary: Autobiography of an Olympic Champion* (1969), pp.33–34, 109–115; *Daily Express*, 22 September 1961, 9 May 1961; *Daily Mail*, 14 August 1961; *Times*, 15 October 1964; *Sunday Times*, 27 December 1964.

10 Peters, *Mary P: Autobiography*, p.43; pp.84–93; Smith and Porter, *Amateurs and Professionals*, p.87; p.105; *Guardian*, 7 March 2020;

Butcher, *The Perfect Distance*, ch.18; British Library oral archive, interview with Mary Peters, 24 January 1997.

11 Jeremy Crump, 'Athletics', in Mason (ed.), *Sport in Britain*, p.48; Smith and Porter, *Amateurs and Professionals*, pp.89, 103; BL oral archive, interview with David Hemery, January 2000; David Hemery, *Another Hurdle* (1976), pp.6–20, 101–131; Rider, *BBC Sports Personality of the Year*, pp.72–73; Holt and Mason, *Sport in Britain*, p.47; David Goldblatt, *The Games: A Global History of the Olympics* (2016), pp.281–286; *Daily Mirror*, 15 December 1972.

12 Brendan Foster and Cliff Temple, *Brendan Foster* (1978), pp.112–123, Holt and Mason, *Sport in Britain*, p.143; Goldblatt, *Games*, p.290; *Daily Express*, 3 August 1974.

13 Pat Butcher, *The Perfect Distance*, chs.2, 13; *Times*, 11 August 1984; Dominic Sandbrook, *Who Dares Wins*, pp.625–626; Alwyn Turner, *Rejoice, Rejoice*, p.22; David Renton, *Lives: Running, 'The Grimace'*; Sebastian Coe and David Miller, *Running Free* (1981), p.51; Steve Ovett and John Rodda (1984), *Ovett: An Autobiography*, pp.72, 96; Sebastian Coe, *Running My Life* (2012), p.80; Randolph Northam, 'We will never see their like again' (June 2008), www.sportsjournalists.co.uk/sja-news/sja-1948-2008/we-will-never-see-their-like-again/; Rider, *BBC Sports Personality of the Year*, pp.118–122.

14 Butcher, *Perfect Distance*, chs.4, 11, 16, 18, 22; *Daily Mirror*, 18 July 1979; LWT, *Ovett*, dir. John Sheppard (1982); *Daily Mail*, 16 December 1978; Renton, *Lives: Running, 'The Grimace', 'The Red Vest'*; Sandbrook, *Who Dares Wins*, pp.626–628, 718–720; Observer, 27 July 1980; Ovett and Rodda, *Ovett*, pp.168–170; Coe, *Running My Life*, p.88; *Daily Express*, 3 November 1979; Skip Rozen, Daley Thompson: *The Subject is Winning* (1983), pp.7–8.

Chapter 2

Athletics: The Professionals

Daley Thompson (1982) – Steve Cram (1983) – Fatima Whitbread (1987) –

Liz McColgan (1991) – Linford Christie (1993) – Jonathan Edwards (1995) – Paula Radcliffe (2002) – Kelly Holmes (2004) – Mo Farah (2017)

AT THE 54th Academy Awards in 1982 there was something of a surprise. A British film, seemingly suffused with a sense of nostalgic patriotism, defied all the odds and the crowd-pleasing heroics of action-man archaeologist Indiana Jones in the *Raiders of the Lost Ark*, to take the best picture award. *Chariots of Fire* told the story of two little-known British athletes, Harold Abrahams, the son of a Jewish immigrant, and Eric Liddell, a devout Christian, as they prepared for the 1924 Paris Olympics. But for all its scenes of rugged public-school alumni training on windswept beaches or careering round gothic Cambridge cloisters, *Chariots* was not meant to be a paean to an imagined glorious past. Rather it was, at least in the eyes of the film's Labour-supporting director David Puttnam, and 'romantic socialist' screenwriter Colin Welland, the story of two outsiders who found the courage to take on Establishment hypocrisy.

The reviewer for the *Evening Standard* may have thought the film championed 'love of country, fear of God, loyalty to team … and becoming modesty in the moment of victory', but the screenplay's pivotal scene delivered a very different message. Abrahams, who has taken on the services of a professional coach in the pursuit of Paris gold, finds himself unable to control his temper as he is berated by two Cambridge dons for betraying sport's amateur ideals. 'Yours,' he snaps at his dinner-suited hosts, 'are the archaic values of the prep school playground. You deceive no one but yourselves. I believe in the pursuit of excellence and I will carry the future with me.' It was a sentiment that would have had any budding British Olympians huddled in their local Odeon silently cheering in support.

As athletics entered the 1980s, the reactionary ideals of the sport's administrators, which had so angered Abrahams 60 years earlier, were becoming increasingly untenable. As ever, money was at the heart of the problem. The growing demands of the international circuit required athletes to train full-time if they were to have any chance of success. A few airline tickets and the occasional brown envelope stuffed with cash was no longer enough to persuade young men and women to devote their lives to athletic excellence.

With demands for professionalism becoming ever louder, the first step on the road to reform occurred in 1982 when the IAAF sanctioned trust funds for athletes. After that the whole amateur edifice quickly collapsed. Within five years the IOC had removed the word 'amateur' from its charter, and by 1995 the organisers of the top 15 Grand Prix meetings were offering over £10m in appearance fees alone.

Although this money did not extend much beyond the very best, the incentive was still enough to open up the sport to a new demographic.

In particular, as the sports historians Richard Holt and Tony Mason have noted, without the introduction of professionalism it was hard to see how athletes from poorer backgrounds, especially those of Afro-Caribbean heritage, could have afforded to compete at the highest level. The statistics appear to confirm this view. Only two of the British team for the 1969 European Athletics Championships were black. By contrast, at the 1987 World Championships in Rome, over a third of the British contingent were of Afro-Caribbean origin. The same pattern can be discerned in SPOTY. Before the advent of trust funds, nine athletes topped the poll and all were from white, British backgrounds; the same was true for only four of the nine winners after 1982.[15]

The first athlete to win SPOTY in the professional era was very much a standard-bearer for this new wave of young talent that was reinvigorating athletics from the 1980s onwards. Born to a Nigerian father and a Scottish mother, Daley Thompson was one of the first black British athletes to break through as a global star.

Even more remarkably, he did it in an event at which the country had never won an Olympic medal. The decathlon was, according to Steve Ovett, 'nine Mickey Mouse events and a slow 1,500m'. It was a view with which many of the public at the time, uninitiated in the complexities of multi-event scoring tables, would have had more than a little sympathy.[23]

Even the sport's administrators seemed to share Ovett's opinion. The decathlon was rarely included in the programme for international fixtures and was invariably relegated to a separate day and an empty stadium for the AAA championships. It was hardly surprising, then, that Thompson bridled when the authorities tried to interfere with his training programme and dictate his competitive schedule. Told, in 1981, that his sports aid grant was conditional on competing at the European Combined Events Cup in Birmingham, he chose 'to cut my nose off to spite my face' and not attend. The dispute soured his relations with the sport's governing body for the rest of his career.

Thompson's relationship with the press was equally strained. Journalists, he felt, 'simply don't do their homework'. 'Most,' he told one biographer, 'don't know what the decathlon's ten events are; even fewer can list them in the order they are contested.'[24] In return, the press pool regarded Thompson as 'objectionable, charmless and rude'. The *Sunday Times* ranked him No. 8 in 'Sporting Awkward Customers', one place ahead of Steve Ovett but (small mercies) a few slots behind 'Super Brat' John McEnroe and Eric 'Kung-Fu' Cantona.

Yet, although Daley was undoubtedly shabbily treated by many sports correspondents, much of the negative coverage was

23 Thompson himself was a reluctant decathlete. It was only when he won the decathlon at the AAA Junior Championships in 1975 that he was persuaded by his coach to abandon sprinting in favour of multi-eventing.

24 Should any journalists be reading, the events are (in order): 100m, long jump, shot put, high jump, 400m, 110m hurdles, discus, pole vault, javelin and 1,500m.

self-inflicted. His 'athleticism and competitiveness are unrivalled', observed Jon Rodda of *The Guardian*, 'but when he leaves the arena he runs-up a points record in disaster'. This was never more apparent than during the Los Angeles Olympics in 1984. Having won over the crowd with a mesmerisingly nonchalant world-record performance, he then proceeded to undermine all his good work. He first contrived to turn a trackside chat with Princess Anne into a joke about starting a family together and hoping the baby would be white. This was swiftly followed up by telling a straitlaced American news reporter that he had not been 'this happy since my grandmother caught her tit in a mangle'. And, to cap it all off, he arrived at the obligatory press conference sporting a T-shirt with the slogan: 'Is the world's second greatest athlete gay?' – a not so veiled reference to rumours that Carl Lewis might (perish the thought!) be homosexual.[25] The media was distinctly unimpressed. 'Champ Chump' was the *Daily Mirror*'s headline, while the usually forgiving Chris Brasher of *The Observer* felt Thompson's behaviour amounted to no more than a 'third-rate cabaret act … in the poorest taste'.

Even in retirement, the unerring knack of hitting the wrong note was never lost. 'This isn't meant to be derogatory,' he told his fellow pundits after seeing a poorish javelin throw from Katarina Johnson-Thompson at the 2015 World Championships, 'but she throws like a girl.' 'You run like a decathlete' was Paula Radcliffe's withering response.

---

25 Thompson remained unrepentant about the T-shirt. 'You have to differentiate yourself,' he told the *Mirror*'s Mike Walters some years later. But the explanation did little to appease Richard Smith, the associate editor of *Gay Times*, who bluntly insisted the slogan was proof that Thompson was a 'homophobic cunt'.

Yet, for all his missteps with the media, Thompson remained a favourite with the wider public. His combination of irreverence and brilliance, determination and relaxation was, for many, irresistible. Although held up as a role model for other young black men, he refused to be anything other than himself. 'What do you want to talk to me for?' he told one researcher on black sports people. 'I'm not black. I'm just Daley Thompson.' And it was as Daley that he seemed to capture the mood of the times so perfectly – confident, ambitious, unfettered by tradition.

But, of course, his popularity was dependent on his ability. He may not, *The Guardian*'s Rob Bagchi noted, 'always have been as warm as he seemed but he was always as good as he looked'. Having made his breakthrough with victory at the Commonwealth Games in 1978, he announced his arrival on the global stage two years later with a world record in Götzis, followed by gold at Moscow. A natural showman, Thompson revelled in his newfound status as Olympic champion. He hosted TV shows, offered advice in fitness magazines, starred in his own computer game (*Daley's Decathlon*), and even managed a third-place finish in SPOTY behind two other Olympic champions, Robin Cousins and Seb Coe.

With the Commonwealth and Olympic titles secured, Daley's stated ambition for the 1982 season was to 'search for perfection'. He found it in Athens at the European Championships. Having exchanged world records with the 6ft 7in West German Jürgen Hingsen early on in the season, Athens was billed as the ultimate showdown between the world's two best all-round athletes. Such was the interest back in Britain that the BBC took the unprecedented step of delaying *To the Manor Born* by 17 minutes to show the clash's climactic denouement, the 1,500m. Needing to run the last lap in under 67 seconds to take back the world record, Thompson, for once, sacrificed appearance for effort and came home to beat Hingsen by nearly 200 points and the record by over 50.

Although he went on to win further titles, not least at the World Championships in 1983 and the Olympic Games in 1984, it was in Athens in 1982 that Daley was, perhaps, at his supreme best. It was fitting, therefore, that this was the year he was crowned SPOTY champion. Yet, even as he accepted the trophy from Sir Garfield Sobers, the new people's favourite could not avoid controversy. Modelling what Alan Partridge would call 'the sports casual look', he opened his acceptance speech with: 'The first thing I would like to say is that I feel shit.' It was, undeniably, a break from the usual list of thank yous, but one that the *Sunday Times* estimated cost him £250,000 in potential sponsorship.

But for all the media run-ins and controversial press conferences, the moment that best summed up Thompson's career occurred, appropriately, on the track in Athens at the 1982 European Championships. It was perfectly captured by the sports photographer Steve Powell. Daley is standing at the finish of the 1,500m, hands on hips, looking down on his exhausted rivals lying prone on the track. It is an image of utter supremacy. Predictably, the subject himself will allow no hero-worshipping. 'I was bloody knackered,' he told one interviewer who asked him about the photograph. 'I was just looking for a place to fall, but there wasn't any room.' Brilliance and bathos. It was Daley all over.[16]

The year after Daley's triumph, the public once again looked to athletics for the SPOTY winner, but this time it returned to the sport's traditional roots of distance running. Yet Steve Cram was still something of an outsider. The Coe/Ovett duopoly, which had dominated British middle-distance running since the mid-70s, seemed set to remain unchallenged well into the 1980s. Admittedly, avid readers of specialist running magazines might have been aware of a prodigiously talented youngster from the North East who was smashing age-group records with remarkable regularity, but even they could not have anticipated the speed with which the 'Jarrow Arrow' would break through at senior level.[26] In 1980, aged just 19, he made the Olympic 1,500m final in Moscow, and two years later, with Coe and Ovett sidelined by injury, he took the Commonwealth and European titles for the same distance. It had, by any standards, been a meteoric rise but, as *Athletics Weekly* quickly reminded its readers, 'you know who and the other fellow weren't around to put the young pretender in his place'.

The inaugural World Championships in Helsinki the following year presented the perfect opportunity for Cram to prove he was no Bonnie Prince Charlie. Advised by fellow Geordie Brendan Foster, on the morning of the 1,500m final, that the young Moroccan Said Aouita would go to the front with about a lap to go, the British hopeful executed the perfect race. Mercilessly tracking Aouita down the back straight, Cram hit the front with 200m to go and held off the experienced American Steve Scott and a fast finishing but, for once, tactically naïve Steve

26 Cram broke the British 1,500m record for a 16-year-old in 1977 and the world mile best for a 17-year-old the following year.

Ovett to take the title.[27] The feeling as he crossed the line, the new world champion recalled, was 'just like Sunderland winning the FA Cup'. An allusion that maybe only Bob Stokoe would have fully appreciated.

Cram had now proved, insisted *Athletics Weekly*, that he was not the world's best 'by default'. But not everyone agreed. Ovett's return to form with a new world 1,500m record in Rieti, just three weeks after Helsinki, gave voice to those who demanded a run-off to determine the top spot. To his immense credit, Cram accepted the challenge. 'You can kid yourself as to how good you are,' he told one journalist, 'but you've got to go and put yourself on the line.' It was a refreshing change after the Cold War of the Coe and Ovett era. The venue for what was billed as 'the mile of the year' was the end-of-season Coca-Cola meeting at Crystal Palace. The race was a classic. As the starter's pistol fired and the pacemakers disappeared into the distance, Cram and Ovett eyed each other like two wary sprint cyclists. Steadily working their way through the field, the duo caught the leaders with two laps to go before Cram, shadowed by Ovett, finally hit the front with 400m remaining. Ovett seemed poised to strike at any moment but could not quite draw level. A last despairing lunge at the line cut the gap to less than a metre, but the world champion had finally proven himself worthy of his title.

The press was in raptures. It was, thought *The Guardian*, 'a vintage reminder of what racing should be about', while the *Daily Mirror* hailed the clash as 'one of the greatest head-to-head races

27 Scott finished second, Aouita third and an out-of-sorts Ovett fourth. A viral infection had ruled Coe out for the whole season.

in track history'. 'The real winner,' insisted Neil Wilson in the *Daily Mail*, 'was the sport.' Not according to Cram. 'I've won!' was the *Daily Express*'s front-page headline above a picture of the jubilant Jarrow athlete.

The *Sunday Times* was keen to quantify exactly what success meant for 'Britain's new golden boy'. 'Temptingly lucrative offers' must now be pouring in, suggested the paper's chief athletics correspondent, Cliff Temple. 'Well, the guy in the newsagents said I could have the papers for free. Oh, and I've been bought a couple of pints' was all Cram was prepared to concede. But, of course, his breakthrough had come at just the right time. He was, estimated one journalist, earning upwards of £100,000 a year from racing alone. Indeed, such was his pulling power in this period that his wedding, in December 1983, was televised live on ITV's *World of Sport* (where it must have made a pleasant change from the wrestling with Big Daddy and Giant Haystacks) and covered from inside the church by BBC Radio Newcastle's outside broadcast team. The *Daily Mail*'s Elizabeth Cowley might not have been a fully paid-up member of the Cram fan club, but maybe the 'bland innocence', which she found so unappealing, was in fact the secret to his popularity. After the wearing showmanship of Daley Thompson, Cram's down-to-earth approach to the sport was, for many, a welcome change. Certainly, that seems to have held true for SPOTY voters, who relegated Daley, our only other world champion from Helsinki, to third place behind Cram in first, and Torvill and Dean in second.[28]

28 The Nottinghamshire pair won gold at the World Figure Skating Championships in 1983.

Although Cram continued to compete at the highest level for a few more years, winning silver at the Olympics in 1984 and breaking three world records in just 19 days in 1985, he never again won a global title.[29] According to Chris Brasher, his final titles in 1986, at 800m and 1,500m in the Commonwealth Games in Edinburgh, and 1,500m at the European Championships in Stuttgart, marked the last hurrah of 'the golden age of men's British distance running'. SPOTY reflected this. It was to be over 30 years before a male endurance athlete again lifted the trophy. In the meantime, it was up to others to carry the flag for track and field.[17]

Underlining the shift away from male middle-distance running, the next athlete to win SPOTY was a female field eventer. Abandoned as a baby by her Turkish Cypriot mother, Fatima Whitbread (née Vedad) spent a 'nightmare of a childhood' in a series of children's homes. Her fortunes changed, aged 13, when she met, and was later adopted by, Margaret Whitbread, a PE teacher and former international javelin thrower. Encouraged by her adoptive family to channel her all-round sporting prowess into javelin throwing, Whitbread quickly revealed her true potential, making her senior international debut in 1976 when only 16.

Her inspiration in these formative years was Tessa Sanderson, the Ghanian-born, Wolverhampton-based European and Commonwealth javelin champion. But such was the rapidity of Whitbread's progress that, by 1983, she had managed to surpass her childhood idol to take silver in the World Championships.

29 The records were: 1,500m (3:29.67) in Nice on 16 July, mile (3:46.32) in Oslo on 27 July, and 2,000m (4:51.39) in Budapest on 4 August.

Unfortunately, but possibly not unsurprisingly, once equals, the relationship between the two did not flourish. Sanderson felt Whitbread's connections to Andy Norman, the controversial athletics promoter and her future husband, and Margaret Whitbread, by now national javelin coach, gave her an unfair advantage. In return, Whitbread was fed up, one Sunday broadsheet claimed, that she 'trailed behind Sanderson in the muscles-can-be-beautiful stakes'. Whatever the reason, by the mid-1980s the two had, Cliff Temple observed, developed 'a hate-hate relationship that has become one of the most enduring of British sport'. The excessive tears whenever Whitbread lost out to Sanderson were testament to the bitterness of the rivalry. Even in victory, Fatima found it difficult to put the enmity to one side. 'Tessa, if you're watching,' she gloated after winning European gold in 1986, 'thank you for your inspiration. They will have to call me number one now.'

Admittedly, Whitbread had good reason to claim the number one spot. Not only had she become European champion in Stuttgart but she had also taken the world record, albeit in the qualifying rounds at 8am in front of a few sleepy sports reporters and some bussed-in schoolchildren. She was, nonetheless, the first British woman to hold a world record in a throwing event, an achievement impressive enough to merit second place in SPOTY.

But, to confirm her pre-eminence, she needed to win the World Championships in Rome the following year. A throw of 76.64m, the third-longest ever, proved good enough to defeat the new world-record holder, Petra Felke of East Germany. As the nation's only gold medallist, Whitbread had, declared the *Daily Mail*, 'saved Britain's face'. The tears were now banished. Instead, the newly crowned world champion celebrated, one startled trackside reporter noted, 'with the sort of belly dance that in turn amused and embarrassed onlookers'. The victory meant she became the highest-paid European athlete of the late 1980s, and was able to buy 'a house on one of the most sought-after roads in Brentwood'.[30] It may not have been Beverly Hills but it was still quite something for a young woman who had started life as a ward of court.

To round off a superb year for Whitbread, BBC viewers voted her Sports Personality of the Year ahead of Steve Davis and Ian Woosnam. The trophy was, she later recalled, 'the icing on the cake, and the strawberries and cream as well'.[31] But, for some, Fatima's SPOTY triumph was spoilt by a moment of casual sexism so typical of the period. Channelling his inner Terry Thomas, the BBC's Des Lynam introduced Whitbread with the throwaway comment, '1987 was, in a sense, the year of the wiggle for you.' Adrianne Blue, one of the few female sports editors on Fleet Street, was not impressed. 'This was the year of the win,' Blue insisted, 'not the wiggle. This woman is a champion, not a vamp. Why should it be necessary – and it is necessary – for her to invent a victory wiggle, or pose for fashion photographs in *The Sun*. Why is it enough for Cram or Coe merely to win? Because we don't like muscles on women?' Whitbread was not the first,

---

30 Steve Ovett could not understand why Whitbread earned so much when the javelin 'takes just 4 seconds to throw'. It was, he ill-advisedly suggested, 'like the dolly birds who parade in the ring between rounds getting the same as the boxers'.

31 Indeed, Whitbread remains so proud of the SPOTY trophy that she gives it pride of place on her mantlepiece, right next to the preserved carcass of the cockroach that was flushed out of her nose during her successful stay in the celebrity jungle in 2011.

and she certainly would not be the last, sportswoman to find she would be judged on more than just sporting excellence.[32]

A persistent shoulder injury meant that the heights of the summer of 1987 could never quite be replicated. But a career that delivered a world record, a European and a world title as well as a clutch of other major medals was still impressive by anyone's reckoning. The promotional blurb to her 2012 autobiography claimed the book was an 'inspirational story of a woman who succeeded against all the odds'. For once, the hyperbole was warranted.[18]

Another woman who went on to become a world champion despite a relatively challenging start in life was Liz McColgan. Brought up on the tough Whitfield housing estate on the edge of Dundee, running, she later told an interviewer, had saved her from 'a life on the dole'. One close neighbour felt it had saved her from even worse. 'That,' she informed a TV reporter after McColgan had set the best time for a marathon debutante when winning in New York, 'will show them there's more than just criminal records come out of Whitfield.'

Certainly, McColgan's career only took off after she left Dundee. An athletics scholarship to America – first, to a minor college in Ricks and then to the University of Alabama – ensured all the facilities and backroom support necessary for success were in place.[33]

---

32 In fact, Whitbread is proud of her physique. 'I like my muscles,' she told *The Guardian*, 'and don't care if I get a bit of stick for them. They're who I am.' It is a commendable outlook, but one she should not be forced to justify.

33 In fact, the move to America nearly did not come off. Unable to provide Alabama with proof she had the required qualifications for entry – largely because she had left school with no qualifications – McColgan's former headteacher saved the day by enterprisingly sending off her certificate of entry for 'O' level maths. For once, taking part really was all that counted.

But McColgan still had to provide the discipline and hard work. And this she did to a fanatical degree. An obsessive trainer, even by endurance runners' standards, all aspects of her life were carefully micromanaged. Whenever she travelled to competitions, indignant chefs would be given precise instructions, in five languages, on how to prepare her standard breakfast of porridge and prunes ('it makes you run fast'). Such attention to detail quickly paid dividends, and at the Commonwealth Games in Edinburgh in 1986 she won Scotland's only gold medal in a British record time.

But many pundits questioned whether McColgan possessed the change of pace required to win on the global stage. Losing out to Olga Bondarenko of Russia, after leading for the majority of the 10,000m in the Seoul Olympics in 1988, did little to silence the doubters. With such an evident weakness in her armoury, it did, then, seem foolhardy in the extreme to predict, on the eve of the 1991 World Championships in Tokyo, that she 'couldn't be beaten no matter how the race is run'. But, in what Brendan Foster called, 'the bravest run I've ever seen', she was as good as her word. Leading from gun to tape ('I didn't want to get boxed in'), McColgan became the first British woman to win a world-class title on the track since Ann Packer 27 years earlier.

Victory in the New York Marathon two months later meant McColgan was now, according to the *Daily Mail*'s John Burton, 'the hottest property in women's athletics'. And there was plenty of evidence to support Burton's claim. She was offered upwards of £20,000 per event to race on the roads; she was only the second outsider, after Ronald Reagan, to open trading on the New York Stock Exchange; and, the ultimate signifier of fame, she was ambushed by Michael Aspel for *This Is Your Life* ('I'm too young').[34] One honour she did not receive, however, was a civic reception in her hometown of Dundee. The municipal council, still smarting from a *Radio Times* interview in which McColgan had described her birthplace as 'a dead-end town', understandably chose not to put out the bunting. Perhaps, though, becoming just the third Scot to win SPOTY helped to mitigate the snub.[19]

Underlining the range and depth of athletics talent the nation enjoyed in this period, track and field was to have two more world champion SPOTY winners in the next four years. First up was Linford Christie. By the time he lifted the SPOTY trophy in 1993, Christie held all four major 100m titles. Yet his breakthrough had not come until he was 26, a ripe old age for a sprinter, when he won the 100m at the European Championships. Then the gold medals started pouring in, culminating in victory at the World Championships in Stuttgart in 1993 with a British record time of 9.87 seconds. He had now proved, his coach Ron Roddan claimed, he was 'the world No. 1'. The British public agreed, and it upgraded him from runner-up spot the year before to the top step of the SPOTY podium.[35]

Having arrived on the world stage relatively late, it was unlikely Christie was going to be able to maintain his status

34 Try telling that to Michael Owen.

35 Carl Lewis, who had missed the Olympics in 1992, took a little more persuading that the Briton was now the world's best sprinter. He insisted on a showdown, but a poor third place behind a victorious Christie in 'the Dash for Cash' at Gateshead seemed to settle the matter. The $150,000 Lewis earned for his 10.22 seconds of work must have taken the edge off the disappointment.

as the world's fastest man for very long. Yet he still managed to retain the European and Commonwealth titles in 1994 and, astonishingly, make the Olympic 100m final in 1996 at the age of 36. As he lined up for the final in Atlanta's Centennial Olympic Stadium, the oldest man in the field by five years, the British hopeful realised he would need something special if he was going to win. The aim was, he later recalled, 'to get out before the "B" of bang'. It was an ambitious plan, but, in the age of electronic sensitive starting blocks, also a foolhardy one. Christie's Olympic dream was over before the 'D' of disqualified appeared next to his name on the stadium scoreboard. It was a disappointing end to his appearances in global finals, but it hardly detracted from a career in which he had amassed 24 major medals, including 11 golds.

Yet, for all the titles and records, Christie did not always find it easy to win people over. 'Making friends; I suppose that's why we do it,' he told *The Guardian*'s Tumaini Carayol, but the press pool, in particular, seemed reluctant to buddy up. To many journalists, the British record holder appeared unappreciative of the support he received and too determined to find offence. Typical was Giles Smith's take in *The Times* on the eve of the 1995 World Championships. 'Linford,' Smith wrote, 'enjoys public goodwill of a kind normally reserved for the Queen Mother on her birthday. And she, to my knowledge, has never interpreted all those people waving flags and hankies as a massive surge of resentment. Linford, on the other hand, would probably feel persecuted to discover a hole in his Polo.' The *Daily Mail*'s assessment was rather more direct. 'Christie,' the paper famously commented, 'is the most balanced athlete of all time because he has a chip on both shoulders.'[36]

But Christie's view was that if he did have a chip on his shoulder then 'somebody's got to have put it there'. Although black athletes were increasingly leading the way in Britain in this period, their successes on the track did nothing to shield them from the ongoing discrimination that still blighted the country in the aftermath of the race riots of the early 1980s. Some of the bigotry was shockingly blatant. Christie was pulled over by the police so many times when driving his sponsored Mercedes that he eventually lost all patience: 'Name?' 'It's on the side of the car!' Frequently, however, the racism was much more covert, although no less hurtful for that. Throughout his career, the tabloids insisted on making lewd innuendoes about Christie's genitals, or what they euphemistically termed 'Linford's lunchbox'. Unsurprisingly, *The Sun* led the way. After his victory in the Barcelona Olympics in 1992, the paper chose to celebrate by packing a male model's Lycra shorts with a variety of fruit and veg 'to achieve the Linford look'. The only way to emulate the track hero, the feature concluded, 'is to be born like Linford'. The press pack may have considered the whole thing a bit of 'harmless fun', but, as one black academic pointed out, such stereotyping played into 'a centuries old emasculating discourse of racism which dehumanises and sexualises the Black male body'. To add insult to injury, if Christie complained, he was

36 The quip about having a chip on both shoulders is frequently attributed to Derek Redmond, a former British 400m record holder. Ben Carrington, a sociology professor at the University of Southern California, sees the citing of Redmond, a black athlete, as the source for the quote as an attempt by journalists to distance themselves from accusations of racism.

accused of lacking a sense of humour and seeing racism where it did not exist.

Even in his moments of triumph, there could be insinuations that he did not quite belong. His habit of draping himself in the Union Jack was, one team official cautioned him, 'inappropriate'. For the enormously patriotic Christie, this was a desperately offensive comment. Yet there was little sympathy for him within large sections of the West Indian community. 'When he always wrapped himself in the flag,' the racial justice campaigner Darcus Howe remembered, 'it made many black people squirm. It seemed like he was trying to ingratiate himself with the establishment.' To cap it all, even the flag owners themselves were not always happy. 'I'm a bit upset Linford didn't give it back,' complained Penny Morris after Christie had swathed himself in her homemade Union Jack during his lap of honour at the Barcelona Olympics. 'I spent two weeks making the flag by hand from a double bedsheet. And I used a Brownie handbook to make sure I got the colours and design just right.'

As if all this was not enough, throughout his career Christie was also plagued by rumours that he was a drugs cheat. His late flowering – he was 28 before he made the Olympic team – inevitably raised suspicions. Despite his penchant for wearing T-shirts proclaiming he was '100% natural' and a 'Drugs Free Zone', allegations to the contrary seemed to have been proved true when he tested positive for the banned stimulant pseudoephedrine after the 200m final at the 1988 Seoul Olympics. In a Games already rocked by the disqualification of Ben Johnson in the 100m, this was bleak news indeed. Christie claimed the result was a consequence of the ginseng tea he had been drinking, and a hastily convened adjudication committee gave him 'the benefit of the doubt' by 11 votes to 10.[37] Christie was furious that he hadn't been fully exonerated, and his mood was hardly improved when Professor Arnold Beckett, a leading member of the IOC medical commission, offered up the opinion that 'Linford was lucky to hold on to his silver medal'.[38] Although Mum proved endearingly supportive ('If they told me Linford had taken an overdose of roast chicken and baked potatoes, I would believe it. But drugs? Never.'), the press remained sceptical. 'Christie escaped all sanctions by the narrowest of margins,' Steve Downes wrote in the *Sunday Times*, and then only because 'one of the disciplinary panel fell asleep and failed to vote'.

The whispers never entirely went away during the championship-winning years, but there were no more positive tests. And then, unbelievably, at a minor indoor meeting at the very end of his career, Christie was found to be 100 times over the limit for nandrolone, a synthetic anabolic steroid. It seemed to make no sense. He was only competing, he claimed, 'for fun', to prove to the athletes he coached that he could still beat them. But there was to be no benefit of the doubt this time. As news broke that the IAAF had imposed a two-year ban, the reaction was swift and devastating. Puma refused to renew his £100,000 sponsorship deal, the BBC withdrew him from their commentary team for the Sydney Olympics and, most wounding of all, the

37 Asked why he had drunk so much ginseng tea, Christie was reported to have replied, 'Because the 200m is twice as far as the 100m.'

38 After Johnson's disqualification in the 100m, Christie was upgraded to second place, sandwiched between the two Americans, Carl Lewis in first and Calvin Smith in third.

IOC prohibited him from having any contact with the British Olympic team. It meant he could play no part in Britain's bid for the 2012 Games. It was a desperately sad way for an outstanding servant of British athletics to end his career.[20]

Although, at first glance, the triple jumper Jonathan Edwards, an 'ordinary skinny guy' brought up in the comfort of a vicarage in rural Devon, appeared to face none of the challenges Christie had to confront, he was still something of an outsider. A devout Christian in an increasingly secular country, he firmly believed he was 'a witness to God in running spikes'. Perhaps inevitably then, rather like Eric Liddell in the interwar years, he found himself in conflict with the athletics authorities over the issue of Sunday competition. It was not until 1993, by which time he was already a Commonwealth Games silver medallist, that he announced that God had finally given him permission to jump on the Sabbath. The fact that all the major triple jump finals that year were scheduled for Sundays did not escape the tabloids' notice. Yet even *The Sun* thought it would be wrong to be cynical, as Edwards was 'so genuine and obviously a nice young man'. God certainly did seem to work in mysterious ways.

Divinely sanctioned or not, the change of heart certainly paid immediate dividends. A bronze medal at the World Championships in August brought in some much-needed sponsorship, and by 1995 Edwards was in spectacular form. After two astounding, but wind-assisted, jumps in excess of 18m at Lille in the European Cup, he became the first British male since C. B. Fry in 1893 to break a world jumps record, with a legal mark of 17.98m in Salamanca. Although now favourite going into the World Championships in Gothenburg, Edwards recalled that his overriding feeling on the eve of competition was 'fear – I felt if I didn't win or break the record my season was a failure'. He need not have worried. He not only demolished the world record in the first round, but jumped so far beyond the pit-side ruler that *The Independent*'s trackside reporter saw spectators 'in the front rows of the stands flinching in their seats'. *The Guardian*'s Stephen Bierley was lost for words as he watched Edwards's 'speed, rhythm and balance'. Unfortunately, the BBC's Paul Dickenson wasn't. 'Oh! It's huge! It's massive! And it's legal!' he screamed much to the delight of *Private Eye*'s 'Colemanballs'.[39]

Unbelievably, Edwards managed to jump even further in the second round. His distance of 18.29m still stands as the record today. It was an incredible feat. In just two leaps, the new British world-record holder had seemingly achieved the near impossible. He had turned an event, which one commentator 'fondly assumed … came in the athletic schedule somewhere between the sack race and the 4x40m potato and spoon race', into a fan favourite. The *Sunday Times*' man in Gothenburg found it all equally bemusing. The morning after the final, he was astonished to see an excited gaggle of schoolchildren demanding Edwards's autograph while Donovan Reid, the newly crowned 100m champion, strolled by unnoticed. 'When was the last time,' he rhetorically asked, 'someone from a Cinderella event like the triple jump made more of an impact than the world's fastest man?'

But Edwards's appeal lay as much in his unassuming manner as his athletic accomplishments. 'He is,' thought David Miller of

39 'Colemanballs', named in honour of the inestimable David Coleman, was a regular column in *Private Eye* that showcased commentators' gaffes.

The Times, 'as far removed from a typical ego-driven superstar as it is possible to get.' Even at the post-event press conference, the world champion cut a winningly modest figure. 'I can see no harm in the occasional glass of wine,' he said, when asked how he intended to celebrate. 'After all, it says in Psalms that God gives wine, which makes glad the heart of man.' This pronouncement, *The Telegraph*'s Paul Hayward wryly noted, was 'met with much sage nodding'. The *Mail on Sunday* was completely won over. Gothenburg, the paper declared, 'proved that nice guys could come first'.

And SPOTY proved it again. The only other real contender for the trophy in 1995 was another self-effacing world champion, Frank Bruno. Although Edwards had to endure the humiliation of losing out to rugby league's Martin 'Chariots' Offiah in a studio-based attempt on the standing long-jump record, he still looked genuinely delighted when the victorious Ryder Cup captain, Bernard Gallacher, announced he was the public's favourite sports personality.[40] In contrast, when it dawned on Bruno that he had finished runner-up to 'a bashful triple jumper', he looked, the boxing correspondent Kevin Mitchell observed, like he had just been 'king-hit by five Mike Tysons'.

Edwards, not unreasonably, found it difficult to match the heights of Gothenburg in the next few seasons. By 2000 many assumed his chance of Olympic gold had gone. He has, declared *The Sun*, on the eve of the Sydney Olympics, 'had his time'. Even the usually ebullient world-record holder's faith seemed to waver. 'Perhaps,' he wondered, 'I'm not some specially anointed

40 Offiah was the only person to beat Edwards in a jump competition in 1995.

messenger of God after all.' Happily, however, he managed to hold his nerve and, with a relatively modest (by his standards) distance of 17.71m, comfortably take the gold. The world crown the following year meant that, like Linford Christie in 1994, he now held all four major titles simultaneously. Maybe, though, even more remarkable than all the gold medals and world records was the way Edwards achieved the extraordinary while remaining, at least to the casual onlooker, so ordinary. 'I am,' he told the *Daily Mail* with typical humility, 'the sort of guy who makes people think, well, if he can do it, I can do it.'[41]

As the nation entered the new millennium, the public returned to track and field's traditional base of hard-grafting endurance runners to find the sport's final three SPOTY winners. And nobody grafted harder than Paula Radcliffe. Key to her popularity, according to Olympic Games expert Duncan Mackay, was her 'ordinariness and fallibility'. But there was nothing ordinary about a training schedule that involved upwards of 140 miles a week, plus daily conditioning sessions, ice baths and massages. Just possibly the pain that was etched across Radcliffe's bobbing head during races did make her a little more relatable for the Sunday morning jogger, but even then it was a stretch.

Mackay was probably right, however, when it came to fallibility. No matter how hard Radcliffe tried, she seemed unable to secure championship victories. Invariably, she would plug away at the front before being left for dead on the last lap. Simon Barnes of *The Times* found her races almost unbearable. It was, he felt, like watching 'moths fly around candles ... It could only end one way.'

41 You can't.

Fans, though, were enthralled by the courage she showed on the track. Here, it seemed, was another graduate of the Henman school of gutsy British losers. And, as successive East Africans sprinted by to claim global titles, so her popularity grew. Unsurprisingly, the adulation was little consolation to Radcliffe. 'I wanted to show people I was a winner,' she recalled in her autobiography, 'not just some plucky girl who tried hard but couldn't get there.'

In 2001 it seemed she would finally get there. Having won the World Cross Country Championships in March, and set the second-fastest time ever in a 10km road race three months later, she started the World Championships 10,000m track final in Edmonton as one of the favourites. The race, though, unfolded in a worryingly familiar fashion. Relentlessly whittling the field down from the off, Radcliffe hit the bell with only three Ethiopians for company; 400m later, the quartet crossed the line separated by just one and a quarter seconds. Heartbreakingly, Paula missed out on a medal yet again, this time by less than one hundredth of a second. To add to the misery, her husband and coach, Gary Lough, decided this was the perfect moment to showcase some shockingly boorish behaviour. Instead of consoling his distraught wife, he publicly harangued her for failing to follow his tactical plan. Radcliffe pushed him away in disgust. The press was appalled. 'You deserve a medal, Paula' was the verdict of the *Daily Mirror*, 'and that's just for putting up with your hubby.'

As the 'nearly girl' of British athletics, Radcliffe's goals for 2002 were strikingly ambitious. The aim was to retain the World Cross Country title, win the London Marathon, take gold in the Commonwealth Games 10,000m and break the European 10,000m record. She achieved all four and, just for good measure, broke the marathon world record during an impromptu visit to Chicago. It was this transition into the world's best marathon runner that was the most remarkable achievement in a remarkable year. Distance running had become big box office since the road-racing boom of the early 1980s, so there was intense media interest when Paula announced she intended to make her marathon debut in London in April. The interest, though, turned to concern when she forged into the lead as she rounded Cutty Sark with just six miles gone. But this time there were no Ethiopians shadowing her every step. A minute up at Tower Bridge, by the time she came down The Mall she was over three minutes clear. Her time of 2hr 18m 56s was the fastest ever by a debutante and just nine seconds off the world record. It was a performance of such brilliance that even her husband gave her a hug. Maybe he was thinking what he could do with the £180,000 prize money.

Six months later Radcliffe made the world record her own, clocking 2hr 17m 18s at Chicago. 'In just one calendar year,' Matt Lawton of the *Daily Mail* declared, 'she had graduated to the finest, fastest and most successful runner of her generation.' He could also have added one of the richest, as she came away from America close to £500,000 better off. To underline her new position as one of the brightest stars in the sporting firmament, she beat David Beckham into second place at SPOTY.

Another superb performance in London the following year meant Radcliffe went into the Athens Olympics in 2004 with a marathon record of three wins in three outings, two of them in world fastest times. Finally, a global title seemed there for the taking. But the discovery of a haematoma in her left leg two weeks before the Games were due to begin meant she arrived on the marathon start line underprepared. Six miles into the race she knew she was in trouble, but she courageously battled on until forced to abandon with under four miles to go. As she sat on the kerbside and wept, the television cameras cruelly recorded her despair. Back in the stadium, expectant British fans looked on in stunned silence as images of their heroine in tears were beamed on to the giant screens.

Although David Hemery, in the *Sunday Times*, gamely insisted that Paula was still 'everything you could ask for in an athlete', the dailies were less forgiving. *The Star* supportively opened a poll entitled 'Is Paula a quitter?', while the *Daily Mail*'s Jeff Powell suggested that 'Radcliffe had lost her self-respect' by not emulating Pheidippides, the ancient Greek messenger, who had 'kept going to the end before dropping dead'.[42] It seemed a mercilessly exacting standard to hold anyone to. Eventually, the media coverage became so intrusive that Radcliffe felt compelled to relocate her family to Monaco.[43] It was proof, if proof was needed, that although the rewards in the professional era were higher than ever, so too were the pressures.[22]

The penultimate track and field athlete to win SPOTY also struggled with the pressure of being cast as a gallant loser. Although Kelly Holmes was an immensely talented youngster – she won the English Schools 1,500m in 1983 – her focus in her early 20s was on forging a career as a PT instructor in the army. When she eventually made the jump to full-time athlete in

42 Accusations that Radcliffe was a quitter were given a further boost when she dropped out of the 10,000m five days later.

43 The memory of Athens was, at least in part, exorcised in August 2005 when Radcliffe won the marathon at the World Championships in Helsinki.

1997, at the age of 27, a series of injuries and illnesses prevented her from fulfilling her true potential. 'Her body,' Simon Barnes of *The Times* commented at the time, 'is like a temperamental Formula One car; if it isn't giving trouble here, it is breaking down there.' Yet another forced lay-off in the pits, on the eve of the Sydney Olympics in 2000, meant a hard-won bronze medal in the 800m was regarded as an overachievement. Indeed, she was so proud of her third-place finish that she decided to buy a replica of the SPOTY trophy when the British Olympic medallists secured the team award at the end of the year. After all, she thought, 'It's probably the only chance I'll ever get to have one of these'.

By the time the next Olympics came along, few gave the by then 34-year-old Kent athlete much chance of success. 'Kelly is one of those eternal good eggs of British athletics,' was *The Times*' rather patronising view, 'always there, always busting a gut, usually somehow scraping a minor medal; a talent renowned more for hard work and honesty than for speed blessed by the gods.' Even Holmes herself was gloomy about her prospects. She made 'Eeyore sound like Kriss Akabusi', thought Brian Viner of *The Independent* after a bleakly introspective interview on the eve of the Games.

Holmes was particularly worried about doubling up in the middle-distance events in 2004. Uncertain that her fragile body would hold out, she only decided to do the 800m three days before the first-round heats. But the gamble paid off, and in the tightest possible finish she took the title by just 0.05s. Although receiving the gold medal from Seb Coe was the 'best moment of my life', the impending 1,500m heats restricted her celebrations to a stroke-threatening plunge in a wheelie bin full of ice. Released, now, from her self-imposed fear of failure, her plan for the metric mile was to 'just try and be awake on the start line'. It was unconventional but it worked a treat, and Holmes became the first British woman to take two titles at the same Games.

She was now, the *Daily Star* proclaimed, 'the country's most high profile sports star', and could expect to 'rival David Beckham for earning power'. That may have been overstating it, but she certainly got to enjoy a taste of the celebrity high life, appearing on *Parkinson*, *EastEnders* and the *Royal Variety Show*, as well as rubbing shoulders with Tom Cruise, the Queen and even Nadia from *Big Brother*. But more special than all of that, she confided to a reporter from the *Independent on Sunday*, was the open-top bus parade through her hometown of Tonbridge followed by a knees-up at her local Beefeater.[44] It was this winning combination of stardom and homeliness that made almost inevitable, despite a line-up that included four-times gold medallist Matthew Pinsent, her coronation as Sports Personality of the Year for 2004.

Although her body finally succumbed to injury the following year, her place in sporting immortality was already secured. Her double in Athens was, according to Brendan Foster, 'the most outstanding performance in the history of British distance running'. Yet, perhaps, her greatest achievement was still to come. In 2022, in the ITV documentary *Kelly Holmes: Being Me*, she publicly came out as a gay woman. It was, she said, 'really hard … to be open and honest with the true me'. The programme was difficult viewing but, thought the *Daily Mail* reviewer, would

44 Holmes later conceded that receiving a damehood from the Queen in March 2005 pushed the Beefeater close.

undoubtedly serve as an 'inspiration' for others. In a career already filled with remarkable moments, maybe this was the most remarkable of all.[23]

The final athlete to win SPOTY not only matched Holmes's achievements on the track but also her courage in retirement. When Mo Farah was knighted by the Queen in 2017, the two-time double Olympic champion's journey from child refugee to sporting royalty seemed the stuff of Hollywood films. But a 2022 documentary, *The Real Mo Farah*, revealed the truth was even more astonishing. Rather than arriving in Britain with his mother and two brothers, Farah had, in fact, been trafficked and spent his early childhood in domestic servitude. Such an appalling introduction to life in his adopted country only served to make what was to follow all the more inspirational.

As is so often the case, it was meeting the right people at the right time that helped Farah's career flourish. A sympathetic PE teacher at Feltham Community College resolved his desperate domestic circumstances, the Head of Endurance for UK Athletics secured a vital sports scholarship at St Mary's University and, albeit more controversially, Nike Oregon Project's Alberto Salazar offered 'scientific' solutions to the apparent invincibility of the East Africans.[45] In particular, Salazar's input seemed to pay immediate dividends and, at the 2011 World Championships in Daegu, Farah broke into the global elite with a silver in the 10,000m and gold in the 5,000m.

---

45 Alberto Salazar, a former marathon runner turned coach, was banned for doping violations in 2019, and his training group, the Nike Oregon Project, was closed down shortly after. There was never any suggestion Farah had been involved in drug-taking, but naturally his association with Salazar left him exposed to some uncomfortable questioning.

After his breakthrough in South Korea, the global titles started to pour in, most memorably at the London Olympics in 2012. Already billed as the greatest celebration of Britishness since 1951, Danny Boyle's quirkily patriotic opening ceremony for the 2012 Games, which featured cameos by (among others) Mary Poppins, Mr Bean, James Bond (and the Queen), Dizzee Rascal, David Beckham and the Sex Pistols, even managed to win over world-weary members of the press corps. 'I felt a strange stirring inside,' recalled Simon Kuper of the *Financial Times* as he watched the extravaganza in the Olympic arena. 'At first I thought it the dodgy chicken sandwich bought in the stadium, but I eventually identified the feeling: British patriotism. This was new to me.'

Eight days later, in what would be dubbed 'Super Saturday', the mood of national self-congratulation went into overdrive when the country won three track and field gold medals in the space of just 46 minutes. For the press, the victories were evidence of British openness and inclusivity. 'Saturday evening,' the *Daily Telegraph*'s Jim White proclaimed, 'demonstrated that anyone from any minority can succeed in a country as tolerant as this: Jessica Ennis, Mo Farah, and Greg Rutherford, the mixed-race woman, the refugee, and the ginger kid.' But most papers wondered whether hair colouring really had any part to play in multiculturalism and instead focused on Farah exclusively. His victories in London were, thought Tom Peck in *The Independent*, 'an affirmation of who we are' in a post-imperial world.[46] Even for readers of the *Daily Mail*, Farah could be held up as a 'a success

46 Of course, Farah followed up his victory in the 10,000m on Super Saturday with the 5,000m gold a week later.

story made in Britain'. Yet, for all the acclaim, he still failed to make the top three in that year's SPOTY awards.

At Rio in 2016, despite falling in the 10,000m, Farah managed to do the double again. But he still failed to place on the podium in SPOTY. *The Telegraph* considered the snub 'a disgrace', while both the triathlete Alistair Brownlee and the veteran showjumper Nick Skelton, who had finished second and third respectively in the SPOTY poll, insisted they would have cast their votes for Mo. The *Daily Mail* speculated that Farah's continued association with the increasingly beleaguered Alberto Salazar, who was facing intense scrutiny by the US Anti-Doping Agency, might have put people off. It was a possible explanation, but the oversight still seemed hard to fathom.

After a relatively quiet season in 2017 (only one global title!), Farah, although nominated again for SPOTY, decided not to bother turning up for the ceremony in Liverpool's Echo Arena. He was, after all, a 50-1 outsider in the betting. Inevitably, he won. As Kenny Dalglish announced the result, the shock that many were feeling but had the good grace not to articulate was summed up by Mo's new coach, Gary Lough, who mouthed to Paula Radcliffe, 'Fucking joke!' Even the video link seemed affected by the upset. Just as the trophy was about to be presented, the feed to Farah's Twickenham hotel cut out. 'Not since Princess Anne beat George Best and Barry John in 1971,' moaned the *Daily Telegraph*, 'had there been such unexpected, if not bizarre, voting.' *The Guardian*, though, thought the result was simply the most recent example of electoral fickleness. What else could you expect, reasoned the paper's chief sports reporter, from a 'British public who had voted for Brexit just 18 months ago and given

Jeremy Corbyn a dramatic uplift in the final days of the general election'? In fact, the only thing wrong with the result was that it was so long coming. And, belated though the award was in 2017, it was still a fitting tribute to a man who had provided his adopted country with so much pleasure and who was, by any measure, the greatest athlete the nation had ever possessed.[24]

Chapter Notes

15 Dominic Sandbrook, *The Great British Dream Factory* (2015), pp.100–101; *Who Dares Wins: Britain 1979–1982* (2019), pp.622–623; Pat Butcher, *The Perfect Distance: Ovett and Coe, the Record-Breaking Rivalry* (2012), ch.17; *Chariots of Fire*, dir. Hugh Hudson (1981); Steve Downes and Duncan Mackay, *Running Scared: How Athletics Lost Its Innocence* (1996), p.16, 213; Richard Holt and Tony Mason, *Sport in Britain, 1945–2000* (2000), p.47; *Observer*, 13 July 1987.

16 Skip Rozen, *Daley Thompson: The Subject is Winning* (1983), pp.6, 81 179–181; Neil Wilson and Steve Powell, *Daley: The Last 10 Years* (1986), p.84; *Independent*, 27 July 2008; *Sunday Times*, 30 October 2005, 19 December 1982; *Guardian*, 4 April 2012, 11 August 1984; Rob Steen, *Floodlights and Touchlines: A History of Spectator Sport* (2014), p.477; *Daily Mirror*, 13 August 1984; *Observer*, 12 August 1984; Sandbrook, *Who Dares Wins*, p.630; *Daily Express*, 24 September 1982; *Times*, 13 August 1983.

17 Norman Barrett and Mel Watman, *Steve Cram* (1984), p.56; Roger Tames, *Steve Cram: The Making of an Athlete* (1984), pp.104–109, 142; *Athletics Weekly*, 18 August 2023; *Daily Mail*, 9 September 1983, 10 September 1983, 15 August 1983; Pat Butcher, *The Perfect Distance: Coe and Ovett: The Record-Breaking Rivalry* (2004); ch.21; *Guardian*, 10 September 1983; *Daily Mirror*, 19 December 1983, 10 September 1983; *Daily Express*, 10 September 1983; *Sunday Times*, 21 August 1983; Downes and Mackay, *Running Scared*, p.124; *Observer*, 11 September 1983.

18 *Observer*, 25 September 2012, 28 October 1990; *Daily Express*, 30 August 1986; Fatima Whitbread, *Fatima Whitbread: Survivor* (2012), pp.2, 198–205, 246; *Daily Mail*, 7 September 1987; *Times*, 30 December 1987, 7 September 1987; Holt and Mason, *Sport in Britain*,

p.86; Sports Hub Video, *Fatima Whitbread: Full Interview* (2021); *Sunday Times*, 20 December 1987; *Guardian*, 6 July 2012.

19 ITV, *This Is Your Life: Liz McColgan* (1991); Adrianne Blue, *Queen of the Track: The Liz McColgan Story* (1992), pp.57, 153–161; *Daily Mail*, 5 November 1991.

20 ITV4, *Sports Life Stories: Linford Christie* (2015), dir. Adam Maynard; Linford Christie, *To Be Honest with You* (1995), p155; *Times*, 29 August 2011, 9 August 1995; *Guardian*, 13 May 2021, 22 August 2000; *Daily Mail*, 25 July 2009, 5 August 1999, 15 October 1988, 1 October 1988; Ben Carrington, 'Double consciousness and the Black British Athlete', in Kwesi Owusu (ed.), *Black British Culture and Society* (2000), p.135; *Sun*, 6 August 1992; *Observer*, 4 September 2005; *Sunday Times*, 8 August 1999, 20 December 1992; Downes and Mackay, *Running Scared*, p.29.

21 *Sunday Times*, 13 August 1995; Jonathan Edwards, *A Time to Jump: The Authorised Biography of Jonathan Edwards* (2000), pp.232–233, 2; *Independent*, 9 December 1995, 9 August 1995; *Guardian*, 8 August 1995; *Times*, 9 August 1985; *Telegraph*, 9 August 1995; *Observer*, 24 December 1995; 17 December 1995; *Daily Mail*, 9 August 1985.

22 *Guardian*, 25 April 2015, 31 December 2002; *Times*, 23 August 2001; ITV4, *Sports Life Stories: Paula Radcliffe* (2015), dir. Luke Mellows; Paula Radcliffe, *Paula: My Story So Far* (2005), p.171; *Daily Mirror*, 8 August 2001; Paul Owen, *For the Love of Running: A Companion* (2017), n.p; *Daily Mail*, 23 August 2004, 14 October 2002; BBC, Paula Radcliffe: *The Marathon and Me* (2015), dir. Jamie Gavin; *Sunday Times*, 29 August 2004; *Daily Star*, 24 August 2004.

23 Kelly Holmes, Kelly: *Black, White and Gold: My Autobiography* (2011), ch.3, 15; *Times*, 30 August 2004, 24 August 2004; *Independent*, 18 December 2004, 13 December 2004; *Guardian*, 20 December 2004; *Star*, 30 August 2004; *Independent on Sunday*, 29 August 2004; *Daily Mail*, 24 June 2022, 13 December 2004 ; ITV, *Kelly Holmes: Being Me* (2022), dir. Lucy Rogers; *Metro*, 20 June 2022.

24 BBC, *The Real Mo Farah* (2022), dir. Leo Burley; Mo Farah, *Twin Ambitions: My Autobiography* (2013), p.108, 232–233; *Mo Farah: No Easy Mile* (2016), dir. Joe Pearlman; *Financial Times*, 27 July 2012; *Telegraph*, 18 December 2017, 19 December 2016, 6 August 2012; *Independent*, 13 August 2012; *Daily Mail*, 7 August 2012; *Guardian*, 18 December 2017, 19 December 2016; *Times*, 18 December 2017; *Daily Express*, 18 December 2017.

Chapter 3

Team Games: Football, Cricket, Rugby

I. Football

Bobby Moore (1966) – Paul Gascoigne (1990) – Michael Owen (1998) –

David Beckham (2001) – Ryan Giggs (2009) – Beth Mead (2022)

LATE ONE spring morning at Liverpool's Melwood training ground, John Barnes took a break from training to make an unusual media appearance. With the Winterburn Heights tower blocks looming in the background, England's star striker stared down the camera lens and broke into song. 'You've got to hold and give, but do it at the right time,' he rapped while professional provocateur Keith Allen cavorted impishly behind him. The year was, of course, 1990 and the occasion was the recording of the official video to accompany yet another FA-sponsored World Cup anthem. But this time things were different. Barnes had style. The music was hip. The song topped the charts. Something strange was going on.

The last time the England team had found itself with a No. 1 on its hands had been 20 years earlier. Then, though, the tub-thumping 'Back Home' had seemed to have taken its inspiration from the wartime morale boosters of Flanagan and Allen rather than the psychedelic rock of The Doors and Jimi Hendrix. An appearance by the dinner-suited squad on *Top of the Pops*, half-heartedly miming with all the enthusiasm of an under-rehearsed schoolboy choir, had done little to counter the notion that football was out of touch with the mood of the times. Nobby Stiles was no Jim Morrison.

But New Order's 'World in Motion' was not just a break from football's execrable musical past, it was also a signal for a new cultural dawn. 'We ain't no hooligans,' the song proclaimed. The message was clear. The game was no longer, as the *Sunday Times* would have it, a 'slum sport played in slum stadiums by slum people', but instead a modish entertainment for John Major's classless society; an essential component of the new loved-up Hacienda scene. Barnes was right when he insisted, 'This ain't a football song.' 'World in Motion' was, rather, an anthem to an evolving celebrity culture; a culture in which the nation's elite footballers (and to a lesser extent cricketers and rugby players) were destined to be the new rock stars.

'World in Motion' not only distanced football from the mob violence of the 1980s but it also managed to integrate the patriotism of the terraces into the wider face-touching chemical-induced, love fest of the rave scene. The song made supporting or, even better, representing the national team cool. And, of course, it transcended the bitterness of local rivalries to unite listeners in a heady fusion of fashion and football. No matter how hard

Chas and Dave might try, this was a feat that just could not be replicated with club anthems. Invariably released to celebrate FA Cup Final appearances, club songs found it almost impossible to shrug off the grip of 1970s easy listening and gain traction within wider youth culture. Even Manchester United's chart-topping 'Come on You Reds' in 1994, the only club single to reach No. 1, had a hook and video so bland that it made 'Back Home' look dangerously post-modern.

For players of team sports with ambitions to win SPOTY, the success of 'World in Motion' served as a useful guide. To be in with a shout of lifting the trophy, they would have to reach beyond the unfashionable confines of parochial rivalries and enter the borderless uplands of hip celebritydom. Only a select few would manage it. Gascoigne and Beckham in football, Botham and Flintoff in cricket, Wilkinson in rugby – all for individual moments of brilliance in World Cups (or the cricket world's equivalent, the Ashes).[47] The exception to this rule, once again, came from the red side of Manchester, with the ageless Ryan Giggs's triumph in 2009.

The first four footballers to win SPOTY were recognised for their exploits in World Cups, and for the first two these occurred in matches against England's arch-rivals, Germany. SPOTY success began for football in (when else?) 1966. Prior to this, British football was in the doldrums. On the international stage, having finally deigned to participate in the FIFA World Cup in 1950,

47 Of course, since Sky's takeover of cricket, the ODI World Cup has assumed greater importance and Ben Stokes's SPOTY win was on the back of England's dramatic victory in 2019, although a standout performance in the Ashes later in the year helped to seal the deal.

none of the home nations managed to go beyond the quarter-finals in the tournament's four iterations before England's great Wembley triumph. Domestically, the situation wasn't much better. The game was beset by the problems the modern fan has become all too familiar with – corruption and hooliganism – and attendances were in freefall, down by nearly a third in the 20 years since the end of the war. In an otherwise bleak picture, the only glimmer of hope for the FA was television's embryonic interest in the sport. The BBC negotiated a deal to show league highlights in the early 1960s, and in August 1964 *Match of the Day* was first aired.

Expectations were not high, therefore, on the eve of England's World Cup. Ramsey's stuttering start as national team manager, a 5-2 trouncing by France in the European Championships in 1963 followed up by defeats against Argentina and Brazil in the 'Little World Cup' of 1964, had done nothing to raise hopes. A general air of public resignation was reflected in the muted press build-up. Thankfully, the theft of the Jules Rimet trophy and its subsequent discovery eight days later under a suburban garden hedge in Croydon by Pickles, a black-and-white mongrel dog, afforded the tournament some desperately needed publicity. From this small beginning, interest slowly began to build as England started to progress through the early rounds, and a fiery quarter-final victory over Argentina provided the requisite drama to ignite public interest.

By the time of the final, World Cup fever had finally taken hold in the country. And the fact that the opponents were West Germany only added to the excitement. Although more restrained than they would be two decades later, the tabloids still gleefully indulged in a bit of German-baiting. 'If Germany beat us this afternoon in our national game,' announced the editor of the *Daily Mail*, 'we can always point out to them that we have recently beaten them twice at theirs.' Proving that it is not just great minds that think alike, *The Sun*'s Peter Lorenzo reminded his readers, as if they needed any reminding, that 'England have never lost to Germany – at soccer either'. With the game billed as a sporting rerun of the Somme and El Alamein, it was hardly surprising that 32 million tuned in to watch the match. And, of course, they were not to be disappointed.[25]

Victory against the West Germans that July afternoon was viewed by many as a miracle. Just as Britain seemed to be drifting into global obscurity, the nation's footballers had shown that England could, once again, lead the world. And the hero of the hour was team captain Bobby Moore. Voted Player of the Tournament, he led by example on the pitch. Moore, David Miller of the *Daily Express* admiringly noted, spent the final 'moving among opponents like a bank manager among junior clerks, correcting, re-directing and discreetly scolding'. His calming presence was no better epitomised than during the last frantic seconds of extra time as England defended a 3-2 lead. While the referee, whistle in mouth, checked his watch, a speculative cross was floated into the England penalty area. 'Get fucking rid! Put it three tiers up!' Jack Charlton screamed at his captain. Instead, Moore, the only composed person in the whole of Wembley, coolly chested the ball down, exchanged passes with Ray Wilson, before striding forward and pinging an inch-perfect 40-yard pass to set up Geoff Hurst's famous third goal.

Such equanimity had always been a feature of Moore's play. An intensely private man – a diagnosis of testicular cancer in 1964 was shared with only his immediate family – his reserve on the pitch was balanced by a magnetic mixture of self-possession and natural authority. His leadership potential was quickly recognised by team managers. In 1962, when only 21, he was made captain of West Ham, and the following year he became the youngest player ever to lead England. A perfectionist, he set himself the highest of standards and expected the same from his team-mates. Yet any aloofness was offset by a wry sense of humour. Gordon Banks's 'save of the century' against Brazil in the 1970 World Cup, an astounding dive to one-handedly flail Pelé's powerful downward header over the bar, was met with a droll, 'Catch those, Gordon!'[48]

In July 1966, Moore was, then, the watching public's ideal of a triumphant England captain: talented but modest, unyielding but gallant, ambitious but humble. And to cap it all, on his way up the Wembley steps to receive the Jules Rimet trophy, he proved himself to be a gentleman as well, carefully wiping his hands on the velvet balcony cover to avoid dirtying the lilywhite gloves of the young Queen. The country was in raptures. London ground to a standstill as people flocked into the streets to celebrate. 'It was,' one presumably overworked AA repairman was quoted as saying, 'like VE Night, election night and New Year's Eve rolled into one.' 'Everyone,' the *Sunday Express*'s man on the street observed, 'unashamedly gripped by emotion and patriotism, danced, wept and hugged each other.' Well, not quite everyone. It was, Scotland's star striker Denis Law morosely recalled, 'the blackest day of my life'.

48 This anecdote may well just be part of Geoff Hurst's after-dinner repartee, but it still helps to reveal a wider truth about Moore's character.

Moore's celebrity status now transcended football. The abolition of the wage cap and reform of the retain and transfer system in the early 1960s had enormously increased the earning potential of professional footballers and propelled an elite few into the glamorous celebrity culture of Swinging London. The England captain was now mixing with the likes of Joan Collins, Sean Connery, Tom Jones and Mick Jagger. He was in demand for society events and commercial endorsements. He and wife Tina modelled for *Vogue*, appeared on *This Is Your Life* and urged the British public to 'look in at the local'. To popular acclaim, in December 1966, he became the first footballer to win SPOTY. Yet fame did not bring the sort of financial rewards the cosseted superstars of the modern era have come to take for granted. Morlands, Moore's neo-Georgian house in Chigwell, was undoubtedly one of the more substantial properties in Essex's stockbroker belt, but it was no Beckingham Palace, and the £250 fee he received to open a garage in Weybridge may have been more than his weekly wage at West Ham, but it was hardly on a par with the £25m David Beckham would earn for being seen in a pair of Emporio Armani Y-fronts.

When Moore lifted the Jules Rimet trophy in July 1966 he was 25 years old and in his prime. To reach such heroic heights again was always going to be a challenge. Although he came close in Mexico in 1970, with a commanding performance against Brazil, encapsulated by a sublime dispossession of Jairzinho ('that tackle by Moore'), much of what followed was inevitably anticlimactic. His international career ended in disappointment when an uncharacteristic error saw England lose to Poland and fail to qualify for the 1974 World Cup. At club level it took a move to Second Division Fulham in 1974 to provide one last chance of lifting a trophy. But the 1975 FA Cup Final against, ironically, West Ham ended in defeat, and from then on England's World Cup-winning captain became a bit player at a succession of overseas teams.[49]

In retirement things didn't get much better. Poor business decisions left him financially insecure, and brief spells as manager of Third Division Southend and Oxford City of the Isthmian Premier League both ended in relegation. Shamefully, the FA never found a role for him. The administrators at Lancaster Gate, oblivious to the burgeoning culture of celebrity surrounding the stars of the game, still viewed players as little more than waged employees. It is telling that Andrew Stephen, FA Chairman 1967–76, and Denis Follows, FA Secretary 1962–73, were knighted in 1972 and 1978 respectively, while it took until 1994 for Bobby Charlton to become the first World Cup-winning player to be similarly honoured. Moore, meanwhile, had to settle for an OBE, and for five of his team-mates it was not until the 21st century that they were deemed worthy of MBEs.

Bobby Moore was, in many ways, a pioneer. Signed by West Ham at a time when professional footballers were effectively owned by their clubs, he went on to become one of the game's first true celebrities as football moved into a new era of small-screen commercialism. For the majority of his career he was as much a feature of the front pages as the back pages. Long before

49 The most bizarre of the overseas teams Moore played for was Herning of the Danish third division. He made just nine appearances, in front of crowds numbering in the hundreds rather than thousands, before being released for being 'too good'. It was the only club to ever sack him.

Posh and Becks, Bobby and Tina were the sport's golden couple. Lacking the teams of PR advisors and image consultants that have now become fixtures of an international footballer's retinue, Moore had to navigate his own way through the largely uncharted waters of an evolving media celebrity culture. He did so with characteristic composure. His was a career, then, that served as a blueprint for the multi-millionaire prima donnas of later generations. As journalist and fellow East Londoner Tony Parsons astutely observed, 'Before anyone did anything, Bobby Moore did everything.' And, what's more, he won the World Cup.[26]

Just as Moore struggled to recapture the glory of lifting the World Cup, so too English football found itself in an inexorable downward spiral after 1966. Despite unparalleled success in European club competitions, domestically attendances declined throughout the 1970s and 1980s. Internationally things were no better. A sign of just how far the country had fallen since 1966 was England's record against West Germany. The two teams had met 13 times before the 1966 final and England had never lost. In the ten matches between the Wembley victory and Italia 90, England only won twice. 'No Englishman,' Hugh McIlvanney of *The Observer* bemoaned after a particularly abject 3-1 home defeat in a qualifier for the 1972 European Championships, 'can ever again warm himself with the old assumption that, on the football field if nowhere else, the Germans are an inferior race.' The tabloids found all this particularly hard to take. Having magnanimously given the game to the world, it was assumed we would always be its master.

To further underline the dreadful state of the game in these years, a series of appalling tragedies shockingly exposed decades of government neglect and owner underinvestment. Fifty-six people died in a fire at Bradford City's rickety Valley Parade ground during the last match of the 1985 season; 18 days later, 39 mostly Juventus fans were killed when a wall collapsed in the Heysel Stadium as they tried to escape rampaging Liverpool fans before the European Cup Final kick-off; and finally, in 1989, a mixture of poor planning and police incompetence resulted in 97 Liverpool supporters being crushed to death in the Leppings Lane end of Hillsborough at the start of their team's FA Cup semi-final against Nottingham Forest. If, as many believed, football acted as a barometer of the state of the nation, then by the end of the 1980s the situation was dire indeed.

The game's rehabilitation began with the start of the new decade. English football teams were allowed back into European competition following a blanket ban in the aftermath of the Heysel Stadium disaster, and Lord Taylor's report into the Hillsborough tragedy proposed a series of reforms, the most significant of which was the introduction of all-seater stadia. Central, at least from a British perspective, to this new dawn for football was the 1990 World Cup. Italia 90 introduced the idea of the beautiful game into the popular consciousness. In particular, the BBC's choice of Puccini's 'Nessun Dorma', sung by Italian tenor Luciano Pavarotti, as its World Cup theme tune coated the people's game with a balm of high culture.[50] Although the sport's rough edges were still on show, with England fans involved in pitched battles against the Italian police during the country's opening group

50 On the back of the World Cup, 'Nessun Dorma' went to No. 2 in the British charts, and in 1991 the rock promoter Harvey Goldsmith staged a Pavarotti concert in Hyde Park in front of 125,000 people.

matches in Sardinia, this was not enough to undermine the tournament's broad appeal to a cross-class viewership.

'The standard bearer,' according to *The Guardian*'s David Lacey, 'for this regeneration of English football's appeal' was the next footballer to win SPOTY, Paul Gascoigne. Having helped propel an unfancied England side to a spot in the semi-finals of Italia 90, this sublimely gifted but emotionally impulsive young midfielder from Gateshead was about to have his moment of destiny. Once again, the opponents were Germany. Once again, the tabloids looked to the World Wars for inspiration. 'Herr we go again!' declared *The Sun*. 'We beat them in 1945. Now the battle of 1990.' 'The Kaiser puts troops on full alert,' cautioned *The Mirror*. The 25 million viewers who tuned in for the Turin showdown were steeled for an emotional rollercoaster. And, as the first period of extra time drew to a close with the teams locked at 1-1, their worst fears were realised. Overrunning the ball, Gascoigne lunged to retain possession and in the process brought down the German right-back Thomas Berthold.[51] Even before Berthold hit the ground, Gazza's hands were up pleading for leniency. But to no avail, and the resultant booking, his second of the tournament, ruled him out of the final should England win. It was all too much. His eyes welled up, his bottom lip quivered and the tears came. 'Have a word,' the England captain, Gary Lineker, signalled to the bench, but the young Geordie was beyond consoling.

---

51 Gascoigne later claimed, 'I hardly touched him,' but the replays suggest otherwise, and by today's standards he would be lucky to get away with only a booking.

Although the incident was ultimately rendered academic as England (inevitably?) lost the match on penalties, Gascoigne weeping was immediately seized on as the defining moment of the tournament. 'Gazza's tears' resonated with the viewing public, the poet and literary critic Ian Hamilton suggested, because they were 'an unequivocal spot-on depiction of our own distress'. The *Daily Mirror* agreed. A two-page spread of a blubbing Gascoigne was captioned 'The emotional moment that captured the feelings of a nation'. And for readers keen to wallow in their misery, a 'full colour poster of the picture that moved a nation' was obligingly made available for the bargain basement price of £1.50. If possible, *The Express* was even more taken by the whole occasion. Gascoigne's performance in extra time, the paper declared, epitomised 'old English values – values of heart and cussed belief that something stirs in the nation, something that forbids any easy bending of the knee'. The match, it insisted, 'ranks with Agincourt [for] we were present to cry God for Gazza! England! And St Bob!' After such passion it would have taken a cold-hearted subscriber to point out that Agincourt had actually been a victory.

There was the usual celebrity round for Gazza in the following months: an appearance on *Wogan*, a waxwork in Madame Tussauds, a trip to meet (and hug!) Mrs Thatcher at Downing Street.[52] Such was his fame at this time that he even sought to prevent the publication of an unauthorised biography

---

52 For the meeting with Thatcher, Gazza chose to wear a mustard-yellow suit matched with a floral beach shirt. His receipt of the Menswear Association's award for 'Britain's Best Dressed Man' tells you all you need to know about fashion in the early 1990s.

by claiming the proposed title, *Gazza*, was so well established it was effectively a trademark. Possibly, though, court was not the best place to test the limits of celebrity. 'Rugby or association?' Mr Justice Harman asked on being told the plaintiff played football. The case was dismissed. But, shockingly, for once the judiciary was out of touch with the mood on the ground. Gazza's fame crossed class boundaries, fusing popular and high culture. He could simultaneously be acclaimed, by one leading academic, 'the weeping, doomed, inarticulate idol of the working-classes', and proposed, 'alongside holders of peerages and baronetcies', for inclusion in Debrett's *People of Today 1991*. Perhaps the most astute dissection of his appeal came from (of all people) the Australian feminist intellectual Germaine Greer. '[Gascoigne] may be an idiot,' Greer told readers of *The Independent*, 'but he is an idiot savant. His genius is for football, and football is an art more central to our culture than anything the Arts Council deigns to recognise.' His coronation as Sports Personality of the Year in December 1990 was easier to explain. He won, *The Times* reported, because 'the public fell in love with him'.

Yet the public did not always find it easy to sustain their love for Gazza. The endearing innocence of the Turin tears was frequently offset by a crass boorishness. It was hard to know exactly what response a Norwegian television crew expected when they asked England's star player if he had a message for their country on the eve of a crucial World Cup qualifier in October 1992, but 'Yes, fuck off Norway!' must have been pretty low down the list. If the red tops' coverage had been limited to this sort of minor indiscretion, then all might have been fine, but more and more frequently the headlines focused on drink-fuelled nights out, brawls in pub car parks and his alarmingly volatile and ultimately abusive relationship with partner Sheryl. It was becoming increasingly clear to even the most casual observer that Gazza's errant behaviour stemmed from deep-seated mental health issues rather than some maverick propensity for mischief-making. But such a realisation did nothing, of course, to restrain the tabloids.

On the pitch things were little better. A wild challenge on Nottingham Forest's Gary Charles in the opening minutes of the 1991 FA Cup Final resulted in a shattered cruciate ligament and 16 months out of the game.[53] It was a sad way to end his career with Tottenham Hotspur. Although, on his return to fitness, there were occasional reminders of the free-flowing brilliance that had captivated the viewing millions during Italia 90 – most notably a magnificent goal against Scotland in Euro 96 – these were all too fleeting. For too much of his time with Lazio, Glasgow Rangers and, finally, Middlesbrough, Gazza was either injured or out of condition. In the course of his career, he underwent 27 operations, endured ten months in hospital and spent four and a half years recuperating from injuries. The tragedy was that these lay-offs were often self-inflicted. Ian Wooldridge's unforgiving verdict for the *Daily Mail* that Gascoigne was 'a fat ill-mannered Geordie who urinated a glorious God-given talent against numerous walls' was almost certainly too harsh. More revealing, perhaps, was Gazza's own assessment: 'I fulfilled my dreams but I didn't fulfil my potential.'

---

53 In his autobiography, Gascoigne admitted to behaving like 'a mad bastard' in the match. And when Gazza labels behaviour mad you know that means something.

Gascoigne was the first football celebrity of the big-money era. With satellite broadcasting companies such as BSB and Sky putting football at the centre of their business models, the game grew dramatically in reach and wealth. When Sky acquired BSB in 1992 it ploughed £305m into the sport to secure the television rights to the new Premier League. Suddenly the top stars could command astronomical fees. Gascoigne's first professional contract, in 1985, was for £120 per week. By the time he signed for Lazio in 1992 he was earning £22,000 per week. Yet, despite all the riches and fame, Gazza's public image remained largely unmediated. Throughout his career he appeared, at heart, to have stayed true to the unspoilt boy from a Gateshead council estate who just happened to have a gift for kicking a football. When he turned out for the 1990 World Cup homecoming parade sporting a pair of gigantic tie-on plastic breasts accompanied by a pendulous beer belly, he may have left even his most devoted fans momentarily bewildered, but he was simply being himself. He was, he told the documentary-maker John Pettman, most at home in the Dunston Excelsior Working Men's Club, where he still had to put his name up on the board to play snooker when he went out for a beer with the lads.

But the cost of authenticity was mockery. Gascoigne's peak coincided with a press war between the country's two bestselling dailies, Rupert Murdoch's *Sun* and Robert Maxwell's *Daily Mirror*. Between them they had a readership in excess of 15 million. With 'Gazzamania' sweeping Britain in the aftermath of Italia 90, the two papers engaged in a bitter contest to print ever more salacious material about the nation's new favourite. 'I just hope the tabloids will be kind to him,' confided the chat-show host Terry Wogan. He might as well have been hoping for the tides to halt. As press interest intensified, so Gascoigne seemed compelled to fuel it. 'He suffered more than anything,' Michael Henderson of *The Spectator* shrewdly noted, 'from being Gazza, a showbiz character designed to keep his name before the public.' For the future stars of the game, the lesson was clear. Football's ascent to cultural hegemony meant what happened off the pitch had become as important as what happened on it.

The news of Bobby Moore's death from cancer in February 1993 only added to the sense that the sporting landscape had somehow irrevocably changed. If Moore embodied the glories of the past, then Gascoigne represented the failings of the present. The aptly named Peter Tory of the *Daily Express* was just one of many columnists who found the urge to compare the two England heroes impossible to resist. Gascoigne, he wrote, 'wears kiss-me-quick hats, bongo-drum underpants, sticks his tongue out at camera lenses and no doubt lifts his leg at lampposts. If it's fogeyish in these matters to yearn for the old days, then God stand up for Fogeys. And let us shed a tear for the untimely passing of Bobby Moore.' Even a future home secretary felt obliged to contribute to the moralising. 'Surely nothing could illustrate more starkly the sorry state we have now reached,' David Blunkett informed the editor of the *Daily Mirror*, 'than the contrast between the attitudes, actions and behaviour of the much-loved late Bobby Moore and the present so-called heroes, such as Paul Gascoigne.' Clearly a new type of footballing icon was needed for the age of media celebrity.[27]

The next SPOTY winner from the people's game seemed to fit the bill perfectly. Although Michael Owen viewed Gazza as 'an absolute hero', he couldn't have been more different. Born into a stable and supportive family in the leafy Flintshire village of Hawarden, his formative years were a far cry from the chaotic, poverty-stricken upbringing Gascoigne endured. As he rapidly progressed through the youth system to break into Liverpool's first team before his 18th birthday, his father, Terry, a former professional with Everton, Bradford City and Chester, among others, ensured self-belief never spilled over into cockiness. Respect for the hierarchy of the dressing room was a lesson the neophyte Owen had taken to heart. In his most recent autobiography, he recalled always being anxious 'never to overstep the mark … or be at the core of all the fun and games'. It was hard to believe such concerns ever kept Gazza awake at night.

Yet, of course, on the pitch Owen and Gascoigne were not so dissimilar. Like all truly great players, they shared the ability to light up a match with a moment of sublime skill. For Owen, that moment came on 30 June 1998 in Saint-Étienne's Stade Geoffroy-Guichard. It was again a World Cup knockout match but, for once, the opponents were not Germany. Argentina, though, were the next best thing. With Maradona's 'Hand of God' goal from 1986, not to mention the Falklands War from four years earlier, still fresh in the minds of England fans, passions were running high. A penalty apiece in the first ten minutes warned ITV's record audience of 26.5 million viewers that it was going to be a long night of high drama. Then, just six minutes later, Owen produced the goal of the tournament. Receiving the ball inside the centre circle, he ran directly at the Argentinian defence, shrugged off a challenge from José Chamot, left Roberto Ayala for dead, before slotting past Carlos Roa in goal to put England 2-1 up. He was the youngest England player to score in the knockout stages of the World Cup.[54] The six seconds from receiving the ball to scoring were, he said, 'life-changing'. Unfortunately for England, such heroics were not enough to reverse what was now 32 years of hurt. In the inevitable penalty shoot-out, David Batty, who had only once before taken a spot kick (a missed one at that!) when a junior, blasted his effort straight at Roa, and Argentina were through.[55]

Despite the defeat, the press was in raptures over Owen's performance. 'He made you proud to be English,' raved *The Mirror,* while *The Express* settled for a front-page picture of the young star under the banner headline 'Hero'. Even the usually restrained *Guardian* expressed relief that 'an 18-year-old from Chester had finally buried memories of the Hand of God [with] the supreme moment of 1998'. But, by the time Owen was pronounced Sports Personality of the Year six months later, some commentators were ready to reassess just how much had really been achieved that night in Saint-Étienne. Both the *Daily Mail*'s Neil Wilson and Giles Smith for *The Times* worried that the public seemed fixated with gallant losers. Owen's award, thought Smith, 'bore sturdy witness to the nation's magnificent ability to dramatize itself in defeat'. The racehorse trainer, Jenny Pitman, was rather more blunt. She could not comprehend how the great National Hunt jockey A. P. McCoy could be overlooked

54 He had already become the youngest England player to score in the World Cup, with a goal against Romania in the group stage eight days earlier.

55 Even Batty's team-mates were surprised when they saw him step forward for the crucial fifth penalty. David Seaman recalled thinking, 'Hang on a minute, I've never ever seen him take a penalty, even in training.'

in favour of 'some 18-year-old kid who's been around for a few minutes. It's a joke.'

Perhaps it was just as well that Owen won SPOTY at such a young age, because his career never quite reached the same heights again. A ruptured hamstring playing against Leeds in April 1999 left him injury-prone and, although he continued to play at the highest level for another 15 years, he found it difficult to recapture the electrifying form he had shown against Argentina that June night in the Stade Geoffroy-Guichard. Probably the closest he came to it was in September 2001. The occasion was a crucial (aren't they all?) World Cup qualifier away to Germany. In an astonishing evening for English football, Owen scored a hat-trick in a scarcely believable 5-1 victory.

Back home the mood was ecstatic. Having honed their skills in comically antiquated stereotyping during Euro 96 ('We blew their jocks off' for Scotland; 'We gave 'em a good clogging' for the Netherlands; and, my personal favourite, 'We kicked 'em in the castanets' for Spain), the tabloids leapt at the chance to unleash their full range of anti-German taunts. 'Oh, mein Gott! It's their wurst nightmare,' crowed *The Sun*, having already dispatched an oompah band to play outside the German team hotel. 'Our Finest Hour' declared *The Mirror*, which had thought fit to reinforce the oompah band by mobilising a vintage armoured car. Disdainful of such glib headlines and cheap gimmicks, the *Daily Mail* chose instead to provide readers with a Cook's tour of Anglo-German flashpoints. The 'antagonism' between the two countries, the paper lectured, stemmed from 'the Archduke Franz Ferdinand, Field Marshal Haig, the Versailles Treaty, Chamberlain, Colditz, Bomber Harris and Dresden'. Yet not even this level of joyous

German-baiting was enough to secure Owen a second SPOTY triumph. He had to settle for third place as his team captain David Beckham lifted the trophy.[28]

In many ways it was not so surprising that Beckham was voted the nation's favourite in 2001. He, more than an unassuming young lad from Deeside who didn't even have his own bank account until he was 35, epitomised the expansive celebrity culture of Cool Britannia. Whether it was in the run-down estates of East London or the rarified corridors of Westminster, football now mattered more than ever. When Tony Blair reworked Baddiel and Skinner's 'Three Lions' England anthem at the Labour Party Conference in 1996, telling delegates '17 years of hurt never stopped us dreaming, Labour's coming home', he was not only referencing a new mood of political optimism but also tacitly acknowledging the cultural reach of football in the Premier League era. The beautiful game was now an ever-present feature of our national story. And, like all good stories, a tragi-heroic lead was required. In David Beckham the country had the ideal candidate. His public life, the Poet Laureate Carol Ann Duffy explained, was 'like a Greek myth, it contained both triumph and tragedy and in a way we could all learn from it'.

For Beckham, as the narrative arc of a collective fairy tale demands, the tragedy came before the triumph. On the same night that Owen was sanctified, he found himself vilified. With the second half of that pulsating clash against Argentina in the Stade Geoffroy-Guichard just seconds old, he was sent clattering to the ground by a clumsy challenge from Diego Simeone. All would have been fine but, inexplicably, the prostrate England midfielder chose to petulantly flick out his right leg and bring down the Argentine. The ensuing red card left England's hopes in tatters. Co-commentating for ITV, Kevin Keegan did his best to put everything into perspective. 'I had a player sent off in the play-offs against Grimsby,' he chirpily reminisced. But it wasn't enough to assuage the anger of the masses back home. The public mood was unforgiving. Beckham was condemned as a 'spoilt brat with more millions than common sense' by the cultural commentator Tony Parsons, while over two thirds of respondents to a Talk Radio poll felt he should never be allowed to play for England again. But maybe the general feeling of outrage was best captured by the *Daily Mirror*. 'Take your fury out on our cut-out David Beckham dartboard,' the paper urged readers. Needless to say, the villain of the hour was the bullseye, but should passion trump accuracy, the angry subscriber could still obtain some satisfaction by landing General Galtieri (13), Maradona (10), Ossie Ardiles (8) or, as a special bonus, Paul Daniels (7).

Although, in the aftermath of his red card in the World Cup, the level of media vitriol was shocking, constant press attention was something Beckham had long become used to. With catwalk good looks and a gift for the spectacular free kick, he had rarely been out of the news since making his debut for Manchester United in 1992. Interest only intensified in 1997 when he started dating Victoria Adams, Posh Spice from the hugely successful all-female pop band the Spice Girls. The alliance of football, fashion and music catapulted the pair to global celebrity. Beckham's lifestyle choices now received as much attention as his footballing skills. When he chose to wear a Jean Paul Gaultier sarong on a night out during of the World Cup in 1998, it made front-page news, although a junior reporter from *The Mirror* who was dispatched to the West End's pubs and clubs dressed in a similar outfit remained distinctly unimpressed. 'With Posh Spice on one arm and a gold Rolex on the other Becks can afford to look stupid,' he complained, 'and is unlikely to get beaten up.' But, to most, Beckham was now a 'metrosexual icon'. 'He might be gay, straight or bisexual,' Mark Simpson of *GQ* magazine mused, 'but this is utterly immaterial because he … has a way of asserting a new aesthetic power in an aestheticized world.'

And there was no better example of that new aesthetic power than Posh and Becks' wedding in July 1999. Held at Luttrellstown Castle in Ireland, and exclusively covered by *OK!* magazine for the exorbitant price of one million pounds, the event took ten months to organise and had a cast of over 300 to look after the 225 guests. Themed as 'romantic Sherwood Forest', the vibe was baroque royal. There were gilded thrones for the happy couple, a fanfare to announce their arrival, and flags with a specially designed crest to mark their union. The wedding planner was Peregrine Armstrong-Jones, Lord Snowdon's half-brother, the flowers were arranged by John Plested, a veteran of royal events, while Slim Barrett, the Queen's jeweller, supplied Posh with a diamond-and-gold tiara. This was as much a coronation as a wedding. They were, claimed the newlyweds' biographer, Andrew Morton, 'royalty for the common man'. Yet, despite the ostentation of the ceremony and the lavishness of the wealth on display, the Beckhams' appeal lay in the glamour of the everyday. By 'combining a common touch with the exoticism of fame', they had, thought the historian Alwyn Turner, managed to pull off the same trick as Princess Diana nearly 20 years earlier.

Although, by the turn of the 21st century, Beckham was the most recognisable footballer on the planet, he had yet to convince everyone that his prowess on the pitch fully warranted his level of celebrity. He was, it was generally agreed, unrivalled at set-piece plays but lacked the touch of genius required to dictate open play. Not only was Becks not the best midfielder in the world, argued team-mate Gary Neville, in a reworking of John Lennon's famous quip about Ringo Starr's drumming, but he wasn't even in the top three of Manchester United's midfield quartet.[56] It would require, therefore, a single act of brilliance to propel him to the top of the BBC's SPOTY poll. That moment arrived in the last minute of England's final qualifying match for the 2002 World Cup. With 93 minutes on the clock, and a stubborn Greek team resolutely hanging on to a 2-1 lead, the capacity crowd inside Wembley seemed resigned to their nation missing out on the desperately needed draw that would mean automatic qualification for Korea/Japan 2002. But then Sheringham was brought down on the edge of the Greek penalty area, and Beckham stepped up and stepped into sporting immortality.

From being the most hated man in Britain just three years ago, he was now, insisted the *Daily Star*, 'a national treasure'. And to underline the point, readers were provided with a 12-page 'Becks-tasy' special, charting the England saviour's rise to sainthood. The *Daily Mirror* considered it necessary to go all the way back to the dark days of the Second World War to find a comparable example of one man saving the nation from

56 At the time, United enjoyed an embarrassment of riches in the centre of the park with Ryan Giggs, Roy Keane and Paul Scholes.

international dishonour. 'You really want a new Churchill?' it rhetorically asked, 'then take a look at David Beckham, who didn't stop fighting when all around him his team-mates had given up the ghost.' To the delight of all, the man who 'single-handedly took England into the World Cup Finals' duly won SPOTY at the end of the year. Well, nearly all. *Top Gear* presenter Jeremy Clarkson was unable to forgive and forget. 'How do we reward round-the-world sailor Ellen MacArthur, the bravest and most talented sports person this country has ever produced?' he mused in his regular *Sunday Times* column. 'By telling her in front of ten million TV viewers that the man who cost us the chance of victory in the 1998 World Cup is somehow better.'

Although Beckham fell out with the Manchester United manager, Sir Alex Ferguson, in 2003, over the impact his wider fame was having on his commitment to the club, he still continued to enjoy success on the pitch as one of Real Madrid's *galacticos*. Even as late as 2010, by which time he was on loan with AC Milan, the nation was still sufficiently invested in his footballing fortunes that a torn Achilles tendon was enough to move the poet laureate to write a consolatory verse.[57] But Beckham was more than just a footballer. Rather like Paul Gascoigne, his fame reached far beyond the boundaries of the beautiful game. But, whereas Gazza found the media glare of global celebrity too much to bear, Becks flourished to become a recognised brand in his own right and an accepted member of the super-rich. Yet Beckham's celebrity should not be allowed to overshadow his achievements as a footballer: 394 appearances and 85 goals for

57 Carol Ann Duffy, *Achilles (for David Beckham)* (2010).

an all-conquering Manchester United team was an impressive tally by anybody's standards. Except, possibly, those of the next SPOTY winner.***29***

Ryan Giggs made his league debut for Manchester United in March 1991 as a 17-year-old and, astonishingly, remained a fixture of the first-team squad for the following 23 years. In that time he made 632 league appearances and 963 appearances in all competitions, breaking Bobby Charlton's previous record by over 200. This achievement was all the more remarkable for having taken place in the post-Bosman era, when restrictions on player movement across the European Union had been lifted.[58] As an influx of highly paid foreign imports started to raise questions about commitment and club identity, Giggs's fidelity seemed all the more commendable. In the dislocated landscape of post-industrial Britain, the Manchester United man was a nostalgic reminder of a time when a job was for life.

And what made Giggs's story even more inspiring was that he was a local boy made good. Although born in Cardiff, he was brought up in Manchester where his father played rugby league for Swinton. From an early age it was clear he was a unique talent. Sir Alex Ferguson first saw Giggs play in a schoolboy match. 'He was 13 and just floated over the ground like a cocker spaniel chasing a piece of silver paper in the wind,' the Manchester United manager recalled with uncharacteristic lyricism. Even his peers singled him out as exceptional. 'No disrespect to Beckham and

58 A 1995 test case, brought by a little-known Belgium player, Jean-Marc Bosman, resulted in the European Court of Justice ruling that all restrictions on foreign EU players within national leagues were illegal, and that players should be regarded as free agents when their contracts expired.

Scholesy,' Steve Bruce told *The Sun*'s Frank Worrall, 'but Ryan was the only one who was always going to be a superstar.'

However, in 1991, it wasn't so obvious that the road to superstardom lay with Manchester United. It had been 24 years since the club had last been crowned champions, a fact not lost on Liverpool fans who, when hostage negotiator Terry Waite was released after nearly five years in captivity in Beirut, had commemorative T-shirts commissioned emblazoned with Waite's face and the slogan, 'What, Manchester United still haven't won the league?' Even consecutive titles in 1993 and 1994 did not convince everyone that Giggs and his new young team-mates – the Class of '92 – would become world-beaters.[59] 'You can't win anything with kids,' *Match of the Day* pundit and former Liverpool defender Alan Hansen intoned, after United had lost 3-1 to Aston Villa on the opening day of the 1995 season. But, of course, he could hardly have been more wrong. By the time Giggs decided to hang up his boots, he had become the most decorated British player ever, having won the Premier League 13 times, the FA and League Cups four times and the Champions League twice.

Although one biographer felt his longevity counted against him when it came to individual awards because fans simply took his success for granted, in 2009 he, nonetheless, won both the Professional Footballers' Association's Player of the Year award and, the acid test of public popularity, SPOTY. Certainly there was a feeling among some commentators that, at 36, Giggs was

59 The 'Class of '92' was a group of young academy players at United who went on to achieve success with the first team. As well as Ryan Giggs, Paul Scholes and David Beckham, the group included Nicky Butt and the Neville brothers, Phil and Gary.

past his best and these honours were, as *The Guardian* put it, merely 'an exercise in nostalgia'. But most believed the recognition was fully deserved, not just for his talent on the pitch but for his conduct away from it. He was, thought the *Sunday Express*, 'a fabulous role model in a gaudy sport not entirely filled with such characters'. In a rare moment of harmony across the political divide, the *Daily Mirror* agreed. Giggs was popular, the paper's award-winning sports columnist, Brian Reade, claimed, because he was an 'anti-modern footballer' who had not allowed the money of the 'Sky Super Sunday Premier League' to 'skew his values and turn his head'. And for those who wanted one of the modern wastrels who had allowed their values to be skewed and their head to be turned to be named and shamed, Reade was happy to oblige: 'A vote for Giggs,' he acidly noted, 'was a vote against the Ashley Coles of this world.'[60]

But Giggs's reputation as a model professional was tarnished in 2011 when news broke that he had been having an affair with his sister-in-law for the past eight years.[61] The revelation was a bitter disappointment. It appeared to many that the people's game was no longer able to furnish the nation with heroes in the mould of Bobby Moore. The London Olympics, the following year, served to further underline the sense that football was a sport that had sacrificed its soul. The contrast seemed stark between 'the loyalty and fair play of our cyclists, rowers and runners [and]

60 The Chelsea defender, Ashley Cole, whose turbulent relationship with Girls Aloud singer Cheryl Tweedy provided endless copy for the tabloids, was often held up as all that was wrong with the modern game.

61 Giggs's reputation took a further knock when he was charged with assaulting his ex-girlfriend and her sister. A jury, in 2022, was unable to reach a verdict and the CPS subsequently chose not to go to retrial.

the vast carnival of cheating, brutality and avarice known as the Premier League'. Maybe it was inevitable, then, that the next footballer to win SPOTY should come not from the cash-bloated ranks of male players but instead from the relative purity of the women's game, where the sport was unspoilt by billion-pound TV and sponsorship deals.[30]

But the apparent innocence of women's football had, of course, nothing to do with some idealistic attachment to Corinthian values. It was simply the result of straightforward sexism. Worried by the growing popularity of 'munitionettes' matches during the Great War, the men who ran the Football Association had, in December 1921, reasserted what they considered to be the natural order by banning all women's teams from league and association affiliated grounds. The ban remained in force for half a century and prevented any meaningful development of the women's game. The second feminist wave of the 1960s onwards did manage to bring some gains. The prohibition on using FA grounds was lifted in 1971 and, the following year, England women played their first international match against Scotland at the Ravenscraig Stadium in Greenock. Over the next couple of decades progress was steady, although it wasn't until 1995 that England made their debut at the World Cup. Media coverage in this period was minimal, with only Channel 4 deigning to air a brief highlights package. Even this was too much for Scottish sports commentator Archie Macpherson. 'I'm not saying a woman's place is purely in the home,' he combatively began a piece for the *Sunday Times* in 1990, '[but] if Ch4 wants to show us how entertaining football can be outside the senior game then let them put the cameras at other places like any school playground.'

Unfortunately, Macpherson's antediluvian views were all too common. Ron Atkinson's blunt assessment that 'women should be in the kitchen, the discothèque and the boutique, but not in football' was shocking only inasmuch as it revealed that the bluff Aston Villa manager apparently had a passing acquaintance with dance-club culture and high-end couture. The extent to which sexist views continued to pervade the game was most starkly illustrated during a match between Wolves and Liverpool in 2011. Wrongly assuming they were off-mike, Sky pundits Andy Gray and Richard Keys took assistant referee Sian Massey to task for allowing Liverpool's first goal to stand. 'Somebody better get down there and explain offside to her,' a condescending Keys suggested. Gray was equally contemptuous. 'Female linesmen,' he spluttered, '... they probably don't know the offside rule ...Why is there a female linesman? Somebody's fucked up big.' Predictably, replays proved Massey's judgement to have been spot on.[62]

Something of a turning point occurred a year after the Keys and Gray incident. Inspired by a summer of Olympic sport, 70,000 turned up at Wembley to watch Team GB defeat Brazil in the group stages of the women's football tournament. Continued success for the English national squad saw the profile of the women's game rise even higher. The semi-final defeat by Japan in the 2015 World Cup drew a television audience of 2.4 million, despite a midnight kick-off, and four years later over 11 million tuned in to see more semi-final heartache as the Lionesses went down 2-1 to the USA. On the back of this progress, the domestic game was overhauled in 2017, with a fully professional Women's

62 Keys and Gray were sacked by Sky in January 2011.

Super League attracting an £8m-per-season broadcasting deal from the BBC. All it needed now was England to go all the way in a major tournament for popular support to reach the critical point where a female footballer would be in with a chance of being crowned Britain's favourite sportsperson.

The staging of Euro 2022 in England could not, therefore, have come at a better time. Although, rather like the World Cup in 1966, it took a while for public interest to build, by the knockout stages the nation had become fully invested in the fortunes of Sarina Wiegman's England team. Over nine million watched the Lionesses overwhelm Sweden 4-0 in the semi-final at Sheffield United's Bramall Lane, while nearly twice that number sat nervously in pubs, clubs and front rooms as Germany finally succumbed after extra time in the final at a sold-out Wembley Stadium. Emblematic of a country in thrall to the sheer joy of the occasion was eight-year-old Tess Dolan. Dressed in the full team kit, and clutching an England scarf, the television cameras caught her as she unselfconsciously danced her heart out while jubilantly belting out 'Sweet Caroline'. Women's football had truly arrived.

Just as had been the true for Moore in 1966, the figurehead of the victorious England team in 2022 was voted Player of the Tournament. And, just for good measure, Beth Mead also took home the Golden Boot. It was no real surprise, therefore, when the England striker again matched Moore with the award of the Sports Personality of the Year trophy in December. Yet, although it was predictable, it was also startling. Mead's victory showed just how far women's football had come in such a short time. In many ways her career mirrored those of any number of male professionals. Scouted at a young age, she joined her local academy before being signed up by a league club on leaving school. But it was during her spell at her first senior team, Sunderland, that the additional challenges faced by elite female footballers became most evident. With the men's team facing imminent relegation in 2017, the board looked for ways to reduce expenditure. Although the women's team was enjoying a period of top-flight success, having just been promoted to the Super League and reaching the FA Cup semi-final, it was here that the financial axe fell. To support the men, the women were all reduced to part-time contracts. It was a cruel reminder of the subordinate status of the female game. Having overcome such obstacles, it was little wonder that a tearful Mead insisted her SPOTY triumph was 'for women's sport and for women's sport heading in the right direction'.[31]

* * *

II. Cricket

Jim Laker (1956) – David Steele (1976) – Ian Botham (1981) – Andrew Flintoff (2005) – Ben Stokes (2019)

FOOTBALL MAY have a long way to go as it heads off in the right direction, but at least it has set out on the journey. By contrast, cricket still appears to be waiting to depart. In June 2023, an independent commission, tasked by the English and Wales Cricket Board to look into equity in cricket, found that the sport was riven with 'structural and institutional racism' and laboured under 'a culture of sexism and misogyny'. As if this was not bad enough, the commission's report also noted that, at all levels, the game was blighted by 'elitism and class-based discrimination'. This last criticism, in particular, pointed to a sport that still seemed to be stuck in the high Victorian period when gentlemen amateurs ruled the roost. Two World Wars and the advent of mass democracy had done little to alter the social composition of cricket's governing elite, which still looked to retired army generals, the landed gentry and men of private means to fill its ranks. Compared with the Marylebone Cricket Club (MCC) committee, Lord Monckton thought Harold Macmillan's cabinet in 1959 (a third of whom were Old Etonians and all of whom were public-school alumni) 'looked like a band of pinkos'.[63] And Monckton was well placed to know, having been a member of both. Even at the beginning of the 21st century, 'Freddie' Flintoff, Ashes hero and SPOTY winner in 2005, believed you had to be either 'lucky or privileged to play men's cricket'.

For the first cricketer to win SPOTY, this elitism was especially galling. Born in the West Riding of Yorkshire, educated at the local state grammar and raised in a household where his father's abandonment made finances tight, Jim Laker bridled at what he called 'the traditional Oxbridge axis' that dominated the game. The distinction between professional 'players' and amateur 'gentlemen', which still held fast in the immediate post-war years, was, he felt, an affront to his dignity. 'I would rather doff my cap,' he confided to one team-mate, 'to a professional

63 The MCC was formerly the governing body of cricket and still holds a role as the custodian and arbiter of the laws and spirit of the game.

like Len Hutton than an undeserving amateur.' And it wasn't just a matter of principle. Money was at stake as well. An arcane expenses system meant amateurs could claim for a whole range of incidentals. Indeed, as *The Observer* wryly noted, 'The only thing that amateur cricketers may not receive money for is playing cricket.' Laker was so outraged by the injustice of it all that, on the eve of the 1958–59 Ashes, he leaked to the press that he was thinking of turning amateur for the duration of the tour so he could earn more money.

It hardly helped matters that Laker played for Surrey. Despite the new meritocratic public mood in the wake of the People's War, the authorities at The Oval clung tenaciously to the old ways. Surrey's amateurs had their own entrance to the ground, padded up in separate changing rooms, enjoyed first-class travel to away matches and stayed over in the most prestigious hotels. Throughout Laker's time at the county, the captaincy was the preserve of the amateur. Professionals, so the thinking went, whose livelihoods depended on winning, could not be trusted to play the game in the right spirit. With the pool of gifted amateurs dwindling in the aftermath of the war, Surrey's determination to eschew the professional captain led to some unfortunate decision-making.

In 1946, the county rather surprisingly announced that the team would be led by Major N. H. Bennett, a moderate club cricketer with no first-class experience. Bennett had been appointed having popped down to The Oval to renew his membership and ask whether there was any chance of a knock with the 2nd XI. Although no one would subsequently admit to having made a mistake, it seems almost certain that the selectors had got their Bennetts confused. A. C. L. Bennet, who captained the BBC 1st XI and had occasionally led Northamptonshire, never did find out why an initial approach by Surrey was not followed up. N. H. lasted just one disastrous season. His successor was only marginally better. E. R. T. Holmes, an Old Malvernian and Oxford Blue, may have possessed 'great charm and sweetness', but even Surrey's official historian had to admit that he was 'not a master tactician'.[64] It was hardly any wonder that the ultra-professional Laker thought the abolition of amateur status in 1962 was the 'best thing to have happened in the game in my lifetime'.

Laker's career at The Oval began after demobilisation in 1946. Although he enjoyed enormous domestic success, helping Surrey to seven consecutive county titles between 1952 and 1958, he could not replicate this form at international level. His first taste of Ashes cricket, in 1948, was a severe disappointment. The nine wickets he took across three of the five matches in the series cost 472 runs, and he found himself out of the squad for the subsequent tour of South Africa. By 1956, then, the 34-year-old Laker was a relatively inexperienced Test player, having been out of the England line-up more often than he had been in it since his debut in 1947.

However, continued good form at county level persuaded the selectors to issue a recall for the Australians' visit in 1956. Laker's moment had finally arrived. In direct contrast to 1948, he played in all five Tests and took 46 wickets in total as he helped England to a 2-1 win. In the fourth Test at Old Trafford his

64 Cricket is particularly fond of initials and used to deploy them to denote the status of a player – before the surname for an amateur and after for a professional.

figures were 19-90, with one remarkable 22-ball spell resulting in seven wickets for just eight runs. His bowling over those five days in Manchester remains unmatched in first-class cricket. Although the dailies were duly impressed, '10 Little Aussie Boys Lakered in a Row' was *The Express*'s distinctly of-its-time headline, the public acclaim was considerably more muted than that experienced by Test heroes in the age of live television coverage. Customers in a Lichfield pub, happily watching the evening highlights of the final day's play from Old Trafford, remained blissfully unaware that the man of the moment had broken his journey home to have a quiet beer and sandwich in the corner of the snug. Thankfully, by the end of the year, Laker's face had become recognisable enough for the public to vote him in as the first cricketer to win SPOTY.

The financial rewards for Laker were equally less extravagant than they would be for the small-screen sporting stars of later years. He managed to supplement his £75 Test fee with commercial deals worth about £1,000. A tidy sum but hardly life-changing. It was to be expected, therefore, that on his retirement in 1960 he would cash in on his celebrity by publishing a memoir. Equally expected were the frank views expressed in *Over to Me*. Writing an autobiography, Laker felt, was a chance 'to offer criticism of what I think is wrong with the game'. And he certainly took full advantage of that chance. Directly in his sights were the blazered administrators who maintained the sport's class apartheid. Officials, Laker complained, treated the professional as if he was no more than a 'paid lackey'. By today's explosive standards the book was candid rather than scandalous, but it was still enough for both the MCC and Surrey to revoke their former star's honorary membership on the grounds that he had 'done the gravest misservice to cricket'.[65] Worryingly, though, for the authorities, Laker's views elicited some unanticipated sympathy. *The Times*, usually a pillar of the cricketing status quo, gently mocked the MCC, hoping its ban would 'not apply to all honorary members. After all, the forthright Duke of Edinburgh is one and, like Laker, he bowls off-breaks.'[32]

The press' largely unsympathetic response to Laker's censure in 1960 was a sign of a game in crisis. Crowds at county matches had been in freefall since the late 1940s. Peaking at 2.2 million in 1947, they had fallen to 700,000 by the time of Laker's Ashes triumph, and then bottomed out at just 160,000 by the start of the 1980s. So dire was the situation that Anthony Eden's Conservative government felt obliged to exempt cricket from entertainment tax, although this could easily be viewed as a damning comment on the county game's defensive drudgery as much as its financial precarity. The real problem for the sport was that it had failed to move with the times. With the Empire collapsing, satire flourishing and the counter-culture in full swing, by the late 1960s cricket seemed pitiably out of date. To make matters worse, at the start of the 1970s the England team went on a losing streak. For the first time, a home Test series was lost to India, with further humiliation being doled out by the West Indies and Australia, including a 4-1 Ashes thumping in 1974–75.

As far as the old guard in the committee rooms at Lord's was concerned the rot had set in with the advent of sponsored

65 Both the MCC and Surrey later reversed their decisions.

limited overs competitions in the 1960s.[66] The need to satisfy the meritocratic demands of commercial partners and live television had resulted in the abolition of the divide between gentlemen and players. The *Daily Mirror* might have been excited that the inaugural one-day Gillette Cup Final between Sussex and Worcestershire in 1963 had turned 'Lord's, the temple of tradition, into a reasonable replica of Wembley', but for the purist this was cause for deep regret. The problem, the Tory peer Lord Trafford thought, was that cricket was now played in a 'red brick manner by red brick characters with red brick outlooks'. Maybe it wasn't quite as bad as being branded 'a slum sport played in slum stadiums by slum people', but it was still pretty damning.

What was needed was a new Test hero to reignite the public's passion for the sport's traditional format. And in 1975, in the midst of all the sporting and economic gloom, an unlikely saviour was found. David Steele was 33, although his grey hair made him look older, and was in his benefit year with Northamptonshire when he was called up for the second Ashes Test at Headingley at the end of July 1975. England had been brushed aside by an embarrassing innings and 85 runs in the first Test, and the selectors were desperate to find someone who could shore up the batting. As Steele prepared to walk out of the pavilion at Lord's and on to the international stage, few thought he was the man to resurrect English cricket. Certainly not the caretaker who had to point him in the direction of the pitch when he took a wrong turn and ended up in the basement toilets, nor Jeff Thomson,

66 The Gillette Cup was set up in 1963 and the John Player Sunday League in 1969. Both were limited overs competitions.

the fearsome Australian fast bowler, who greeted the eventual arrival of the bespectacled debutant with a dismissive, 'Bloody hell, who've we got here, Groucho Marx?' Even normally loyal MCC members could be heard muttering to each other, 'Who's this grey old bugger?'

And the members had good cause to be concerned. This was the era of the bouncer wars, when fast bowlers would attempt to intimidate batters with short-pitched deliveries. There were real fears that the practice would result in fatalities. Just six months before the second Ashes Test at Lord's, New Zealand tailender Ewen Chatfield had to receive on-the-pitch mouth-to-mouth resuscitation after he had been struck on the temple by a bouncer. Facing Steele, as he prepared to make his debut, were two of the greatest-ever proponents of fast bowling, Jeff Thomson and Dennis Lillee. The intention, said Lillee, was to 'hit a batsman in the ribcage … so he doesn't want to face me anymore'. Thomson set his sights slightly higher. 'I thought, stuff that stiff-upper-lip crap,' he told one journalist, 'let's see how stiff it is when it's split.' Even more alarming from an English supporter's perspective was Steele's nonchalant approach to personal safety. He refused to encumber himself with thigh pads and chest protectors, and instead simply stuffed a few strategically placed towels inside his kit. He did, though, thank goodness, 'make sure his glasses were clean'.

But, of course, it was this undemonstrative courage that was the secret to Steele's popularity. He might not have been a 'glamorous batsman', admitted his county captain, Mushtaq Mohammad, but he refused to back down and 'he got the job done'. An average of just over 60 across the three Tests he played helped England to some unlikely draws, and meant the series resulted in a disappointing, but by no means humiliating, 1-0 defeat. In the context of 1970s Britain, it was really the best that could be hoped for. The doughty veteran from Northamptonshire had managed to restore some pride to the country and in the process tap into a powerful national trope. He was, the renowned cricket historian Derek Birley noted, universally celebrated as 'the quiet unassuming chap who stands up to the bully'. Or, as Clive Taylor of *The Sun* famously put it, he was 'the bank clerk who went to war'.

Just like the everyman heroes of the People's War, Steele's rewards for his efforts in the summer of 1975 were honorific rather than pecuniary. He won both the *Daily Express*'s and the BBC's Sportsman of the Year awards. But these accolades didn't mean he could afford to give up his job as a sales rep for a printing company in the close season, nor did they guarantee him continued employment as a Test cricketer. Despite a good showing in the home series against the West Indies in 1976, he was dropped for the subsequent tour of India and never regained his place in the Test squad. His brief spell in the sun was over and all that there was left to do, as *The Guardian*'s Frank Keating observed, 'was to waddle back to the county grind'.[33]

If Steele was a throwback to the unsung heroes of wartime, then the next cricketing SPOTY winner was very much a creature of his time. Ian 'Beefy' Botham presented as the brash icon of Thatcher's Britain. A state-educated individualist whose talent and bloody-mindedness took him to the very top of an establishment world, he had a self-confidence that bordered on arrogance. 'I sometimes got called big-head,' he recalled, 'but I used to think, "No, I'm not, I'm just very good at this, a lot better than you."' Opponents on the field and in the committee rooms were dismissed with the same savage brutality that Thatcher reserved for the 'wets' in her cabinet. Botham, the *Daily Express* approvingly declared after his Ashes triumph at Edgbaston in 1981, 'forgot he was British and played to win'. But maybe that was the new normal in Thatcher's aggressively ambitious Britain.

When Botham took over from Mike Brearley to become England's youngest-ever captain, in 1980, it seemed to signal not simply a change in leadership but a complete cultural shift. Proud of his working-class roots and intolerant of the 'gin-slinging dodderers' who ran the sport, Botham was the antithesis of the quietly intellectual, public-school and Cambridge-educated Brearley. For Botham, cricket was a simple game: 'Three sticks in the ground and a ball to knock them down, a big stick to protect them by hitting the ball.' He had no time for the teams of psychologists, nutritionists and sports scientists who tried to control every aspect of the professional sportsman's life. Cricket was about enjoying yourself. The best way to prepare for a big match, he told one interviewer, was not in the practice nets but in the bath, with a copy of the *Sporting Life* and a cigar, followed by a pork pie for breakfast.

And relaxing post-match, whether celebrating a victory or nursing a defeat, was equally important. On tour, his most recent biographer noted, Botham 'invariably shoved people into swimming pools … singed their hair with cigarette lighters and, with breathtaking predictability, turned up to Christmas fancy-dress parties as a gorilla'. For a public emerging from the gloom of the strike-hit 70s, such larger-than-life antics came as a welcome distraction. If Botham was a drink, Jonathan Margolis of the *Sunday Times* asserted, 'He would be a six-pack of strong lager: brash, powerful, popular and in thoroughly bad taste.'

If Laker defined the 1956 Ashes series and Steele the 1975 series, then Botham's moment came in 1981. Born in Yeovil, he left school at 16 and, after a spell as what was effectively an apprentice at Lord's, he joined Somerset when he was just 17. From there his progress was rapid, and by 1978 he was being widely touted as the future of the national team. Over the next couple of years he played in 20 Tests, scoring over 1,000 runs and taking 112 wickets. His new standing as a sporting man of the people was officially confirmed when he was invited to join the likes of Mick McManus and Harvey Smith as a *Sun* columnist. But then it all seemed to fall apart. Having been appointed captain in the summer of 1980, his form collapsed. His batting average dropped from 40 to 14, and his England team failed to win a single Test match.

Although the selectors backed their new captain when the Australians arrived in England for the 1981 Ashes, it simply seemed to make matters worse. England fell behind 1-0 in the series after the first two Tests, with Botham managing only 34 runs in total.[67] And, to add insult to injury, the nation appeared to be collapsing in sympathy. Rioting, which had initially started in Brixton and spread to Toxteth, was now breaking out in impoverished inner cities across the country. It all seemed symptomatic of a society on the brink of failure. Desperate to

67 The second Test at Lord's was a personal disaster for Botham as he failed to trouble the scorer in both of England's innings.

revive a team that was woefully short of confidence, the selectors brought back Brearley as captain and the stage was set for what the *Daily Express* wearingly dubbed 'the greatest comeback since Lazarus'.

After the first three days of the third Test at Headingley nothing much seemed to have changed. England had been forced to follow on after collapsing to 174 all out in their first innings, 227 behind the Australians, and although Botham had recovered some form, with a solid 50, nobody was expecting anything other than another victory for the tourists. Both Ladbrokes and the Australians were confident the match would be done by the fourth day, with the former offering 500-1 against an England victory and the latter ordering in a case of celebratory champagne. Even some of the England players believed the cause was lost, and checked out of the team hotel on Monday morning, assuming their misery would be over before the final day.

As late as the afternoon of the fourth day, with England seven wickets down and well behind the Australians' first innings total, Ladbrokes' odds still looked to have been the right call. Then in came the young fast bowler Graham Dilley, who decided he might as well have a bit of fun and hit out. Recognising a fellow risk-taker, Botham followed suit, and his 149 not out gave England something to play for in the final day. With Australian confidence seeping away by the minute, Warwickshire's Bob Willis took a superb 8-43 to give England the unlikeliest of victories. It was the first time a team had won a match after following on since 1894. The fourth and fifth Tests followed much the same pattern. England got off to dreadful starts before inspired passages of play by Botham – five wickets in 28 balls at Edgbaston and 118 runs from 102 balls in the final Test at Old Trafford – turned the tables. Against all the odds, England, driven on by their former captain, had retained the Ashes.

Botham may have been the sporting embodiment of Thatcherism, but the press was keen to place his Test heroics in a long tradition of English indomitability. The *Daily Express*, ever predictable, struck a Churchillian note, proclaiming, 'Never in the field of cricket conflict between England and Australia can one team have owed so much to one man,' while *The Mirror* looked to the sport's golden era, insisting Botham was 'a throwback to the days of Grace, Hobbs and Empire'. But, for jingoistic nostalgia, they were both trumped by *The Independent*'s Derek Hodgson. 'There are dates and times,' Hodgson rhapsodised, 'forever connected to one name: William and 1066; Nelson and 1805; Wellington and 1815. In the English consciousness, 1981 will be Ian Terence Botham.' Even the man himself got caught up in all the hype. 'Out on the field,' he told a feature writer for *Esquire*, 'it's you against them. It's similar to guys being in their Spitfires in the Battle of Britain.' It was a good soundbite, but it didn't convince the great Australian all-rounder and former RAAF flying officer Keith Miller. 'Pressure,' Miller told Michael Parkinson when asked how he dealt with the stresses of a Test match, 'is a Messerschmitt up your arse, playing cricket is not.' Maybe the heroics of 1981 were not quite on a par with those of 1940, but it was still generally agreed that Botham had only to turn up to win SPOTY. In fact, he did not even have to do that, and he duly received the trophy (or at least a replica) from Mike Brearley in Bangalore during England's tour of India.

But, as is so often the case, winning SPOTY proved to be a turning point, and Botham never quite reached the same heights again. In fairness, being tagged the saviour of hopeless causes was just not sustainable, although there was a feeling among some that 'Beefy' had allowed the balance between hard work and self-confidence to tip in the wrong direction. Too often, after 1981, the headlines were made by exploits off the field rather than heroics on it. There were tabloid stories of liaisons with glamour models, drunken punch-ups in bars and illicit drug-taking. The nadir came in 1986 when Botham admitted to being a 'casual' user of cannabis. It was pretty tame stuff, but the Test and County Cricket Board still banned him from all forms of the game for two months. A novelty T-shirt slogan – 'From Ashes to Hashish' – said it all.

Despite the indiscretions, Botham remained immensely popular. In part, this was due to his indefatigable efforts raising money for leukaemia research through a series of gruelling long-distance walks, but mostly it was down to the enduring legacy of that summer in 1981. His unwavering will to win, while living life to the full, proved to be an irresistible combination. He may have been thought to capture the *zeitgeist* of the times, but he was also regarded as an ageless symbol of British invincibility and exceptionalism. He would, held one former president of the Cricket Writers' Club, have been instantly recognisable to 'Regency England … as the man who could ride to hounds from dawn, fight twenty-five rounds bare-knuckle of an afternoon, dine on a mountain of boiled mutton, roast beef, plum duff and Cheddar cheese, washed down by ale and claret, and top it off with a bottle of brandy: a man who proclaimed one Englishman worth ten scurvy foreigners. For Ian Botham read John Bull.'[34]

It was to be 26 years before a cricketer again topped the SPOTY poll. And, once again, the setting was a dramatic home Ashes victory. Indeed, the parallels between 1981 and 2005 were striking. Both series began shockingly for the hosts, and both were played out against a backdrop of civil turmoil – in 2005 the country was still reeling from the London bombings of 7 July when the first Test at Lord's opened. But, of course, it was the match-winning exploits of yet another swashbuckling all-rounder that really fuelled the comparisons. In Andrew 'Freddie' Flintoff the sport seemed to have found a Botham for the new millennium; another working-class icon whose talent and exuberance provided copy for the feature writer and gossip columnist as well as the sports journalist. Like Botham, Flintoff drove England to an unlikely Ashes victory in 2005 with passages of sublime play. Indeed, with typical modesty, 'Beefy' felt the 'highest compliment' he could pay 'Freddie' was to point out 'he plays like me'.

But there was also a vulnerability to Flintoff that was not there in Botham. Rather like Paul Gascoigne, Flintoff was a complex personality. A swaggering, rumbustious presence on the cricket pitch and in the dressing room, he was quietly spoken and self-effacing when away from the sport. 'Are you now the best player in the world?' asked one interviewer, once all the excitement of 2005 had died down a little. 'No, am I 'eck. I'm all right,' replied a clearly embarrassed Flintoff. Whereas Botham was a cricketing colossus to be admired from a distance, a superman whose feats on and off the field ordinary mortals could not hope to emulate,

Flintoff came across as a normal bloke who just happened to be very good with a bat and ball, a sporting icon with the common touch. He was, essentially, one of us. Just like Freddie, surely we all secretly wanted to have fish fingers, chips and beans at the kids' table on our wedding day rather than 'confit chicken something'? His agents may have seen him as cricket's answer to David Beckham, but, if he had to be the face of a brand, it was always going to be budget-friendly George at Asda and not Dolce & Gabbana.

Flintoff's early career was typical of the gifted cricketer from a humble background. He left school at 16 to join his local county squad, Lancashire, and from there progressed through age-group teams to make his international debut when he was 20. But much of this period of professional development was blighted by back and knee injuries, neither of which were helped by weight issues.[68] Although he gradually secured his position as a key member of the Test squad over the next few years, another injury requiring an operation to remove a heel spur provided unwanted pressure on the eve of the 2005 Ashes. The opening Test at Lord's did nothing to ease the strain. His contribution to a 239-run defeat was just four wickets and three runs. It was a terrible disappointment for the record crowd anxious to witness a first Ashes win in 18 years.

But then the series turned in the second Test at Edgbaston. On the fourth day, needing 107 to win with two wickets remaining, the Australians fell short by just three runs. It was the narrowest victory in Ashes history. This time Flintoff's contribution had

68 It was only after he retired that Flintoff revealed he had struggled with bulimia for much of this period.

been crucial. He had ended the match as England's top scorer with 141 runs and, in one devastating spell, had taken three wickets in only four balls. Even more remarkable, as far as the press was concerned, had been the England star's magnanimity in victory. His emotional embrace with the despondent Australian batsman Brett Lee was declared by the *Daily Mirror* to be 'one of the greatest acts of sportsmanship in Ashes history'. For *The Guardian*'s chief sports photographer, the moment brought back memories of Moore and Pelé exchanging shirts in the heat of Guadalajara in 1970.

By the time of the fifth Test at The Oval, with England just needing to avoid defeat to win the series, the country was well and truly in the grip of Ashes fever. A pair of tickets for the second day's play sold on eBay for over £1,000, while a flat with a view of the ground cost £20,000 for the week of the match. On the final day, a Monday, the streets were eerily quiet. The Confederation of British Industry urged employers to 'be flexible in allowing staff to keep tabs on the score'. A clerk at Southwark Crown Court used an elaborate system of display cards to make sure those in attendance did not miss out on the excitement. Even Tony Blair, during a speech at the City of London Academy, felt obliged to apologise for dragging people away from their television sets, before ruining the day for anyone who had set their video recorder by announcing the match result. Those lucky enough not to be at work, on trial or listening to Blair were able to settle down with a record eight million other viewers and enjoy Channel 4's coverage.

With so much invested in the result, even an anticlimactic draw in the final match, which secured England's 2-1 series victory, was enough to ensure the team was the focus of unprecedented celebrations. At the insistence of Ken Livingstone, who was desperate to prove to the world that London was still open despite the 7 July bombings, a victory parade was held along the Strand, while receptions were given at Buckingham Palace, Mansion House and 10 Downing Street. The whole squad appeared on the New Year Honours List and became the first identifiable living people, outside the royal family, to be depicted on a set of stamps. As 'man of the series', Flintoff was singled out for attention. He got to sing with Elton John at a charity gig in Battersea Park, was honoured by Danilo with its 'official Andrew Flintoff calendar', and, of course, received the ultimate tribute of being presented with the SPOTY trophy by Ian Botham.

Like Botham in 1981, it was all but impossible for Flintoff to live up to the hype after 2005. Assuming the role of England captain in early 2006 merely added to the pressure, and a string of poor results, including a whitewash in the Ashes of 2006–7, seemed to act as the catalyst for some increasingly indiscreet alcohol-fuelled behaviour. Matters came to a head after defeat by New Zealand in the opening match of the 2007 World Cup in the West Indies. A post-match eight-hour drinking spree ended up with the England all-rounder having to be 'rescued' by hotel staff from a pedalo.[69] Although gran Elsie thought it a 'poor do' when a young man 'can't go on a binge every now and then', the selectors were inclined to agree with the *Daily Star*'s assessment that Flintoff had been caught 'keg before wicket', and insisted on a public apology and a suspension. Happily, though, this did not mark the end of his career, and he was able to help

69 Inevitably, the *Daily Star* immediately dubbed the pedalo the 'fredalo'.

England reclaim the Ashes in 2009, despite being hampered by a serious knee injury that ultimately forced him into retirement the following year.[35]

The television landscape changed for cricket after Flintoff's *annus mirabilis* in 2005. Despite the excellent ratings for the Ashes series, Channel 4 chose not to challenge Sky's bid of £220m for a four-year deal, and live coverage of home Test matches and one-day internationals disappeared behind a paywall. Just as cricket was embedding itself in the nation's sporting psyche, it was to be hidden away from the reach of the casual viewer. The subscription barrier, the journalist Martin Kelner felt, would result in cricket becoming 'even more the preserve of the corpulent and the corporate than it already is'. That may have been a touch unfair, but what the migration to Sky undoubtedly meant was that for the wider public to vote in another cricketer as the BBC's Sports Personality of the Year, it would require something, and someone, exceptional. Ben Stokes and the 2019 ICC Cricket World Cup provided just that combination.

Stokes's sporting history is written on his body. The silver fern on his left arm points to his New Zealand heritage. It was not until he was 11 that the family moved from Christchurch to Cumbria when his father accepted the role of head coach with the Workington Town rugby league team. It was probably inevitable, therefore, that New Zealand would be the opponents in that dramatic World Cup Final in 2019. 'Kiwi born; English at heart,' Stokes reassured fans on the eve of the match. But Dad, Ged, was not quite so diplomatic. 'I support any team my son is in,' he tweeted, 'unless they are playing against the Black Caps.' Luckily, Ben was able to reassert the family's loyalty to their adopted home when he was nominated for New Zealander of the Year in the aftermath of the match. He withdrew his name and considerately put forward 'all-round good bloke' Kane Williamson, the Kiwi captain, as a better option.

In 2016, Stokes had inked on to his right arm a phoenix rising from the ashes. The spur for this new tattoo was the final of the 2016 Twenty20 World Cup. Tasked with bowling the final over, he needed to restrict Barbadian all-rounder Carlos Brathwaite to fewer than 19 runs. Four balls and 24 runs later, the trophy was in the hands of the West Indies. It was a devastating blow for Stokes. 'Ben Chokes' was the *Daily Express*'s assessment, and it was hard to disagree. The following year, matters got worse for the newly appointed England vice-captain. A night out with a team-mate in Bristol descended into an ugly street brawl and a charge of affray. The CCTV footage of the incident did nothing to lessen tabloid outrage. Rehabilitation, let alone investiture as the nation's favourite sporting personality, seemed a long way off.[70]

Offsetting the silver fern on his left arm, Stokes has an English rose tattooed on his upper right arm. His commitment and importance to the country's cricketing cause had been evident long before he took to the field for the ICC World Cup Final in July 2019. At Lord's, in 2015, he had scored the fastest Test century by an English batsman, and the following year, in Cape Town, he had racked up the nation's quickest double hundred. But the showdown against New Zealand on 14 July 2019 was still special. It was a chance for redemption after the humbling

70 Stokes had, in fact, been defending a couple from homophobic abuse, and he was acquitted when the case eventually came to trial in August 2018.

at the hands of the West Indies three years earlier. And this was the ICC World Cup, the most prestigious of the knockout tournaments. England had not reached the final for over 25 years, and had never won it. To the surprise of no one, it all came down to the last over. This time, though, Stokes was looking to emulate Brathwaite, with 15 required to win. Two sixes, two singles and two run outs later and the scores were tied. It meant a super over (who knew?). Even then the teams could not be separated and England were deemed to have won on boundary countback. Stokes, who had scored 84 not out, then 8 in the super over, was declared Player of the Match. It was, said the film director and opening bat for Wychwood village cricket club, Sam Mendes, 'a story you could not script'. The viewing public clearly agreed, and Stokes and the England team were rewarded with SPOTY wins at the end of the year.[71]

One of Stokes's greatest achievements, thought the ghostwriter of his most recent autobiography, was his ability to 'make non-cricket lovers fall in love with the sport'. And, although the 'Bible of cricket', *Wisden*, might have snootily 'compared one-day cricket to pop music and the standard game to Mozart', the truth was that, for the uninitiated, the simplicity of one team trying to outhit another was immensely appealing. To enjoy Test matches, one aficionado explained, you had to accept 'the possibility of boredom', but in the new digital world of televised sport, the small-screen fan demanded instant gratification. What Stokes,

71 Stokes had capped his match-winning performance against New Zealand with some Ashes heroics later in the season. An amazing last stand with Jack Leach at Headingley saw England secure an improbable draw. It was not enough, though, to prevent Australia retaining the urn.

along with Botham and Flintoff, managed to do was not only provide that gratification but also demystify cricket. To Stokes, cricket was 'a simple game' that should not be 'over-analysed'. It was a view echoed by Mendes. The secret to the sport, he contemplatively shared with Stokes as they both gazed across the pitch at Cockermouth Cricket Club, was to remember that, in essence, it was 'nothing more or less than a slow trek to rediscover those great and simple images in the presence of which [a man's] heart first opened'. Then again, maybe Stokes's response suggests that such introspection does not hold the key to cricket after all. 'I've got,' he told Mendes, 'no idea what you just said.'[36]

* * *

III. Rugby
Jonny Wilkinson (2003)

AFTER THE founding of its governing body in 1871, rugby consistently promoted itself as a bastion of middle-class amateurism. 'Even cricket,' sports historian Tony Collins noted, 'did not carry the same moral character or cachet of exclusivity.' Although the Rugby Football Union was reluctantly forced to embrace professionalism in 1995, by the time of the World Cup in Australia eight years later much remained unchanged. The players may now have become full-time athletes, but they still played for a trophy named in honour of a rule-defying public schoolboy from the high days of the Victorian cult of the amateur; the tournament's official anthem, 'World in Union', persisted with the claim that 'win, lose or draw, it's a victory for all' (try telling that to football fans!); and the two teams contesting the final, Australia and England, continued to be dominated by the privately educated.[72] To cap it all, the man of the match in that pulsating final, Jonny Wilkinson, the scorer of the dramatic drop goal 28 seconds from the end of extra time that gave England an historic victory, was, if the British press was anything to go by, Tom Brown reincarnated.

Proof that England's new star was a model of sporting rectitude cropped up again and again in match reports. His first thought, the *Daily Express* pointed out, after scoring the winning points was not to whip his shirt off in celebration but to calmly prepare for the restart. He refused, *The Times* noted, to have his picture taken alone with the trophy. He was quite simply, the *Daily Mail* insisted, 'a good old-fashioned British sporting hero'. Indeed, finding themselves running short of superlatives, some journalists thought it easier to define Wilkinson by what he was not. And critically, of course, he was not a football player. The *Mail*'s Geoffrey Wansell was thankful that the England fly-half 'demonstrated none of the preening histrionics of those overpaid, over-indulged stars of soccer', while the editor of the *Sunday Times* was relieved that, unlike the regulars of the Premier League, he did not wear 'Tiffany diamond earrings and drive a Yank tank bigger than a council house'. Inevitably, unpleasant class-conscious comparisons with David Beckham were made. Unlike the 'studious' Wilkinson, who 'gained A Levels in French, biology and chemistry and earned a place at Durham University',

72 Over half the players from the two squads had attended fee-paying schools.

Beckham, the *Daily Mail* snootily observed, 'barely managed a GCSE'. Curiously, no mention was made of the prestigious private school that Wilkinson had attended.

With the World Cup triumph still fresh in the public's mind, and having already won *The Guardian*'s 'Smile Moment of 2003' ahead of Dirty Den's return to *EastEnders* and American illusionist David Blaine's pelting with eggs while hanging over Southwark's Potters Fields Park in a plexiglass box, Wilkinson was quickly installed as the bookies' favourite for SPOTY. Although a brief challenge arose when disgruntled Australian fans tried to rally support for eternal British 'loser' Tim Henman, to the relief of the BBC, who had already shelled out two grand to ITV for permission to show a clip of the winning drop goal, the public stayed loyal to its rugby heroes. The World Cup-winning squad won Team of the Year, Coach of the Year and, in Wilkinson, Personality of the Year.

Perhaps, *The Guardian* suggested, the country had briefly become a rugby-loving nation. But that was the problem. It was only briefly. With the bulk of the sport's supporters coming from the middle- and upper-middle classes, rugby's moment in the sun was only ever going to be fleeting, and by the start of the new year the entitled show-offs of the Premier League were once again hogging the back pages (and, not infrequently, front pages).[73] The truth of the matter is that rugby union at club level has never had the reach to engage public interest (and, more crucially, media interest) for any length of time. The financial fragility of top-tier

---

73 A 2003 report, commissioned by rugby's elite clubs, found that 61 per cent of Premiership crowds described themselves as middle- or upper-middle class. This compared to just 27 per cent for the British population as a whole.

clubs in the professional age has made this all too apparent.[74] Seventy years after the nation first started voting for its favourite sporting personality, Wilkinson remains the game's only winner.

Rugby union may struggle with an elitist image but, for the game's rival code, it has proven all but impossible to break free from the ties of a parochial, working-class history. For much of the 1970s and 1980s, with football priced out of the market, rugby league was a mainstay of the BBC's flagship sports show, *Grandstand*. The sport's authorities, though, were not entirely happy with the coverage. Rugby league, a viewer survey from 1971 concluded, is 'widely held to be a sport for northern heavyweights with a leaning towards brawn rather than brains, played against a backdrop of pithead slagheaps in a steady drizzle and watched by a sparse flat-capped crowd'. The *Daily Mail* did nothing to help matters. The main features of the game were, the paper's cricket correspondent superciliously declared, 'Tetley's Ales, black-pudding, Lowry paintings, busted noses and huge white thighs'. Confronted by such prejudices, it is little wonder Kevin Sinfield's second place in 2015 continues to be the only time the sport has graced the SPOTY roll of honour.[37]

---

74 A clear sign of rugby union's struggle to carve out a niche in the modern, commercially driven sporting landscape was the collapse, in 2023, of three Gallagher Premiership clubs: Wasps, Worcester and London Irish.

Chapter Notes

25 *Sunday Times*, 19 May 1985; Brian Glanville, *The Story of the World Cup: The Essential Companion to Brazil 2014* (2014), pp.43–130; Martin Polley, *Moving the Goalposts: A History of Sport and Society in Britain Since 1945* (1998), p.70; Kelner, *Sit Down and Cheer*, p.81; Martin Taylor, *The Association Game: A History of British Football* (2008), p.284; Roger Hutchinson, *It Is Now! The Real Story of England's 1966 World Cup Triumph* (1995), p.108; *Daily Mail*, 30 July 1966; *Sun*, 30 July 1966; 'Britain's most watched TV: the 1960s', www.bfi.org.uk/features/mostwatched/1960s.html

26 Percy Young, *A History of British Football* (1973), p.278; *Daily Express*, 1 August 1966; *Bo66y* (2016), dir. Ron Scalpello; *Sunday Telegraph*, 31 July 1966; *Sunday Express*, 31 July 1966; David Goldblatt, *The Game of Our Lives: The Meaning and Making of English Football* (2014), p.228; Matt Dickinson, *Bobby Moore: The Man in Full* (2014), pp.128–129, 270–271, 305; *Guardian*, 28 March 1999; *GQ*, 12 January 2017.

27 Goldblatt, *Game of Our Lives*, pp.10–18, 284; John Ramsden, *Don't Mention the War: The British and Germans since 1890* (2006), p.354; *Observer*, 30 April 1972; Taylor, *Association Game*, p.293; Kelner, *Sit Down and Cheer*, p.260; *Guardian*, 29 December 1990; *Sun*, 4 July 1990; *Daily Mirror*, 27 February 1993; 6 July 1990, 4 July 1990; *Irish News*, 6 July 2018; Paul Gascoigne, *Gazza: My Story* (2005), pp.22, 79, 109, 139, 283, 309; Ian Hamilton, *Gazza Agonistes* (1993), pp.52, 148; *Daily Express*, 26 February 1993, 6 July 1990, 5 July 1990; *Times*, 27 December 1990, 22 December 1990, 13 October 1990; *Independent*, 27 June 1996; Roger Domeneghetti, *From Back Page to the Front Room: Football's Journey Through the English Media* (2017), p162; Alwyn Turner, *A Classless Society: Britain in the 1990s* (2014), pp.69–70; *Daily Mail*, 3 June 1998; LWT, *Gazza: The Real Me*, dir. John Pettman (1990); BBC2, *Gazza*, dir. Sampson Collins (April 2022); BBC1, *Wogan*, (3 September 1990); *Spectator*, 25 January 2003.

28 Michael Owen, *Reboot: My Life, My Time* (2019), p.50, 59, 67; Kelner, *Sit Down and Cheer*, p.183; *Daily Mirror*, 1 July 1998; *Daily Express*, 21 December 1998, 1 July 1998; *Guardian*, 24 December 1998; *Daily Mail*, 1 September 2001, 14 December 1998; Giles Smith, *Midnight*

in the Garden of Evel Knievel: Sport on Television (2000), p.291; ch4, *Beckham and the Battle with Argentina*, dir. Dermot Lavery (2002); Goldblatt, *Game of Our Lives*, pp.230–235; *Sun*, 1 September 2001; Ramsden, *Don't Mention the War*, p.414.

29 Turner, *Classless Society*, p.571; *Guardian*, 2 October 1996; *Daily Mirror*, 16 March 2010, 8 October 2001, 3 July 1998, 1 July 1998, 5 June 1998; *Times*, 2 July 1998; Smith, *Midnight in the Garden*, p.261; *Daily Express*, 1 July 1998; *Independent*, 4 January 2007; *OK!*, 8 April 2022; Pirro Markula, 'Cute with a vague gender shift', in David L. Andrews (ed.), *Manchester United: A Thematic Study* (2004), p.168; Domeneghetti, *From the Back Page*, p.290; Andrew Morton, *Posh & Becks* (2003), p.213; Turner, *Classless Society*, p.517; *Daily Star*, 8 October 2001; *Sunday Times*, 16 December 2001.

30 Goldblatt, *Game of Our Lives*, p.286; Frank Worrall, *Giggsy: The Biography of Ryan Giggs* (2010), pp.11, 133; Turner, *Classless Society*, p.68; *Class of '92*, dir. Ben and Gabe Turner (2013); *Guardian*, 27 April 2009; *Sunday Express*, 13 December 2009; *Daily Mirror*, 12 December 2009.

31 *Daily Mail*, 6 June 2011; *Guardian*, 16 August 2012; Jean Williams, *A Game for Rough Girls: A History of Women's Football in England* (2003), p.89; Suzanne Wrack, *A Woman's Game: The Rise, Fall, and Rise Again of Women's Football* (2022), pp.98, 169–174; Domeneghetti, *From the Back Page*, p.318; *Guardian*, 25 January 2011; Carrie Dunn, *The Pride of the Lionesses: The Changing Face of Women's Football in England* (2019), p.166; Beth Mead, *Lioness: My Journey to Glory* (2022), ch.3.

32 *Holding Up a Mirror to Cricket: A Report By the Independent Commission for Equity in Cricket*, June 2023, pp.6,8,14; Adrian Smith and Dilwyn Porter, *Amateur and Professionals in Postwar British Sport* (2001), pp.40–45, 55; Richard Parry and Andre Odendaal, *Swallows and Hawke: England's Cricket Tourists, the MCC and the Making of South Africa 1888–1968* (2002), p.424; Alan Hill, *Jim Laker: A Biography* (1998), chs. 2, 9, 11; *Observer*, 23 February 1958; Graham Scambler, 'Sociology, Sportization and Cricket: Post WWII', www.grahamscambler.com; *Daily Express*, 19 May 1960, 1 August 1956; Jim Laker, *Over to Me* (1960), p.87; *Daily Mirror*, 19 May 1960; *Times*, 11 July 1960.

33 Derek Birley, *A Social History of Cricket* (1999), pp.282–288, 309, 314–315; *Daily Mirror*, 8 September 1963; Ian Addis, Andrew Radd and David Steele, *The Bank Clerk Who Went to War* (2018), pp.8, 81, 103; Ben Dirs, 'How David Steele became an unlikely England hero', https://www.bbc.co.uk/sport/cricket/33343793, 5 July 2015; *Sunday Times*, 25 July 1993.

34 Simon Wilde, *Ian Botham: The Power and the Glory* (2011), pp.44, 69–70, 111, 261–268; *Daily Express*, 18 August 1981, 3 August 1981, 21 July 1981; *Sunday Times*, 25 July 1993; Dominic Sandbrook, *Who Dares Wins: Britain, 1979–1982* (2019), pp. 633–635; *Independent*, 19 July 1993; *Daily Mirror*, 18 August 1881; Roland Perry, *From Bradman to Border: Australian Cricket 1918–1948* (1990), p.119; Alwyn Turner, *Rejoice, Rejoice: Britain in the 1980s* (2010), p.22.

35 *Daily Mirror*, 9 August 2005, 8 August 2005; *Guardian*, 29 September 2006; ITV, *Piers Morgan: Life Stories*, broadcast 12 September 2014; Andrew Flintoff, *Being Freddie: My Story So Far* (2006), ch.8; *Guardian*, 6 July 2015; Andrew Flintoff and Myles Hodgson, *Ashes to Ashes* (2012), pp.9–11; *Daily Star*, 20 March 2007; *Daily Express*, 20 March 2007.

36 *Guardian*, 17 August 2005; Kelner, *Sit Down and Cheer*, pp.234, 262; Ben Stokes, *On Fire: My Story of England's Summer to Remember* (2019), p.155; *Daily Express*, 4 April 2016; *Ben Stokes: Phoenix from the Ashes*, dir. Chris Grubb and Luke Mellows (2022); *Daily Mail*, 25 July 2023; Birley, *A Social History of Cricket*, p.312; Stefan Szymanski and Tim Wigmore, *Crickonomics: The Anatomy of Modern Cricket*, p.195; Ben Stokes, *Firestarter: Me, Cricket and the Heat of the Moment* (2016), ch.12.

37 Tony Collins, *A Social History of English Rugby Union* (2009), p.212; *Daily Express*, 24 November 2003; *Times*, 24 November 2003; *Daily Mail*, 24 November 2003, 7 May 1976; *Sunday Times*, 23 November 2003; *Guardian*, 15 December 2003; Tony Collins, *Rugby League in Twentieth Century Britain: A Social and Cultural History* (2006), pp.95–95.

Chapter 4

Water – In It, On It, Avoiding It: Swimming, Figure Skating, Rowing, Golf

I. Swimming

Ian Black (1958) – Anita Lonsbrough (1962)

OF ALL the major sports in Britain in the post-war era, swimming was the poor cousin. Although enormously popular as a recreational activity, with over 200 public baths being constructed in the two decades following the Second World War, swimming remained underdeveloped at elite level. In part this was a consequence of the sharp divide that existed between the hobbyist and the competitive athlete. Put simply, splashing around once a week in the local pool was not enough to foster even a passing interest in the gruelling training and racing regimes of club swimmers. But, as ever in the golden years of amateurism, the officials who ran the sport did little to help matters. More interested in politicking than achievement, the Amateur Swimming Association (ASA) managed the near impossible and made the AAA appear a paragon of industry and efficiency. The man in charge of the ASA, retired naval commander Charles Roe, treated the international swimmer with suspicion and the occasional pool-goer with disdain. As a result, the sport failed to capitalise fully on the resurgent peacetime interest in leisure.

For swimming's two SPOTY winners, Ian Black and Anita Lonsbrough, all this meant that even the meagre support that track and field stars such as Pirie, Hyman and Rand received was looked upon with envy. Black, just 17 when he won the BBC trophy in 1958 and still a pupil at the prestigious Robert Gordon's College in Aberdeen, was fortunate that he was able to use the school pool for much of his training. But during the summer holidays he was forced to make alternative arrangements. Aberdeen City Council's refusal to give him special access to the municipal bath meant options were limited. In the lead-up to the Rome Olympics in 1960, the best he and his coach could come up with was a tidal saltwater pool carved into the rocks 500 miles away in Guernsey. Even when school was in session, support was not entirely wholehearted. The college head, clearly a heretic when it came to the public-school games ethic, deplored the 'fuss' over Black's sporting achievements as he felt it gave the pupils the 'wrong set of values'. 'It was a little trying,' he told a meeting of alumni, 'to think of Gordon's College, with more than two hundred years of not undistinguished history, being known as Ian Black's School.' It probably came as no surprise, then, when Andy Robb, a PE teacher at the school, and Black's coach, was denied permission to accompany his protégé to the Olympics in 1960.

Lonsbrough's path to sporting success was equally challenging. A rates clerk with Huddersfield council, she had to fit training around office hours and take unpaid leave when selected to represent the country abroad. And, unlike Black, she had to slum it in the local pool. The worst thing about training, she recalled, was worrying about whether all the cockroaches had been picked out of the water before the session started. 'I kept thinking, is there another one? Am I going to swallow it?' However, implausible as it might sound, such disquiet did occasionally reap unexpected rewards. Positive that a frog had been spotted in the murky water of the pool in Waalwijk, Netherlands, before an international meet in July 1959, the 18-year-old Lonsbrough resolved to swim 'as hard as I could so I could get out as quickly as possible'. Just two minutes 50.3 seconds later she had broken the world record for the 200m breaststroke.

The rudimentary nature of competitive swimming in Britain in this period makes even more remarkable the level of success that Black and Lonsbrough were able to achieve. In the space of just seven weeks during the summer of 1958, Ian Black won a gold (220yds butterfly) and two silvers (440yds butterfly and 4x220yds freestyle relay) in the Empire and Commonwealth Games at Cardiff, as well as three golds (400m freestyle, 1,500m freestyle and 200m butterfly) in the European Aquatics Championships in Budapest. As if this wasn't good enough, two of the medals at Budapest, for the 200m butterfly and 400m freestyle, were won within 40 minutes of each other.[75]

Lonsbrough was equally prolific. Having only switched to breaststroke in 1957, when she discovered she was the sole entrant

75 On the eve of the Aquatics Championships in Budapest, the *Daily Express* had insisted it was a 'blunder' to select Black for both races as it would be impossible to recover in time for the 400m freestyle.

for a 200m butterfly race, within a year she was the Empire and Commonwealth 200m breaststroke champion, and two years later Olympic champion in a world-record time. Still only 21 at the time of the Empire and Commonwealth Games in Perth in 1962, she came away with three individual golds (110yds breaststroke, 220yds breaststroke and 440yds individual medley) and a relay silver (4x110yds medley).[76] She was, thought the Australian team coach, 'the best all-round woman swimmer in the world'. And when an Australian praises any English sportsperson, let alone a swimmer, you know that has to mean something.

Swimming may have been the Cinderella of British sports, but achievements on the scale of those of Black and Lonsbrough were hard for the press and public to ignore. This was especially so in the late 1950s and early 1960s, when FA fears that live televised matches would leave football fans sofa-bound meant the BBC had to scrabble around for minority sports to fill the sporting schedules. Speedway, showjumping and swimming plugged the broadcasting void. With at least one swimming meet a month being televised, elite swimmers quickly became household names. Despite the sport's rudderless leadership, it was not, therefore, so surprising when Black became the youngest-ever winner of SPOTY in 1958, and Lonsbrough the first women to lift the trophy, four years later.

But, as was customary in the amateur sporting world, recognition did not bring rewards – or at least not material ones.

---

76 There was, in fact, some doubt over the 110yds breaststroke result. The electronic timer, which was being trialled at the championships, suggested that Vivien Haddon of New Zealand had touched fractionally ahead of Lonsbrough, but as the final decision still rested with the five poolside judges, victory went England's way by three votes to two.

Where it all started. Chris Chataway with the BBC's 'Sportsview' trophy at the Savoy Hotel in 1954.

Another little Aussie boy lackered. Jim Laker walks off with Australia's Ray Lindwall during the fourth Test, 1956.

The first woman to win SPOTY. Anita Lonsbrough happily shares the trophy with Viscount Montgomery of Alamein in 1962.

'All that and a mother too.' Mary Rand takes gold and the long jump world record in Tokyo, 1964.

Tom Simpson, 'Ambassador of British Sport', in his last grand tour, 1967.

'Immaculate footballer. Imperial defender. Immortal hero of 1966.' Bobby Moore joins the Portuguese star Eusebio at the sports personality awards, 1966.

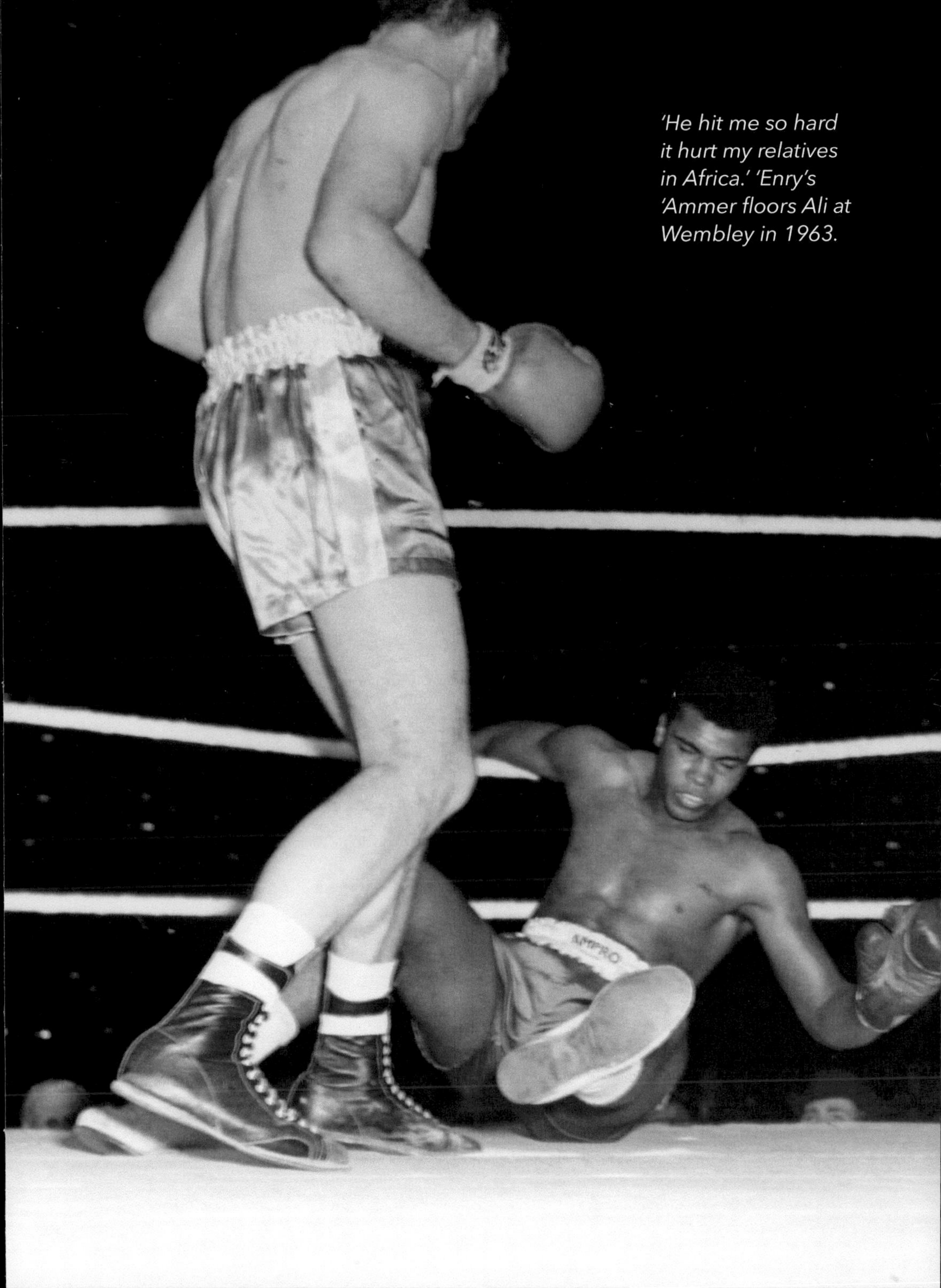

'He hit me so hard it hurt my relatives in Africa.' 'Enry's 'Ammer floors Ali at Wembley in 1963.

Ann Jones lifts the Wimbledon trophy in 1969. British men would have to wait another 44 years.

'A unique example in equestrian history when the Queen had bred not only the horse but also the rider.' Princess Anne and Doublet take the European Three-Day Eventing title, 1971.

Three for the price of one. Coe, Cram and Ovett at the LA Olympics, 1984.

'The greatest comeback since Lazarus.' Ian Botham on his way to 149 not out during the third Test at Headingley, 1981.

Last man standing. Daley reigns supreme as European decathlon champion, 1982.

Perfection. Torvill and Dean produce a performance to die for in Sarajevo, 1984.

Tears of a clown. A distraught Paul Gascoigne in Italia '90.

'His dad would have been so proud.' Damon Hill finally gets to bring the SPOTY trophy home to the Hill household in 1994.

'It's huge! It's massive! And it's legal!' Jonathan Edwards destroys the opposition and the world triple jump record in Gothenburg, 1995.

'You've got my permission to shoot me.' Happily, nobody took Steve Redgrave up on his offer after Atlanta 1996, and he went on to win a fifth gold and SPOTY in 2000.

An inspiration on and off the track. Kelly Holmes takes her second gold in Athens, 2004.

'The only black kid.' Lewis Hamilton wins the F1 Drivers' Championship, 2014.

At last! Beth Mead shows the men what it's like to lift a major trophy.

Beyond a cupboardful of medals and cups, the only prize Black could remember receiving was a 'two foot high statue of a naked man'. It was, he felt, a nice touch for the organisers of the 1958 European Championships to mark his three victories with such a gift, but he could not see his 'mum putting the thing on the mantelpiece'. Promotional offers were equally thin on the ground. The single commercial approach he received after his slew of victories in 1958 came from the temperance charity the Band of Hope, after a picture of the teetotal champion raising a celebratory glass of milk at the Sportswriters' Association 'champagne' dinner appeared in the *Daily Mirror*. Even the Milk Marketing Board remained stubbornly disinterested, Black ruefully observed. Although invitations came through to train in California and Australia, his parents felt he should obtain a degree first because swimming 'could never be his whole life'. Just four years after winning SPOTY, at the age of 21, Black retired.

Lonsbrough's competitive career was just as brief and devoid of financial return. Her gold in the Rome Olympics might have prompted the people of Huddersfield to present her with a silver tea service, but it still was not enough to shame the local council into reimbursing the pay she had been forced to forfeit in order to compete. With money tight, even the pull of international travel started to lose its appeal. 'There is more to do on a Sunday in Huddersfield than there is here,' a disgruntled Lonsbrough complained to the *Daily Express* as she waited impatiently for the 1962 Empire and Commonwealth Games in Perth to end. The organisers must have wondered whether spending over £1m to create the first-ever purpose-built athletes' village had been the right decision after all. Lonsbrough endured one last stretch of athletic purdah, this time in Tokyo's Olympic village two years later, before a seventh-place finish in the 400m individual medley persuaded her enough was enough and she retired from international competition.

Despite individual Olympic golds by Wilkie, Goodhew and Moorhouse in the 1970s and 80s, and Adlington, Peaty and Dean in the 21st century, Lonsbrough remains the last swimmer to claim the SPOTY trophy. One of the reasons for this, Andy Bull of *The Guardian* has argued, is that the personalities in swimming tend to 'get lost beneath all the Lycra, swim caps and splashing water'. Certainly, as the range and frequency of sport available to the armchair fan grew, so swimming's public profile diminished. Even double Olympic gold by Becky Adlington at Beijing in 2008, the first such achievement by a British swimmer for 100 years, was only good enough for a SPOTY third place. As one veteran of the press box bluntly observed, 'Some sports are more popular than others, a fact we all have to deal with until the Olympics, when we can pretend otherwise.' And even then, as far as swimming goes, that pretence only stretches so far.[38]

* * *

II. Figure Skating

John Curry (1976) – Robin Cousins (1980) – Jayne Torvill and Christopher Dean (1984)

RATHER LIKE swimming, figure skating enjoyed a brief spell in the SPOTY limelight before retreating into obscurity. In consecutive Olympic years between 1976 and 1984, skaters beat sportsmen in more well-established sports to come away with the trophy. What made skating's success all the more remarkable in this period was that the sport was not only far removed from the sporting mainstream but, to many, it was not even a sport at all. Reservations centred on whether artistic impression was an appropriate criterion for awarding marks. If applied elsewhere, thought *The Guardian*'s Frank Keating, it would mean 'Rudolf Nureyev beating Daley Thompson in the decathlon because he glides up to the pole-vault pit more artistically'. John Hennessy of *The Times* managed to offend skiers as well as skaters when he raised similar concerns. Pointing out that female figure skaters had to 'display a pretty face and attractive legs in order to prosper', he gracelessly added that, 'almost every girl skier I know would fall out with skating judges on looks alone'.

Curiously, skating's first SPOTY winner, John Curry, agreed with Keating and Hennessy, at least in principle. 'I never thought of figure skating as a sport,' he admitted shortly after his Olympic glory in 1976. 'I always thought of it as a kind of dance.' Fortunately, this was not a view his parents shared. Prohibited when young from going to ballet lessons for, as he later archly recalled, 'the perfectly obvious reasons', he was only permitted to take up skating because his father considered it to be a sport. The Curry household's attitude to what was and was not deemed to be manly was typical of a country in which homosexuality was still illegal. Even after the Sexual Offences Act 1967, it took a long time for public attitudes to catch up with the law. A decade after the act had been passed, a Gallup poll found that 40 per cent of respondents still believed that homosexuality should be illegal, while a majority judged it inappropriate for a gay man to become a doctor or a junior schoolteacher. In all aspects of public life, but especially in sport, homosexuality was all but invisible in 1970s Britain.

The homophobic culture that pervaded Britain in this period was particularly challenging for Curry. Throughout his career he was plagued by invidious attacks on his sexuality. Coverage of his sporting triumphs was frequently underscored by ridicule. Criticisms about the theatricality or flamboyance of his performances were used to cast doubt on his masculinity. Some press reports were less subtle than others. 'Despite his soft curly hair,' began a feature in the *Daily Mail* on the eve of the Innsbruck Winter Olympics in 1976, 'his chiselled lips, gentle voice and the graceful arc he describes with his hands when he talks about skating being removed from the rough world of sport and elevated to the realms of performing arts, he has thick armour plating just below the surface.' As one biographer noted, 'The only word missing was homosexual.'

Skating's governing body in Lausanne was desperate to distance the sport from any hint of effeminacy. To this end, judges were told to ignore artistic nuance, and focus instead on difficulty, strength and athleticism. Physicality, it was assumed, would serve as proof of heterosexuality. Again and again Curry was rebuked by coaches for being too graceful. Don't be so expressive with your hands, one early teacher warned him, it is 'not a movement for a man'. He was urged to emulate the muscular dynamism of his Eastern Bloc rivals. Look how well the Russians can jump, British trainers pointed out. But so can horses, Curry would respond dismissively. 'Judges,' a team-mate cautioned him, 'will not give high marks to someone who makes it look so easy.'

But Curry was not to be dissuaded. The only concession he made to the skating world's obsession with strength was to employ, in the lead-up to the 1976 Olympics, new coaches to help him perfect his jumping technique.[77] Yet, while acknowledging the importance of athleticism, he still remained committed to the belief that figure skating was not a competitive sport. 'When he went on the ice,' the future Olympic champion and SPOTY winner Robin Cousins observed, 'he didn't compete, he performed.' Curry himself insisted that his motivation for participating at Innsbruck was 'to prove skating was a new modern art form'.

And, as he completed his free skate to claim the Olympic crown, he knew he had done just that. 'He gave 10,000 of us not a glance,' the *Daily Mail*'s man in the Olympiahalle reported. 'There, amid the carnations and the gasping recognition of his commanding brilliance, he just looked up with a smile which said: "I told you so."' It was the 'cool beauty of movement' that had most impressed *The Times*, while the *Daily Express* was sure that 'no eye could be so philistine as not to recognise the stunning beauty of the performance'. As ever, though, it was Chris Brasher of *The Observer* who best summed up the importance of what had just taken place. Curry's routine, he declared, 'will break through a barrier of British inhibition: the belief that ballet dancing is not manly'. Even the Olympic judges had to concede that grace had

77 In the lead-up to Innsbruck, Curry also enrolled on a 'self-empowerment' course with Erhard Seminars Training. A hugely popular movement in the 1970s, EST's founder, Werner Erhard, was described by *New Times* magazine as the 'king of the brain-snatchers'. Controversial or not, Curry remained convinced that the course had helped to control the debilitating anxiety he used to feel before competitions.

triumphed over power. The 105.9 points they awarded (from a possible 108) was the highest score ever given in the history of men's figure skating and put the Briton out of sight of the second-placed Soviet skater. It was the British team's first gold medal in the ice rink since 1952.

Yet, sublime though Curry's performance had been, the media remained fixated on his sexuality. An Associated Press (AP) exclusive that the new Olympic champion had 'come out' as homosexual dominated the news agenda in the days following the men's skating final. At the customary post-competition press conference, figure skating was all but forgotten as journalists danced around the AP revelation with euphemistically phrased questions about virility, athleticism and manliness. 'I don't think I lack virility,' Curry responded to one of his inquisitors. 'Do you think that what I did yesterday was not athletic?' On his return to England, matters took a downward turn. At the Sportswriters' Association awards dinner in mid-December, the 'comic' act for the evening, ventriloquist Roger De Courcey and Nookie the talking bear, turned to Curry and unblushingly made a crass joke about a fairy for the Christmas tree. The insult was so blatant that even De Courcey's audience of well-oiled sports correspondents was stunned into silence. It was, therefore, probably some consolation when the British people revealed they cared more about what took place on the ice than what might go on behind closed doors by voting Curry in as the BBC's Sports Personality of the Year for 1976.

Gold at Innsbruck had furnished Curry with enough popular backing to pursue his dream and set up his own professional ice dance company. The mission of the John Curry Theatre of Skating was to rise above the vulgar appeal of the end-of-pier ice spectacular by pioneering a new art form, ballet on ice. It was a worthy ambition, but it sorely underestimated the crude populism of promoters and publicists. Receiving a slot on the Christmas TV schedules was undoubtedly a boost, but it hardly screamed high culture when you were advertised alongside *Rod Hull and Emu's Xmas Special* and a celebrity edition of *Blankety Blank*. Even on tour, idealism could be undermined by commercialism. As Curry's ice dancers took to the rink for a show in Copenhagen, they found the arena surrounded by advertising hoardings. It was more Stamford Bridge than Sadler's Wells. Ultimately, the harsh realities of business forced the Theatre of Skating to close down but, for all the disappointment, Curry had still changed the public perception of his art. His fusion of the aesthetic and the athletic that February evening in Innsbruck in 1976 had set a new standard for the champions of the future and had encouraged the 20 million Britons who had sat mesmerised in front of their televisions to look to figure skating for further glory.[39]

And they did not have long to wait. Robin Cousins, who in 1972 had become the youngest skater ever to win the junior men's British championship, quickly took over from Curry as the nation's darling of the ice. Yet the two could not have been more different. If Curry was the innovator who sought out controversy as he bucked against orthodoxy, then Cousins was the interpreter who looked to appease the establishment as he explored how far conventions could be stretched. 'John pushed people away,' thought Evelyn Kramer, who worked with both skaters, but 'Robin wanted to share himself with others.' The *Daily Mail*'s Brian Jones agreed. Comparing the two champions' Olympic gold medal-winning performances, Jones was struck by how

'Curry, the intellectual, skated with curled lip daring us not to reward him with his medal [while]Cousins looked like everyone's youngest son with his smiling performance'.

The difference between the two was not lost on Cousins. He had respect for Curry's talent, but he never saw him as a friend. 'We had nothing to talk about,' he recollected. 'Nothing in common.' Yet, in seeking out divergences, it is easy to overlook similarities. Both were keen to use figure skating as a vehicle to express their individuality: Curry through classical ballet and Cousins with disco music. And, although the new pretender had none of the brooding intensity of the old master, that did not mean he was any less determined to introduce the masses to skating's artistic merit. Figure skating may be classified as a sport, he told one interviewer, but the aim was to 'make the sport look like an art'. It was a sentiment that Curry would have been happy to endorse.

When Curry relinquished his amateur status to take his professional troupe on tour, Cousins took over as British senior champion. From there he made rapid progress, winning medals at successive European and World Championships before taking the European title in January 1980, just a month before the Winter Olympics at Lake Placid. He now had to carry the burden of being Britain's only realistic medal prospect. Despite the time difference, four million people still chose to sit up through the night to watch the BBC's coverage of the men's free skate programme.[78] Not everyone found the hours passed quickly. 'It takes a lot of free skating,' *The Sunday Times*' television critic

78 The Queen was not among the four million. She chose Cousin's MBE investiture ceremony as the ideal moment to let him know she had gone to bed early on the night of his final.

grumbled, 'to fill the time between midnight and 3am, and not much of it on this occasion was good to watch. Even at Olympic level, when you're not among the leaders you're not a pretty sight. It seemed endless, the sequence of stubby youths, hopping and twizzling from foot to panic-stricken foot while brutally tailored selections from the Candelabra Classics raged and boiled over the Tannoys.' The viewing was hardly made easier when an early mistake by Cousins seemed to jeopardise his chance of victory. After an agonising wait it was announced that, although the second-placed East German had amassed a higher points total, Cousins had been named the winner on six of the nine judges' ballots. It had been such a close call that *The Times* felt the 'throbbing euphoria of 1976' was somehow missing.

But the British public did not appear to see it that way. On his return to Britain, Cousins received all the usual tributes the nation's triumphant sporting heroes had come to expect. As well as winning SPOTY, he was treated to an open-top bus tour of his hometown, offered starring roles in pantomimes, asked to feature on a raft of novelty records and was invited to Bristol's Holiday Inn for a gala dinner, complete with a life-size margarine (!?) sculpture of the man of the moment. It did not get much better than that. Actually, it did. During yet another mayoral reception, he was ambushed by Eamonn Andrews and his little red book before being whisked off to the *This Is Your Life* studio. 'How can I be having a "Life" when I'm still only 22,' a bemused Cousins wondered. And, of course, he was right. It was merely the end of his life as an amateur sportsman. He moved on to have a successful professional career, first in the ice spectaculars so despised by Curry, and then in television as a commentator for

BBC Sport and later as a judge on ITV's long-running *Dancing on Ice*. In his own way, he had helped maintain the high profile of the sport he loved.[40]

The final two skaters to win SPOTY were forced to tolerate, just as Curry had been in 1976, a media fascinated by their private lives. But this time it was slightly different. Jayne Torvill and Christopher Dean, two young skaters from Nottinghamshire council estates, were competitors in the relatively new discipline of ice dancing. Only introduced as an Olympic sport in 1976, journalists, eager for a scoop, inevitably speculated that the pair's sexual chemistry on the ice continued when they came off it. Any interview, *The Times* sniffily observed, was invariably 'worked up into a soufflé of Mills and Boon confection'. The two were 'even closer than lovers', thought Jane Firbank of the *Daily Mail*. It did not help that the day of their greatest triumph at the Sarajevo Olympics in 1984 just happened to be St Valentine's Day. At the obligatory post-competition press conference, Dean's flippant, 'not yet', in response to a query about marriage plans, was hardly designed to cool the media frenzy.

But, of course, the couple knew that any romantic involvement would almost certainly upset the delicate mechanics of their sporting partnership. Dean, the creative force behind the pairing, was an impatient perfectionist. 'If I see a mistake,' he once said, 'and it is Jayne's mistake, I will tell her, and if it's mine, I'll tell her she's made a mistake too.' He was only half kidding. Luckily, in Torvill, he had a partner who possessed both the temperament to cope with his drive and the technical expertise to convert his ideas into reality. The affinity between the two was immediately apparent when they teamed up as teenagers in 1975.

And, although most predicted a successful career, the speed and scale of their progress was still astounding. Within three years they were British champions and, just a year after going full-time following an encouraging fifth place in the 1980 Olympics, they were crowned European and World champions. By the start of 1984, they had not been defeated for three years.

Torvill and Dean were, therefore, under enormous pressure as they headed to Sarajevo for the XXIVth Winter Olympic Games. As far as the British press was concerned, the competition might as well not bother turning up. A near-flawless performance in the compulsory dance, with the British pair's 'Westminster Waltz' achieving an Olympic record of three perfect scores, merely bolstered media expectations. 'The gold medal is as good as won,' the *Daily Mail* crowed. And, for once, the optimism was justified. For the third Olympiad in a row, British skating not only delivered but managed, if possible, to surpass even the most avid fan's wildest hopes. The Nottingham couple's performance in the final round was, Robin Cousins professed, the sport's 'defining moment'.

But the choice of Ravel's *Bolero* for the free dance was a risky one. A single, continuous piece of music, the selection challenged the existing convention that routines should be made up of numerous musical extracts spliced together to allow for random changes in tempo. Instead of crudely signalling a shift in mood by jumping from one track to another, Torvill and Dean opted to follow a solitary narrative arc by allowing the emotional intensity to develop as the music built towards a crescendo. It was a risk. Riskier still was the decision to start by kneeling down gazing intently into each other's eyes. In fact, this was a choice borne of necessity. Even with the most brutal cutting, it had been impossible to edit Ravel's 17-minute-long composition down to less than four minutes 28 seconds, an agonising 18 seconds over the maximum time allowed. But Dean refused to be beaten. A combination of creative ingenuity and close reading of the rule book, which stipulated that the clock did not start until a competitor's blades touched the ice, not only offered up a solution to the problem but provided a global audience with one of the most iconic openings to a skating routine in Olympic history.

On the day of the final, Britain's two medal hopes oozed confidence. An early morning run-through of the routine went so well that even a troop of overworked cleaners put down their mops and buckets to give the British pair a standing ovation. Later, in the group warm-up immediately before the competition, the only preparation Dean considered necessary was a surreptitious scuffing of the ice to make sure it would not be too slippy for their unconventional kneeling start. All that was left was to deliver the perfect performance. And that is exactly what the British favourites did. As the pair fell to the ice in a dramatic concluding act, there was a moment of silence while the audience processed the emotional intensity of what they had just witnessed, before the applause rang out and the bouquets of flowers rained down. It took so long to clear the tributes from the rink that the triumphant couple were still on the ice when a perfect set of scores for artistic impression flashed up on the screen. Even Princess Anne, there in her capacity as president of the British Olympic Association, was caught up in all the excitement. Breaking with protocol, she insisted on staying behind to offer her congratulations at an impromptu celebration held later the same evening. 'Parties usually happen better if they're done on the spur of the moment,' she happily reminisced. And if anyone knows what makes a good party, then surely it is the Princess Royal.

Anne was not the only one partying that night. Some 24 million Britons had gathered round their television sets shortly before 10pm to revel in the moment. One lonely traveller in Cambridgeshire was so desperate not to miss out that, spotting through an open window a family settling down to enjoy the action, he plucked up the courage to knock on their door and ask if he could join them. 'There aren't many moments like that in life,' Jeffrey Archer told his kind-hearted hosts as he took his leave a couple of hours later. 'I can remember when Everest was conquered, I remember when we won the World Cup, and this was another one of those moments.' Maybe, 17 years later, being sent down at the Old Bailey would be added to the list.

As Christmas approached, the country's only Winter Olympic gold medallists were still so popular that when it was announced they had won the BBC's individual SPOTY trophy, to add to their two previous team awards, it came as a surprise to no one. Or nearly no one. *The Sunday Times*, still unhappy about the role of aesthetics in figure skating, considered Torvill and Dean winning a sports award to be up there with George Best being jailed for drunken offences and Mary Decker tripping over Zola Budd as the year's worst sporting moment. But the paper was missing the point. That February evening in the Zetra Olympic Hall in Sarajevo had, the veteran journalist David Miller rightly observed, made discussions about whether ice dancing was a sport or not 'irrelevant'. What was much more important was that, in just four minutes and 28 seconds, Torvill and Dean had 'elevated the Olympics'.[41]

* * *

III. Rowing
Steve Redgrave (2000)

FOR A winter sport like figure skating to enjoy a brief period of SPOTY success was quite remarkable, but for a much more peripheral activity like rowing to top the poll, even once, was truly astonishing. To persuade the public to vote for such a niche pursuit required an athlete of extraordinary determination and talent. In Steve Redgrave, rowing had just that. Between 1984 and 2000, he won gold medals at five consecutive Olympic Games, as well as (and it seems ridiculous just to throw this statistic in as an afterthought) nine world championship titles.[79] Even his SPOTY record is pretty impressive with, complementing his overall first place in 2000, two team awards (1992 and 1996), an individual runner-up spot (1996) and a third place (1997).

Perhaps more surprising still is that the state-educated Redgrave succeeded in a sport that is largely the preserve of the public schools. British Rowing's 'Committed to Inclusion' report in 2021 found that fewer than 10 per cent of its registered schools were from the state sector. 'The evidence shows,' the report concluded with masterly understatement, 'that rowing

---

79 Only one other Olympian has a better record. The Hungarian fencer Aladar Gerevich won six golds at consecutive Olympics between 1932 and 1960. Of course, the Games were not held in 1940 and 1944.

is not currently representative of today's society.' This elitism was certainly reflected in Redgrave's career. Of the eight team-mates who shared Olympic golds with him, seven were privately educated. It was fortunate, then, that the future five-time Olympic champion attended a secondary school in the Thames-side town of Marlow, which not only maintained close links with the local rowing club but also had on staff a rowing enthusiast who encouraged suitably strapping pupils to try the sport out.

By 1996, Redgrave had raised both his own and his sport's profile sufficiently to be installed as favourite for that year's SPOTY award. Having become the youngest rower ever to be crowned Olympic champion, with gold in the coxed fours at Los Angeles in 1984, he had gone on to win the coxless pairs at Seoul, Barcelona and Atlanta, on the last two occasions crewing with the genial Old Etonian Matthew Pinsent. With a quadruple Olympic champion on its hands, the rowing community mobilised to get its man the recognition he deserved. *Regatta*, 'the official magazine of the Amateur Rowing Association', played fast and loose with SPOTY's rules on canvassing and urged subscribers to 'Vote Redgrave!' But it was to no avail. Damon Hill, who had finally managed to win the F1 championship, gave motorsport yet another victory. *The Observer* was sure that 'the wrong man had won', and even Redgrave himself admitted to finding the result a 'bit perverse'. 'We're a nation that seems a bit embarrassed by our successes,' he later mused. Perhaps it was some consolation when Damon Hill's mum sidled up to him after the ceremony and confided, 'I'm delighted for Damon, but you should have won it.' Then again, perhaps not.

Redgrave, nonetheless, managed to put the disappointment behind him. Despite, after the Atlanta row, famously giving the public carte blanche to shoot him if he ever got back in a boat, he decided to press on to Sydney 2000, this time as a member of the coxless fours. Teamed up once again with his trusty lieutenant, Matthew Pinsent, and joined by Olympic bronze medallist Tim Foster and former world junior champion James Cracknell, the prospects looked good. An early victory in the World Championships was encouraging, but from then on matters seemed to go from bad to worse. Foster was sidelined for several months, first with severed tendons in his hand after punching a window during a drunken shindig and then with a long-term back injury that eventually required an operation. Much more worryingly, Redgrave was diagnosed with type 2 diabetes in 1997. Some started to doubt whether an historic fifth gold medal was really possible. These fears seemed to be confirmed when the crew finished in a disastrous fourth place at their last outing before Sydney. Christopher Dodd of *The Guardian* articulated what everyone else had been secretly wondering: 'Is Redgrave over the hill?'

The Olympic final of the coxless fours at Sydney's International Regatta Centre two months later demonstrated that the answer to Dodd's question was 'no'. But it was far from emphatic. One second up with 500m to go, the chasing pack slowly started to reel the British boat in. 'The Italians are coming!' screamed the BBC's Gary Herbert in case the seven million viewers at home were not already anxious enough. By the finishing line the winning margin had shrunk to a nerve-shredding 0.38 of a second. As Cracknell raised his fist in triumph, Pinsent clambered over Foster, hugged the new five-time Olympic champion and gently toppled into the water.

The press nearly ran out of superlatives. Redgrave was 'the greatest Olympian ever' declared the *Daily Mail.* But that was too understated for the *Sunday Times*. 'Not only was [Redgrave's win] the greatest piece of sport in the history of the world,' the paper's chief sportswriter insisted, but the man himself was now 'the greatest athlete in history'. The *Sunday Express* demanded that the Queen 'knight him now!' That would have to wait a few months, but in the interim there was always the satisfaction of being named *Smash Hits* 'Hero of 2000', ahead of teen pop sensation Britney Spears and Geordie pranksters Ant and Dec (who, like Torvill and Dean, invariably came as a pair).

With popular support so high, the bookies sensibly stopped taking bets on SPOTY, and Redgrave finally got his hands on the trophy that many thought should have been his much earlier. The award had 'righted the wrong of 1996' was *The Observer*'s blunt assessment. Even the victor himself felt the public had taken more persuading to arrive at the right decision than should have been strictly necessary. 'Sixteen years I've been coming here,' he told the audience at the BBC's Television Centre, 'and I had to hint this time that I was going to retire.' It was not entirely clear whether he was joking. And a full appreciation of Redgrave's achievements was not limited to armchair sports fans. On the eve of the London Olympics, the *Daily Telegraph* asked the 2,400 surviving British Olympians to nominate their greatest British Olympian of all time. With 53 per cent of the nominations, rowing's most famous son was streets ahead of Daley Thompson in second and Seb Coe in third.[80] It was a fitting tribute to a superb athlete.[42]

* * *

IV. Golf

Dai Rees (1957) – Nick Faldo (1989)

RATHER LIKE swimming, golf has struggled to translate recreational popularity into SPOTY wins. Although modern technology has ensured that the small-screen golf fan can enjoy unrivalled coverage of the majors, for the occasional viewer the sport lacks the immediacy of some of the more high-octane athletic pursuits. The drama during an Open or Masters tends to unfold at a relatively low pitch. No matter how much might rest on a tricky final putt, to the untrained eye the sight of a 42mm ball gently trundling towards the hole on the 18th rarely matches the visceral excitement of a last-minute Beckham free kick or the sublime artistry of a John Curry spread eagle. 'A golfer,' the editor of *Golf Monthly* despaired, 'would need to win the Grand Slam, and then hole the winning putt in a Ryder Cup year, to have a chance of getting on the podium of the SPOTY awards.' Dai Rees and Nick Faldo, the game's only two sports personality winners, never quite managed that, but they did succeed in providing sufficient theatre to capture the imagination of the wider sporting public.

80 Thompson received 13 per cent of the vote and Coe 4 per cent.

Dai Rees, who beat 'Mr Motor Racing' Stirling Moss and world mile record holder Derek Ibbotson to become golf's first SPOTY winner in 1957, not only captained Great Britain to its first Ryder Cup win for 24 years, but did so in a manner that seemed to have echoes of the nation's recent past. Alone against a far superior power, the country, led by 'never-say-Dai' Rees, managed to defy all expectations and recover from a dreadful start to achieve a spectacular victory. And certainly the odds had seemed stacked against Rees. The Americans had only lost the Ryder Cup twice since its first staging in 1927. Indeed, the fixture had become so one-sided that many feared another defeat for the British at Worksop's Lindrick Golf Club, in October 1957, would signal the end of the biennial competition.

Those fears seemed to be fully justified after first-day's play at Lindrick. With victory for Rees and partner Ken Bousfield the only bright spot in a 3-1 trouncing in the foursomes, the *Daily Mail*'s golf correspondent gloomily reported that '15,000 Englishmen had paid 15 shillings a head to attend a wake'. But then the resurrection occurred. Inspired by their captain's record-breaking 7 and 6 win, the British team lost only one of the singles matches on the second day to come out victors by 7½ to 4½. It was, thought *The Guardian*, the 'most remarkable day in the history of golf'. It was the only defeat the Americans would suffer between 1933 and 1985, and the last time they would lose to British golfers unaided by the rest of Europe. They had been so sure of victory that they had not even bothered to cancel the insurance on the trophy. The result even caught out the two millionaire sponsors of the teams. Rather than going to the trouble of writing up new after-dinner addresses for the post-tournament celebration,

Robert Hudson and his British counterpart Sir Stuart Goodwin simply decided to 'change over speeches'.

Rees was universally hailed as the plucky hero of the hour. When all had seemed lost, the *Daily Mirror* reminded its readers, 'The cheery little Welshman, bless his fighting heart, had still thought we could win.' 'His personal contribution to the astonishing victory was,' the *Sunday Times*' venerable golf correspondent Henry Longhurst asserted, 'as great as any I can remember in any team match.' In *The Observer*'s opinion it was, quite simply, 'Rees's finest hour.' And, for the ever-patriotic *Daily Mail*, that hour was all the finer for the fact that it was Americans who had been humbled. 'For far too long,' it raged, 'British golf has cowered before the dollar-chasing, success-inflated Americans, with their arrogance in victory, and belief that British golfers are just a bunch of hard-up country-cousins.' Such venom must have left readers wondering if it really was only the United States' dominance in golf that the paper found so difficult to accept. Whatever the truth, the nation's satisfaction that the new world order had been upended, albeit temporarily and only on the golf course, lasted for another couple of months and, in the plush surroundings of the Great Room at the Grosvenor House Hotel in Park Lane, Rees became the oldest recipient of the SPOTY trophy.[43]

Rees captained the Ryder Cup team three more times after the glories of Lindrick, and continued to be competitive on the professional golf circuit until well into his 50s. For much of his later career, though, he led his peers in demanding a greater eye to commercial opportunities from the sport's governing body, the Professional Golfers' Association. The result of this lobbying was the development of a fully professional golf circuit. In the two decades following Rees's last involvement as a Ryder Cup player in 1962, the reach and scale of international tournaments grew exponentially. Crowds at the Open, for example, expanded by a factor of five in this period, and the total prize money increased a hundredfold.

Golf's only other winner of SPOTY, Nick Faldo, reaped the benefits of these new commercial prospects. Having taken up the sport at the relatively late age of 14, he was instantly hooked and left school at 16 with no ambition other than to be a professional golfer. Two years later he became the youngest-ever winner of the English Amateur Championship and, on the back of that success, signed up with Mark McCormack's International Management Group, the sports marketing firm that had already made fortunes for many of tennis' biggest stars. From there his progress through the professional ranks was rapid. He made his Ryder Cup debut when just 20 and was installed at the top of the European rankings by 1983. However, a crisis of confidence at the 1984 Masters, after a nervy final round saw him drop from third to 15th, drove the fiercely ambitious Faldo to completely restructure his game. It was an incredibly brave decision, and it meant two years of substandard performances.

By 1987, though, he was back, better than ever. Victory in the Open at Muirfield was followed up by a series of encouraging, if frustrating, second places. However, although his improved gameplay was universally praised, his demeanour on the golf course received less favourable coverage. 'If you ever got Nick Faldo as a pairing,' one opponent was quoted as saying, 'you thought, well, this isn't going to be fun tomorrow. We won't be talking about our wives or children.' Invariably, the media portrayed Faldo as cold and aloof, the antihero to his long-time rival, the affable Scot Sandy Lyle. Even worse, a messy separation from his wife allowed the tabloids to present him as a villainous adulterer. To win the necessary public support to claim SPOTY, therefore, would take something spectacular.

The 1989 Masters was just that. Initially, though, it seemed Faldo's bad old days had returned. Joint second after two rounds, he dropped to ninth by the end of the rain-delayed third. The temporary loss of form did nothing to improve his relations with the press. 'Fuck off!' he told an unfortunate course-side reporter as he stormed off to change putters for the final day's play. But happily the change of club brought better fortune, and a near-flawless final round of 65 set up a play-off with the American Scott Hoch. A bunkered approach by Faldo on the first play-off hole left Hoch with a 2ft putt to win the green jacket and secure his first-ever major. As the American took an age to ready himself, the BBC's Peter Alliss ratcheted up the tension. 'He'll be saying,' whispered Alliss, '"Boy, I've got a two-footer downhill for everything, all that we've worked for all the time, all that we think about, all that we dream about. Mom and the babies at home, nervous."' No wonder Hoch missed. That one shot, the *Daily Mail* proclaimed the next day, had earned 'the American miserable immortality among golf's famous losers'.[81] 'Hoch,' readers of the *New York Times* were helpfully reminded, 'rhymes with choke.'

---

81 And if readers wondered just how badly the miss would affect Hoch, the *Mail* was happy to provide a clue. The paper recalled the response of Hoch's compatriot Doug Sanders when asked whether the memory of a missed 3ft putt to win the Open in 1970 still bothered him. 'No,' he had replied, 'sometimes I can go five minutes without thinking about it.'

Hoch was never likely to recover sufficient composure to win the second play-off hole, but Faldo's holing of a 25ft putt for a birdie was perhaps an unnecessary rubbing of salt into wounds. As the jubilant victor went off to the pavilion to become the first Englishman to collect a green jacket, the distraught American was left to face the world's press.[82] 'I'm glad I'm not carrying a gun at the moment,' he gamely quipped. No one was heartless enough to point out that even if he were, with his aim, the danger would be negligible. Back in Britain, the press was in raptures over Faldo's performance. 'The greatest final round of championship history,' *The Guardian* enthused, 'had been capped off with one of the greatest putts in play-off history.' It had been, the wrung-out golf correspondent of *The Express* confided, 'a majestic comeback from the golfing grave on a day that shredded the emotions'. Although not everyone was quite so thrilled. 'It was a wonderful victory,' conceded the new Mrs Faldo from back home in England, 'but the baby has still to be fed. There's shopping to do and I had to go out to keep a doctor's appointment for Natalie.' No doubt golf widows across the country were nodding their heads in sympathy. But, family issues aside, the high drama at Augusta had still been sufficient for Faldo to gain traction with the public and become golf's second and, to date, last recipient of the SPOTY trophy.

That year, 1989, was, of course, just the beginning of a period of sporting dominance for Faldo. He went on to win the Masters and the Open twice more and, between July 1992 and February 1994, spent an astonishing 81 weeks as the top-ranked golfer in

82 Irritatingly, at least for Faldo, arch-rival Sandy Lyle had been fitted for a green jacket the year before.

the world. Yet he never again came close to winning SPOTY. When he lifted the trophy in 1989, second place had gone to Frank Bruno, whose only competitive outing that year had been a swift and brutal defeat at the hands of Mike Tyson, and third place to Steve Davies, a prodigious talent but in the relatively marginal sport of snooker. As footballers, athletes, racing drivers and tennis players once again took over at the top of the SPOTY rankings in the 1990s, so golf found itself pushed back into the shadows. And, with the majors disappearing behind Sky's paywall in the 21st century, there are fears that the sport's long period in the SPOTY wilderness is set to continue. 'Golf broadcasting doesn't suit [the BBC's] demographic,' Matt Chivers of *National Club Golfer* bemoaned after it was announced in February 2023 that, for the first time in 56 years, there would be no live free-to-air coverage of the Masters. 'It seems,' Chivers concluded, 'unlikely there will be a golfing winner of the BBC trophy in the future.' He may well be right.[44]

Chapter Notes

38 *Guardian*, 13 July 2019, 26 July 2009; Holt and Mason, *Sport in Britain*, pp.58–60; *The Scotsman*, 19 December 2012; Robert Philip, *Scottish Sporting Legends* (2011), ch.3; *The Herald*, 16 December 2008; *Daily Mirror*, 6 August 2021, 5 December 1958; *Daily Express*, 8 September 1958, 28 July 1958; *Times*, 1 December 1962, 29 November 1962; Rider and Smith, *BBC Sports Personality of the Year*, p.48; National Film and Sound Archive of Australia, *1962 Games Village* (1962).

39 *Guardian*, 11 February 1984; *Times*, 28 February 1976, 12 February 1976; *Daily Mail*, 12 February 1976, 7 February 1976; *John Curry: The Ice King*, dir. James Erskine (2018); Goldblatt, *The Games*, p.379; Turner, *Crisis? What Crisis?*, p.243; Bill Jones, *Alone: The Triumph and Tragedy of John Curry* (2015), pp.47–52, 130; ITV, *The Real John Curry*,

dir. Ralph Lee, (2003); *Daily Express*, 12 February 1976; *Observer* 15 February 1976; *Daily Telegraph*, 5 February 2018.

40 Martha Lowder Kimball, *Robin Cousins: The Authorized Biography* (1998), pp.39, 134, 140–144; *Daily Mail*, 22 February 1980; Jones, *Alone*, p.129; BBC2, *Gold on Ice*, dir. Margaret Benton (1979); *Sunday Times*, 24 February 1980; *Times*, 23 February 1980; *The Lost Skating Interviews: Robin Cousins* (2005).

41 *Times*, 15 February 1984; *Daily Mail*, 15 February 1984, 11 February 1984; BBC2, *Torvill and Dean: The Perfect Day* (2014); Jayne Torvill and Christopher Dean, *Our Life on Ice: The Autobiography* (2014), pp.80–85; John Hennessy, *Torvill and Dean* (1984), pp.190–194; *Sunday Times*, 30 December 1984.

42 British Rowing, *Committed to Inclusion* (2021), pp.5–6; Steve Redgrave and Nick Townsend, *Steve Redgrave: The Autobiography* (2000), pp.17–28, 222; *Observer*, 24 September 2000, 10 December 2000, 15 December 1996; Rider and Smith, *BBC Sports Personality of the Year*, p.226; BBC, *Gold Fever*, dir. Karen Hamilton (2000); *Guardian*, 17 July 2000; *Daily Mail*, 23 September 2000; *Sunday Times*, 11 December 2000; *Sunday Express*, 24 September 2000; BBC1, *The Rowers Return*, dir. Karen Hamilton (2001); *Daily Telegraph*, 23 July 2011.

43 *Golf Monthly*, 20 December 2022; *Daily Express*, 10 October 1957; *Daily Mail*, 7 October 1957, 5 October 1957; *Daily Mirror*, 7 October 1957; *Sunday Times*, 13 October 1957; *Observer*, 6 October 1957; Rider and Smith, *BBC Sports Personality of the Year*, p.22.

44 Ray Physick and Richard Holt, 'Big Money: The Tournament Player and the PGA, 1945–1975', in Smith and Porter, *Amateurs and Professionals*, p.60; John Lowerson, 'Golf', in Mason (ed.) *Sport in Modern Britain*, p.211; Holt and Mason, *Sport in Britain*, p.5; Rob Steen, *Floodlights and Touchlines*, p.201; *The Incredible Story of Nick Faldo: A Life in Golf* (2022) https://www.youtube.com/watch?v=FAA9_se50IE (accessed 5 September 2023); Dale Concannon, *Driven: The Definitive Biography of Nick Faldo* (2001), pp.66–67, 157; *Daily Mail*, 11 April 1989; *Guardian*, 1 April 2015, 11 April 1989; *Daily Express*, 10 April 1989; *National Club Golfer*, 23 March 2023.

Chapter 5

Horsepower: Motor Racing, Motorcycling, Equestrianism

I. Motor Racing (Formula One)

Stirling Moss (1961) – Jackie Stewart (1973) – Nigel Mansell (1986, 1992) –

Damon Hill (1994, 1996) – Lewis Hamilton (2014, 2020)

MOTOR RACING is one of the world's most popular spectator sports. Formula One (F1), the highest class of international racing, attracts a global audience only bettered by the Olympics and the FIFA World Cup. Such is the sport's reach in the modern satellite pay-per-view sporting age that the latest five-year exclusive rights deal went for an astonishing £1bn. It was a small price to pay, Sky felt, to gain access to the homes of 500 million fans across 185 countries. Yet, despite having the backing of tens of thousands of avid petrolheads across the nation, whenever a racing driver has won SPOTY they have been invariably accused of not quite meriting the honour. And the charge has always been the same. Success, as *The Observer* claimed of Damon Hill in 1996, has been deemed to be the result of 'horsepower not willpower'. Indeed, for the comedian Frank Skinner, even Hill's inclusion on the 1996 shortlist was a travesty. 'When,' he complained, 'is Des Lynam going to say that he's very sorry but it's been decided votes for motor-racing drivers won't be accepted this year because the BBC has realised that motor racing isn't actually a sport. I certainly never remember doing it in games lessons at school.'

For the critics of F1, sporting talent is always trumped by space-age technology. The real star is the car; the driver a mere appendage, little more than an overpaid chauffeur. But, of course, there is more to driving a racing car than there seems. Like all great sportspeople, the best drivers marry genius with dedication to make the supremely challenging look absurdly easy. 'Formula One,' the TV critic Clive James observed, 'is like art – it's the hard work you don't see that makes the difference.' In preparation for the F1 season, Nigel Mansell, Damon Hill and Lewis Hamilton all engaged in gruelling fitness programmes that would have made even the most committed Olympic athlete blanch. Before his debut at the Australian Grand Prix in 2007, Lewis Hamilton swam 2km, cycled 50 miles and did two hours' gym work every day for six months. And, of course, over and above fitness and skill, professional motor-racing demands one extra quality: courage.

Death was ever-present in post-war racing. Between 1945 and 1962, over 180 drivers died in competition. The fatality count in F1 alone reached double figures for each decade from the 1950s to the 1970s. 'To be a racing driver between 1963 and 1973,' triple world champion Jackie Stewart observed, 'was to accept the probability of death.' And he had good reason to think this way. After his close friend, Jim Clark, was killed at the Hockenheimring in April 1968, an F1 driver died each month until the German Grand Prix in August.[83] Indeed, fatal crashes were so common in this period that track officials would invariably insist that racing should continue no matter how serious the accident, compelling drivers to pass the burning wreckage of their colleagues' cars lap after lap. Team bosses, the 1996 F1 champion and double SPOTY winner Damon Hill reflected, simply thought of drivers as light bulbs: 'When one went out you just put another one in.'[45]

Stirling Moss, the first racing driver to win SPOTY, remembered 'the fear of having a serious accident always being there; an ever-present black shadow lurking beside me in the car'. And it was lurking beside him without a seat belt. The cars in the 1950s and 1960s, the great motor-racing commentator Murray Walker stated, were 'mobile death traps'. Not only were they not fitted with safety harnesses, but they had no crush protection of any sort. Even spectating was a dangerous pastime. In 1961, the year Moss won SPOTY, Ferrari's Wolfgang von Trips was killed, along with 15 spectators, as his car careered off the track at Monza and flew up an embankment into the crowd. Moss dealt with the danger by rationalising it. 'It's not a matter of fear,' he explained to John Freeman during the hugely popular BBC show *Face to Face*, 'it's a matter of calculation. If you get the calculation right there is nothing to fear … The only thing to be frightened of is being killed by something over which you have no control.' But the problem was that there were too many uncontrollables. As

---

83 After Jim Clark's fatal crash in April 1968, Mike Spence (Stewart's former team-mate at BRM) died in May, Ludovico Scarfiotti in June and Jo Schlesser in July.

if to underline the point, the week after the Freeman interview, the rear wheel of Moss's car came off while he was cornering at 140mph at Spa. 'Shunt. Back. Legs. Nose. Bruises. Bugger' was the British number one's doleful diary entry.

It was the danger, though, that infused motor racing with glamour. The race that turned Moss into an international celebrity was one of the most hazardous in the world. The Mille Miglia was a thousand-mile open-road race from Brescia to Rome and back. In 1955, driving a Mercedes-Benz 300 and averaging just a fraction under 100mph, Moss beat his great rival, Juan Manuel Fangio, to set a new course record. It was a time that was destined never to be beaten as, just two years later, the event was outlawed after the deaths of three competitors and 11 spectators brought the total fatalities up to an appalling 56 in only 24 outings. But, for Moss, the Mille had served its purpose. He was now firmly established as a star of the international racing circuit. And with his carefully cultivated image of playboy racer – white helmet, nonchalant wave to the crowd, self-deprecating courtesy – he seemed to fit perfectly into the era of the gentleman driver.

But for all his apparent insouciance, what set Moss apart from his rivals was his determination. Peter Collins and Mike Hawthorn, two of the top British drivers of the period, 'had more fun', Moss's manager astutely noted, 'but they were never totally committed'. For Moss, winning was everything. It even eclipsed his much-vaunted patriotism. He may have insisted that his Maserati had two Union flags stencilled on the livery, and thought that 'the rest of the world was a suburb of London', but that didn't stop him signing up for Mercedes when he realised his British team, Hersham and Walton Motors, was no longer competitive.

Unsurprisingly, talent and determination brought success. After his Mille triumph, Moss finished runner-up in the F1 championship four years in a row, and his career tally of 212 wins in 519 races, across all classes of motor racing, is a record as yet unsurpassed. Yet, as the swinging 60s got underway, securing the F1 Drivers' Championship continued to elude him. His unsolicited tag of 'the greatest never to …' may have heightened his popularity by playing into the British public's love of the plucky underdog, but, for the hypercompetitive Moss, it was a sobriquet he could have done without.

The 1961 season seemed destined to be another disappointing one. Moss's outdated Lotus 18-Climax was seriously underpowered in comparison with Ferrari's state-of-the-art 156 'sharknose', with its all-new V6 engine. Yet, in the opening race of the season around the iconic streets of Monaco, he demonstrated astonishing skill as he managed to hold off, for over four fifths of the 100-lap race, not only the Italian challenge but also that of Jo Bonnier's Porsche. It was, said Murray Walker, his 'best drive ever'. The *Daily Express* was in raptures. 'For more than two and half hours,' it enthused, '[Moss] fought a lone battle to keep a British Lotus car in front of a pack of screaming Italian works-entered Ferraris, reinforced by a German Porsche.' An ungrateful Europe may have rebuffed our application to join the EEC, but here, at least, was proof that we still had what it takes to inflict the occasional defeat on the Axis powers. Although it proved impossible for the British favourite to repeat such heroics on less technical circuits and he, once again, finished the season on the podium but not the top step, he had finally done enough for the British public to vote him in as Sports Personality of the Year. It was just as well because next season his luck finally ran out. A horrific crash in the Glover Trophy at Goodwood not only left him in a coma for a month but also ended his career as a competitive driver.[46]

By the time the next F1 driver picked up the SPOTY trophy, just over a decade later, motor racing had changed beyond all recognition. The age of the gentlemen driver had given way to a more commercialised and corporatised operation. No longer was the grid populated by individuals who manufactured their own cars and raced in their national colours. Instead, big works teams, backed by an array of global sponsors, dominated. Britain's new star of the racing track personified this emerging professionalism. Having served his apprenticeship in Formula Three and Formula Two, Jackie Stewart spent his nine-year F1 career as a contracted driver with three major constructors, BRM, Matra and Tyrrell.

But, despite the increasing commercialisation of the racing pit, one aspect of the sport remained unaltered. It was as deadly as it had ever been. This was quickly made apparent to Stewart when he suffered a near-fatal crash on a rain-sodden track at Belgium's notorious Spa-Francorchamps circuit in June 1966. Stuck upside down in a car that was rapidly leaking fuel, he was only freed when his team-mate, Graham Hill, managed to use a spanner borrowed from a spectator to release his steering column. From then on, Stewart not only ensured that he always drove with a spanner taped to the inside of his cockpit, but, more critically, he became an outspoken advocate for driver safety. Why, he would ask exasperated track officials, were there 'grass banks that were launch pads, things you went straight into, trees that were unprotected'? Medical provision, he would point out, was so poor that he was forced to travel to race meetings with his own personal doctor. But the authorities were at best dismissive, at worst hostile when safety issues were raised, and twice the Grand Prix Drivers' Association (GPDA), led by Stewart, was forced to take direct action when it considered circuits to be unacceptably dangerous.[84]

Even then, some fans were less than impressed by Stewart's campaigning. One subscriber to *Motor Sport* angrily informed the magazine's editor that he had 'had enough of this timidity', and suggested Stewart should 'leave motor racing to men' and retire to Switzerland where the only risk he would face would be 'being run over on the way to the bank'. It was an unwarranted attack on a man who had lost nine close friends in racing accidents.

The reason, of course, why Stewart's voice could provoke such passion was because he was one of the best drivers there was. Having signed for Tyrrell in 1968, he finished second in his first season with the Surrey-based outfit, before going on to win the championship the following year and then again two years later. His hat-trick of F1 championships, along with recognition from SPOTY voters, came in his final year in the sport. Yet, although the 1973 season was a professional triumph, it was bookended by reminders of racing's darker side. At the South African Grand Prix at Kyalami in early March, Stewart's brakes failed in practice and he was only saved from what would, almost certainly, have been a fatal collision with a concrete wall by three lines of chain-link safety fencing that, just a few months earlier,

84 The GPDA boycotted the Belgium Grand Prix in June 1969 when officials refused to implement safety modifications, and the following year the German Grand Prix was switched from the Nürburgring to Hockenheim when further strike action was threatened.

had been installed at his insistence. Six months later, however, in qualifying for the last race of the season at Watkin's Glen, New York, the outcome was not so favourable. Stewart's young French team-mate, François Cevert, was killed instantly when his car spun out of control and crashed into the trackside barriers. A visibly shaken Stewart withdrew from the following day's race and announced his retirement. For a man who had fought so hard for driver safety, it was a horrifically ironic way to end his career.[47]

Over a decade passed before another F1 driver was voted in as sports personality. By the time Nigel Mansell won the first of his two SPOTY trophies in 1986, motor racing had undoubtedly become much safer. In part, this was due to the relentless campaigning of Stewart, but it was also a (partially unintended) consequence of the sport's growing corporatisation. Reluctant to have their products associated with the deaths of dashing young men, F1's big commercial sponsors, most of which were tobacco conglomerates, insisted on improved safety standards. Presumably old men succumbing to lung cancer was somehow viewed by John Player's PR department as an acceptable hit.

But the real divergence between Stewart and Mansell was to be found in the personal context of their public image rather than the wider circumstances of racing's commercialisation. Stewart may not have had the post-war drivers' blasé disregard for danger, but he certainly matched them when it came to living life in the celebrity fast lane. And if F1 was about anything, it was about glamour. Yet the world of yachts and casinos, film actresses and private jets never seemed quite the right fit for the new British champion. In a racing pit full of landed Brazilians and dashing Frenchmen, Birmingham-raised Mansell was, in the words of F1 historian Stephen Wagg, 'unashamedly a white-bread, ketchup-sloshing everyman'. While 'Senna was expressive in Portuguese, Spanish, English and Italian, and Prost was fluent in French, delicious in English, comfy after his fashion in Italian; Mansell was', the *Daily Express*'s motorsport correspondent waspishly noted, 'sometimes awkward in English.' Even the Briton's choice of tax haven – the Isle of Man rather than Monaco or Lake Geneva – hardly screamed *joie de vivre*.

Yet maybe Mansell was more in tune with the public *zeitgeist* than the cultural commentators realised. For many, the roots of his popularity lay in his anti-celebrity persona. His story seemed to capture the spirit of the Thatcherite 80s; the ordinary bloke from humble beginnings who, through hard work, sacrifice and persistence in adversity, eventually comes good. Stewart may have tasted Grand Prix victory and finished on the podium in the drivers' standings in his first season, but that was the stuff of fairy tales. Mansell was a grafter. His journey to the world championship was a 16-year odyssey. His first F1 win was not until the European Grand Prix at Brands Hatch in October 1985 – his 72nd start.

The Guardian could easily dismiss Mansell as nothing more than a 'solid plodder', but it could not so readily deny his battling spirit. And if proof of that spirit was needed, then the British public had to look no further than the 1984 Dallas Grand Prix. 'I imagine conditions in those cars are totally unimaginable,' screamed Murray Walker, as the drivers waited in the 110°F heat for the race to start. But 67 laps later, with the chequered flag in sight, the transmission on Mansell's Lotus-Renault gave up the ghost and the chance of a podium finish seemed to have disappeared. However, the plucky British favourite refused to give up. Leaping out of the cockpit on to the rapidly melting tarmac, he pushed his stricken car across the finish line before promptly fainting. He may have only ended up sixth, but he had won British hearts.

Mansell's determination, though, didn't seem to be matched by his luck, and he appeared fated to always fall short of the top spot. This was never more apparent than in the 1986 season. Going into the championship finale in Adelaide, he only required a top-three finish to take his first drivers' title. With just 18 laps of the 82-lap race remaining, he was sitting comfortably in third place, over a minute ahead of the next car, when one of his rear tyres blew as he came into the main straight at 200mph. It was a terrifying moment. For eight heart-stopping seconds he struggled to bring the car under control as it slew crazily across the track in a shower of sparks and flames. The blowout probably cost him more than £3m in sponsorship deals and certainly denied him the world championship, but it could so easily have deprived him of his life. 'He had,' as Clive James astutely noted in *The Observer*, 'cause to bless his fortune while he cursed it.' Mansell's combination of courage and skill that October afternoon on the Adelaide Street Circuit, the *Daily Mail* thought, explained 'why the vicarious were prepared to pay £80 a ticket to witness two hours of turbo-charged chariot-racing'. And it also explained why a 'ketchup-sloshing everyman' was able to pip Fatima Whitbread and Kenny Dalglish to the SPOTY title a month later.

After two more runner-up spots in the drivers' championship (and SPOTY) in 1987 and 1991, the 1992 season looked to hold out the best prospect of at last making it on to the top step of the winners' podium. Driving, once again, for Williams, this time in the newly developed FW14B, Mansell had a mechanical advantage over his competitors that he exploited to the full.[85] Victories in the opening five grands prix, and 14 pole positions in total, both records at the time, meant he was crowned world champion after only 11 races of the 16-race season. Yet the euphoria of finally fulfilling a lifetime ambition was quickly cut short when, just three weeks later, Williams let it be known that they would be signing arch-rival Alain Prost as their number one driver for the following season. The insult was too much for Mansell and he duly announced his retirement from F1.[86] The British tabloids were up in arms at such shoddy treatment of a national treasure. The *Daily Express* devoted a two-page spread to explain how 'our conquering hero' had been 'ousted', while the *Mail* insisted the new champion had been 'appallingly ill-used'. The public clearly agreed, and Mansell was duly installed as Sports Personality of the Year for a second time.[48]

Mansell's replacement at Williams, and the next F1 driver to win SPOTY twice, found it equally difficult to shrug off the charge of not being a 'natural'. But for Damon Hill there was the additional challenge of following in the footsteps of a famous father, whose death just four months after his last race had merely cemented his legend.[87] Throughout his career, Damon found it almost impossible to dismiss the feeling that he

85 Mansell had already had four years with Williams from 1985 to 1988.

86 In fact, Mansell made a brief comeback in 1994 when Williams asked him to act as a stand-in after the death of Ayrton Senna.

87 Graham Hill, a hugely popular and charismatic figure who won the drivers' championship in 1962 and 1968, died in a plane crash in November 1975.

had been 'tasked with a mission to complete'. Even after he had been crowned world champion in 1996 he still felt that he was 'just doing what Graham Hill had done, but had done bigger, better and before'.

It was, no doubt, the fear that his father's legacy would be an impossible one to live up to that initially persuaded Damon to favour motorbikes over cars. Only when he was 24 – a ripe old age in motor-racing terms – did his mother's constant worrying that bikes were even more dangerous than cars finally convince him to swap two wheels for four. And it was not until he was a comparatively geriatric 31 that he belatedly broke into F1, as a stand-in driver for Brabham at the British Grand Prix in July 1992. It was not a debut to remember. Last place, lapped four times by winner Nigel Mansell, was hardly a performance to make people stand up and take note. But it was still enough for Williams, on Mansell's retirement at the end of the '92 season, to promote him from test driver to the number-two seat behind Alain Prost. Although, with typical modesty, Hill later claimed he only got the spot because he was 'cheap and available', his end-of-season ranking of third in the drivers' championship suggested talent must have had a part to play as well.

Initially, it looked as if the 1994 season would follow the same pattern of the year before. But then Ayrton Senna, who had replaced Prost as Williams's first string, was tragically killed at Imola, and Hill, now team leader, found himself in a tooth-and-nail battle with Benetton's young German star, Michael Schumacher. Inevitably, it all came down to the last race of the season. As the drivers waited on the Adelaide tarmac for the green lights, all the ingredients were there for a classic. The arch protagonists were only separated by one point; Benetton were accused by Williams of playing fast and loose with the technical regulations; and Schumacher, the arrogant pretender with a penchant for amassing code violations, was perfectly typecast as the pantomime villain. And the German lived up to his billing flawlessly. As he led Hill into a left-hander on lap 36, he momentarily lost concentration and collided with the trackside wall, wrecking his right rear wheel. Sensing this was his moment, Hill pressed to overtake, but Schumacher suddenly veered sharply to the right and cannoned into the Williams, irreparably damaging its suspension, before being catapulted into the tyre barrier. With both cars unable to continue, the German had, in the most controversial manner possible, secured the title by a solitary point.

But was this simply a racing accident or had there been foul play? The tabloids knew the answer to that one. 'Cheated!' was *The Mirror*'s front-page verdict. It was the 'Hun-acceptable face of motor-racing', *The Sun*, true to form, punned. 'Kraut KOs Damon in Title Storm,' fumed the *Daily Star*, adding for good measure, 'What a Schunt!' But, for once, it was a broadsheet that best articulated the mood on the street. 'Cheating Bastard Robs Damon Hill,' was Giles Smith's blunt take in *The Times*.

Hill may have just fallen short in the drivers' championship, but the high drama at the Adelaide Street Circuit was enough to give him his first SPOTY title – an honour his father had never enjoyed. Yet, delighted though he was by the award, he couldn't quite shrug off the feeling that he didn't really deserve it. It was, he later recalled, 'a bit embarrassing' to have beaten to the title British athletes who had raced to European gold medals – 'after all I hadn't even won the world championship'. He wasn't the only one who felt a bit uneasy. 'How [Australians] would have chuckled last weekend,' observed the *Sunday Times*, 'if they had seen good old Damon Hill, the latest in that long honourable line of plucky British nearly-men, receiving the votes as the BBC Sports Personality of the Year at the expense of Colin Jackson, an athlete who has won every major title going this year and broken a world record to boot.'[88]

After the excitement of Adelaide, the 1995 season was something of an anticlimax for Hill. Most of his time was spent either spinning off the track or crashing into Schumacher – sometimes both at the same time. But the following year a superb start to the season gave him a 25-point lead after just nine races. The chance to emulate his father and seize the drivers' championship finally seemed to be within reach. Then the spinning and crashing started up again. By the last race of the season, in Japan, he was only nine points clear of his young team-mate, Jacques Villeneuve. To make matters worse, Williams had decided not to renew his contract for the upcoming season. In all likelihood this was going to be his last shot at the title. As Villeneuve sat in pole position ahead of Hill, five million sleep-deprived Britons, fearing a repeat of the drama of two years ago, nervously tuned in for the 4am start. For once, though, there was nothing to worry about. Hill led from start to finish and, as he crossed the finish line to take the crown his father had last won 28 years ago, the emotion of the moment rendered a tearful

---

88 Colin Jackson, who had won the Commonwealth and European outdoor 110m hurdles titles as well as the European indoor 60m hurdles gold in a world record, finished third in SPOTY 1994.

Murray Walker momentarily speechless. It truly was a night to remember for F1 fans.

Finally a winner on the track, Hill was quickly installed as the bookies' favourite for SPOTY. Again, he did not disappoint. Although, predictably, there were those who disagreed with the result (when weren't there?), Peter Watts in the *Sunday Times* probably best reflected the view of most sports fans. '[Hill's] transformation,' Watts declared, 'from a typically bumbling British loser to a typically British understated hero is remarkable.' Unfortunately, for the final few years of his career, Hill reverted to bumbling British loser – although this was largely the consequence of driving cars with all the reliability of a 1973 Austin Allegro.[89] But it is the triumph of 1996 that will live in the memory. And, as the *Daily Mirror* remarked at the time, 'His dad would have been so proud.'[49]

No one could accuse the most recent F1 driver to win SPOTY of ever being a loser. Winning was part of Lewis Hamilton's DNA. From when he first started racing karts at the age of eight, Hamilton was rarely off the top step of the podium. Sweeping all before him as he accelerated through the formative ranks of motor racing, he just missed out, in 2007, on becoming the first rookie to win the F1 Drivers' Championship. The following year, normal service was resumed and he became the youngest driver to be crowned world champion.[90] He was just 23. The new, telegenic young star was hailed as the saviour of F1. The recently retired

89 After leaving Williams, Hill drove for Arrows before finishing his career with Jordan. Neither constructor proved to be particularly competitive.

90 In 2010 Sebastian Vettel took over as the youngest-ever champion. Vettel, at 23 years and 133 days, was 167 days younger than Hamilton.

Michael Schumacher may have been 'a serial winner', thought Kevin Eason of the *The Times*, 'but outside Germany and Italy … he was a turn off for millions. Hamilton is pure box office.'[91] The sofa sports fan certainly seemed to agree. ITV's viewing figures for F1 almost doubled when Hamilton arrived on the scene. One of the converts to the sport was *The Independent*'s TV columnist, Chris Maume. Enthralled by the British driver's victory in the Indianapolis Grand Prix in June 2007, he realised that the only other time he had mentioned F1 in his column's ten-year history was when he had written, 'Christ, I'm bored.'

As the victories mounted and public interest grew, so sports journalists, cultural commentators and former champions vied with each other to explain the appeal of Britain's new wonder boy. Yet, although ever-present, what was never quite mentioned in these early profiles was race. Instead, the young champion was described as 'new and exciting', 'a breath of fresh air' or 'irresistibly different'. What was being said, but not said, was that there was finally a black driver on the grid. When the journalist Michael Eboda first went to interview Hamilton, in 1997, at the British junior karting championships, he asked a steward how he could find him. 'That's easy,' he was told, 'he's the only black kid here.' By the time Eboda again interviewed the now seven-times F1 champion (and double SPOTY winner) in 2020, nothing had changed. Over 750 drivers had competed in F1 since its inception in 1950, and Hamilton was still the only black one.

---

91 Schumacher, adhering to the tradition of sporting greats not knowing when to quit, made a brief and largely unsuccessful return to the sport between 2010 and 2012.

Initially, Hamilton's race was regarded as unthreatening. He was, Ben Carrington, a sociology professor from the University of Texas, thought, 'the acceptable face of multi-culturalism. He was from Stevenage not Moss Side. He was mixed-race. He was affable and modest … He represented the difference that is not too different.' But being the only black athlete on a global sporting stage brought extra pressures. Whether he sought it or not, it was Hamilton's destiny to be held up by the press as a representative of his race. And, as Clive James noted at the start of the 2007 season, 'A black destiny can be a tough destiny to have … [Hamilton] had to be perfect. If he behaved like some of the other prima donnas of the grid he would be headline news for a week.'

In fact, even some distinctly suboptimal prima donna-ish behaviour could result in unwelcome press comment. When Hamilton won SPOTY for the first time in 2014, table tennis champion turned *Times* columnist Matthew Syed felt conflicted because, although pleased to see a 'mixed-race kid from a working-class background' succeed, he was disappointed by reports that, 'he shouts at people close to him and lives in tax exile'. It seemed an oddly lopsided balance sheet. Seven years at the very top of a supremely dangerous, ultracompetitive, high-octane sport versus the occasional sharp word and a dislike of paying more tax than absolutely necessary. As Eboda noted, if this was the worst Hamilton's critics could come up with, then he must be 'pretty much a saint'.

Hamilton was always aware that, as an outsider, he would have to adapt if he was going to be accepted. 'The entry point to my sport,' he told *Guardian* journalist and fellow Stevenage escapee Gary Younge, 'was a square and I was like a hexagon, and I thought, "I'm never going to fit through that bloody thing." So, I had to morph my way in order to fit into that world, and then try to get back into the shape I was before.' Certainly, in his early dealings with the media, Hamilton presented as a cautious, conservative and entirely non-controversial figure. It was only after years of success that he felt sufficiently emboldened to give voice to his racial consciousness.

Even in 2014, the year he won his second drivers' championship, his inauguration as Sports Personality of the Year was not greeted with universal approval. There was the usual sniping by golfers who were cross that double major champion, Rory McIlroy had been overlooked. 'Absolutely ridiculous that Rory didn't win SPOTY,' tweeted moaner-in-chief Ian Poulter, '... it would be difficult for any golfer to do better than Rory did this year.' It would have been equally difficult for Hamilton, who had won 11 of the 19 grands prix and finished on the podium in five of the remaining eight races, to have given much more. More insidious was the criticism from Stirling Moss. Writing in *The Telegraph*, Moss complained that Hamilton had become 'whatever you call those superstars and that's not really the way we English go. We're more reserved.' But Hamilton had been born and bred in the Home Counties. What could be more English than that?

Six years later, however, by which time Hamilton had equalled Michael Schumacher's record of seven drivers' championships, the award of a second SPOTY trophy was met with little or no dissent. Six F1 championships in seven years had established Stevenage's most famous son as one of the greatest racing drivers of all time. Perhaps even more importantly, though, his actions away from the track – the support for Black Lives Matter and the campaigning to promote diversity – resonated with the vast majority of the wider public. Giles Richards in *The Guardian* reflected the general mood. 'For once,' he wrote, having watched Hamilton pip Liverpool captain Jordan Henderson to the BBC crown, 'the personality part of the SPOTY award is appropriate … In 2020, Hamilton stood up to be counted. He did not do it for recognition but because it mattered. Reason enough to celebrate a truly great British sportsperson.' Hamilton may have changed but, more crucially, so too had the world.[50]

* * *

II. Motorcycling
John Surtees (1959)

AS EQUALLY talented as Hamilton, and certainly as equally dominant in his sport, was the only motorcyclist to win SPOTY. Like Hamilton, John Surtees started young. He was only ten when he first rode a bike, and just 14 when he became his dad's sidecar partner for a series of grass track races. From then on he never looked back. He won the 500cc world championship in 1956, to become the youngest-ever champion at 22, before going on to retain that title, as well as take the 350cc world crown for three consecutive years between 1958 and 1960. In a career total of 621 races, he won 290 and took a podium spot in a further 103. It was a superb record. Well might the Italians, for whom motorcycling was as much a religion as a sport, dub him *figlio del vento* – son of the wind. He was, thought Raymond Baxter, the

BBC's motoring correspondent, 'one of the finest in one of the finest periods of motorcycle racing'. The public clearly agreed and Surtees beat the late, great Bobby Charlton to the SPOTY title in 1959.

If that had been the end of Surtees's sporting achievements, it would have been impressive enough, but in 1960 he switched from motorcycles to cars. In his debut race at Goodwood, in March 1960, he finished second to future world champion Jim Clark. It was, he mischievously pointed out afterwards, the first time he had watched a car race from start to finish. He took his first F1 Grand Prix win at Spa-Francorchamps in Belgium in 1962, and two years later just edged out Graham Hill and Clark to become the drivers' champion. He remains the only person to have been a world champion on both two and four wheels. But, remarkable though the achievement was, in an Olympic year when Britain's golden girls of the track were sweeping all before them in Tokyo, it was not even enough to feature on the SPOTY podium.[92] It was, perhaps, only after he retired that the sporting public came to appreciate just what a unique talent Surtees was.[51]

* * *

92 Mary Rand (who won SPOTY) took gold and broke the world record in the long jump in Tokyo, while Ann Packer (third in SPOTY) achieved the same double in the 800m. Motor sport did feature on the SPOTY podium, with speedway world champion Barry Briggs coming second.

III. Equestrianism

David Broome (1960, Showjumping) – Princess Anne (1971, Eventing) –

Zara Phillips (2006, Eventing) – Tony McCoy (2010, Horse Racing)

CHRISTOPHER HILTON, the *Daily Express*'s motor-racing correspondent, once remarked that 'good drivers don't win in bad cars'. It is sentiment that can easily be adapted to encompass equestrianism. When Zara Phillips, winner of the World Eventing Championships and SPOTY in 2006, announced she 'couldn't have done it without Toytown [her horse]', she was not just stating the blindingly obvious. Toytown, jointly owned by the Queen, Princess Anne and Captain Mark Phillips, was the equine equivalent of Nigel Mansell's FW14B. Yet, as Princess Anne's close friend Jackie Stewart was keen to point out, riding an expensively bred horse or driving a technically advanced car might confer an advantage, but it did not, by any means, guarantee victory. F1 cars and thoroughbreds are similar, he claimed; they are both 'highly strung' and 'react either positively or negatively to how the driver communicates and functions'. Certainly, few doubted that equestrianism, just like F1, demanded an extraordinary combination of skill and courage, but that still was not quite enough for the sport to shrug off the widely held belief that it was a less than competitive pursuit for the rich and leisured.

A staple of *Grandstand* from its launch in 1958, equestrianism, the socialist academic Raymond Williams argued, was presented by the BBC 'with an ideology on its tail: not just the implication that the horses are one of the better types of Englishmen, but more than the usual chauvinism in commentary and, of course, the social atmosphere of monarchism, army and the sponsoring capitalist corporations'. Quite an indictment! And, as with all good polemics, there was some truth to it. With its roots in the rural culture of the 19th-century landed gentry, which monopolised the British officer class, equestrianism was a sport dominated by the commissioned ranks of the military.[93] This dominance continued well into the second half of the 20th century. In the decades following the Second World War, both the British Equestrian Federation and the Showjumping Association were presided over by a series of seemingly indistinguishable retired colonels, while David Broome, in 1960, the year he won SPOTY, came third in the showjumping at the Rome Olympics behind two Italian cavalry officers.

But where Williams was somewhat wider of the mark was in his insistence that 'most urban democrats have taken against anything to do with horses because of the overtones'. In fact, the BBC's coverage of equestrianism was enormously popular with television viewers until well into the 1970s. The Horse of the Year Show at Wembley Arena held such sway with audiences throughout the 1950s, 60s and 70s that it even managed to turn gruff, professional Yorkshireman Harvey Smith into a national celebrity. Indeed, the SPOTY records serve as testament to the public appetite for showjumping and eventing in this period. Between 1954 and 1973, a showjumper finished in the top-three

93 Eventing was first established as a test for cavalry officers.

places six times and an eventer twice. True, both sports have experienced a downswing in the subsequent half-century, with only Zara Phillips and Nick Skelton managing to make the podium, but this has, almost certainly, had more to do with the expansion of television sports coverage than any sudden anti-equine radicalisation of the urban masses.[94]

The only showjumper to have won SPOTY was well aware that television was responsible for his sport's high public profile. It was, thought David Broome, televised competitions in indoor arenas such as Wembley and Olympia, where competitors rode against the clock, which really drew in the lay viewer. Broome's personal popularity was also aided by his rivalry with the outspoken Harvey Smith. Both men were supremely talented, unforgivingly competitive and, to the public's endless delight, engagingly intolerant of some of the stuffier conventions of their sport – Smith, in 1971, most famously deploying a crude hand gesture to let the judges at Hickstead know exactly where they could go.[95] The two captured the popular imagination, suggested Broome, because 'neither came from typically privileged backgrounds'. That Broome was raised on a 350-acre farm and educated at the elite Monmouth School sheds some interesting light on what was considered 'privileged' in equestrian circles.

Broome, though, won SPOTY long before his rivalry with Harvey Smith really had a chance to take off. An individual

---

94 Skelton won fame as the oldest British Olympic champion in over a century when he took individual gold in the showjumping at Rio in 2016. He was rewarded with third place in that year's SPOTY.

95 On the back of his Hickstead antics, Smith secured a gig advertising Victory V throat lozenges.

bronze at the Olympic showjumping in 1960, along with first in the prestigious (and televised) King George V Gold Cup at the Royal International Horse Show, was sufficient for the 20-year-old rider to top the BBC poll. The *Daily Mirror*, not, admittedly, the paper of choice for the equestrian set, was sure the female vote had swung the result Broome's way. 'Last night's choice in the BBC's Sportsview Personality of the Year,' it insisted, on the basis of absolutely no evidence whatsoever, 'suggests that women viewers polled the majority of the votes.' Probably closer to the truth was the assessment of former Tory minister Lord Brabazon. After presenting Broome with the trophy, he blithely informed those present that 'television must have had a great deal to do with the choice [of winner], for walking was not very thrilling to watch – but a young man on a splendid horse was'. It was a fair point, but possibly one that did not need making when Don Thompson, the Olympic 50km walk champion and that year's SPOTY runner-up, was standing right next to you.

Although 1960 was the last time Broome bothered the individual SPOTY rankings, it was, of course, not the end of his career. He was, after all, only 20. As it turned out, he had nearly three more decades left in the sport, over the course of which he competed at four more Olympics, winning another bronze in 1968, and was crowned European champion three times (1961, 1967 and 1969) and world champion once (1970). And, in 1979, there was another fleeting taste of SPOTY glory as he was beamed into the studio from Bordeaux to join Caroline Bradley, Malcolm Pyrah and Derek Ricketts for the Team of the Year award, in recognition of their gold medal-winning performance at the European Championships.[52]

If Broome was no match, at least by his own estimation if no one else's, for the bluebloods that normally populated equestrian events, then the next two winners of SPOTY more than made up for him. But, as well as being fourth and 11th in line to the throne respectively, Princess Anne and Zara Phillips were also, without a doubt, naturally gifted horsewomen. In the year she won SPOTY, Anne took the European three-day event title at Burghley in what was only her second full-scale competition.[96] So impressive was the performance that the BBC's Clare Balding, who knows a thing or two about such matters, recently suggested that the Princess Royal was, at that time, 'probably the best show jumper in the world'.[97]

Thirty-five years later, Zara Phillips managed to go one better than her mother. Having already become the European three-day event champion at Blenheim in 2005, she went on to collect the world crown in Aachen 12 months later. It was an emotional moment for one of her relatives. The only time, Prince William later recalled, that he had ever cried while watching sport was when Zara won in Aachen – an almost unbelievable claim, one might think, given his lifelong allegiance to Aston Villa.

But Phillips's record was exceptional.

She was only the third rider in history to hold both the European and world titles at the same time. The achievement was sufficiently impressive to persuade the public to make

---

96 After receiving her gold medal from her mum, Anne, momentarily shrugging off her reputation for prickly ill-humour, dryly noted that her win was a 'unique example in equestrian history when the Queen had bred not only the horse but also the rider'.

97 Balding comes from a long line of racehorse trainers. Her father trained the 1971 Derby winner, Mill Reef.

her the first offspring of a previous winner to receive the SPOTY trophy.

Yet for all the talent and accomplishments of the two royals, it was still hard to fully fathom how they had managed to top the BBC poll. Even by equestrian standards, eventing was a niche sport. When Anne won the Europeans there were only nine entrants in total, eight of whom were British; and when Phillips triumphed in Aachen, the title had been shared by only five nations.

It was a world title, but it was far from being a global sport. Even in Britain, where medals of some description were all but assured, eventing was hardly prime-time viewing. Only 45 minutes of live action from the 2006 World Championships made it on to BBC2, with the rest being hidden away on the red button. The Welsh boxer Joe Calzaghe had clearly not been one of the few who had been tempted by the Beeb's coverage. 'Zara Phillips?' was his bemused response on discovering he had finished fourth behind the royal in the sports personality polling. 'I don't know what she does. Ride horses is it?'

Calzaghe was not the only one taken aback by royal eventers being lauded as the nation's favourite sporting personalities. The press also struggled to make sense of it all. In 1971 the general feeling was that with no Olympics or World Cup, and with 400m runner David Jenkins our sole gold medallist in the European Championships, there was a rare opportunity for some of the country's less fashionable sporting pursuits to take centre stage. In an 'unusual summer for British sport', *The Times* noted at the end of the year, more traditional sports had been knocked off the back pages by 'the prime minister's sailing and Princess Anne's horse riding'.[98] The same explanation was resurrected 35 years later. Zara Phillips's SPOTY win, thought *The Guardian*, 'was more a comment on the abject state of the national football and rugby teams'. The *Daily Mirror* agreed. Unhappy that 'the Beeb's silver tripod' would now match 'the silver spoon that was in the Royal show jumper's mouth when she was born', it still took some comfort from the knowledge that 'the prestigious award did not go to one of our useless footballers, Ashes flops or England rugby losers'. Even the normally uber-royalist *Daily Mail*'s verdict on Phillips's success was pretty damning: 'A poor year for British sport was perhaps best summed up by the result of the BBC SPOTY award … the public went for the privileged three-day eventer in a privileged sport ignored by most of the world. It brought back that old Australian jibe about Great Britain winning most of their gold medals sitting on their backsides.'

Whatever the press had to say about the matter, though, did not alter the fact that, twice, a sizeable chunk of the viewing public had bothered to phone in to vote for a royal as their favourite sporting personality. Maybe the *Daily Mail* was right, and Zara Phillips's victory had come courtesy of 'a Middle England who are usually only mobilised by Wimbledon and the Boat Race'. Then again, maybe growing numbers of sports fans had come to see in Zara what Jackie Stewart had seen in her mother. 'The way Princess Anne handles one horsepower,' Stewart had commented in 1971, 'just think what she could do with 450.'[53]

98 In August 1971, Prime Minister Edward Heath skippered his yacht, *Morning Cloud*, to victory in the Admiral's Cup.

The affluent amateurism of showjumping and eventing could not have been further removed from the sporting milieu in which the final equestrian to win SPOTY, National Hunt jockey Tony 'AP' McCoy, made his name. Horse racing has no place for the privileged amateur or the weekend hobbyist. It may be the sport of kings, but any royal involvement is strictly limited to patronage, not participation. A highly professionalised world, the sole function of racing, from punter to owner, is turning a profit. Although hugely popular – second only to football in television coverage – the sport has no real grassroots or fanbase. Just like football supporters, racing enthusiasts may sit at home eagerly awaiting the results service, but, as the academic Wray Vamplew has noted, their concern is 'not about the glory of [their] team but the outcome of [their] bet'. Racegoers might have favourites among the runners and riders, but these invariably stem from financial self-interest rather than tribal loyalty.

In such a hyper-commercialised environment, it is almost impossible for individual jockeys to attract the sort of dedicated personal support required to succeed in sporting popularity contests. Even when, in 2009, McCoy became the first jump jockey to rack up an astonishing 3,000 wins, he failed to make it on to the BBC's shortlist for that year's award. In fact, the closest horse racing came to winning SPOTY before McCoy's triumph in 2010 was when the great steeplechaser, Desert Orchid, retired in 1992. 'Dessie' topped the poll but was disqualified on the spurious grounds that he was a horse, and victory instead went to Nigel Mansell. To many, the decision was further proof that personality clearly played no part in the choice of winner.

McCoy was a perfect fit for racing's win-at-all-costs culture. He was, he once claimed, 'addicted to winning'. It did not matter whether it was a midweek race in Carlisle or the Gold Cup at Cheltenham; if the horse could win, he would ride it. Indeed, for McCoy, it did not matter if it was a horse race or a sack race, the only reason to participate was to win. The idea, he said, that his daughter's primary school sports day should become inclusive and non-competitive was 'the biggest load of bollocks I've ever heard, because no sport is just about taking part – it's about winning'. God knows what happened during the fathers' race.

McCoy's ambition was matched by his dedication. When he was not driving 75,000 miles a year to get to race meetings, he was sitting for two and a half hours a day in the sauna to keep his weight down. Injuries that would have kept most people off work for a month were treated as just 'part of the job'. 'The trick,' he said, 'was to just get yourself treated and get on with it.' Sometimes, getting on with it displaced treatment. Informed, in October 2014, that a punctured lung and dislocated shoulder, suffered in a fall at Worcester, would require a lengthy period of rehabilitation, McCoy's response was to discharge himself from hospital so he could ride (and win!) three days later at Huntingdon. It was the sort of determination few were prepared to match. 'AP,' marvelled Cheltenham Gold Cup winner Andrew Thornton, 'was the man they all struggled to beat but also no sane jockey would attempt to emulate.'

For most sportspeople, success eventually tempers the urge to win. For McCoy, the opposite was true. As soon as he had won a title, he told one interviewer, 'The very next day I wasn't champion anymore; I was back to square one.' He was, thought his wife, 'driven by fear; the fear of not being the best'. As it turned out, he had nothing to be afraid of. First crowned champion jockey (awarded for most wins in a season) in 1996, he did not relinquish the title until he retired 20 years later. In the course of his two decades at the top, he broke Sir Gordon Richards's record of 269 wins in a season (scoring 289), and won virtually every major National Hunt trophy going. In total he rode 4,348 winners in 17,546 rides.

But, for all his achievements, there was one prize he seemed unable to secure: the Grand National. And, of course, it was the one he most wanted. The best-known race in the world, by winning it he would, he thought in 2010 as he prepared for his 15th attempt at the race, be able to prove to the wider public that he can 'ride a bit'. The *Daily Mail* was of the same opinion. Raising the spectre of British sport's favourite loser, the paper's racing correspondent, Marcus Townend, pointed out that the National was the 'haunting omission that tainted [McCoy] like Wimbledon cruelly tainted Tim Henman'. The appalling prospect of forever being lumped together with the hapless Henman was enough to spur AP on, and, as he crossed the finish line five lengths clear on board Don't Push It, he allowed himself a rare smile of triumph. The victory, along with some less than subtle canvassing by the racing community (the most egregious example of which was the staging at Exeter, on the day before the BBC extravaganza was due to be aired, of the 'Vote AP McCoy for BBC's Sports Personality Novices' Chase'), finally delivered horse racing its first SPOTY title.

As far as *The Times* was concerned, McCoy had finally got the award that 'should have been his long ago'. In fact, the only note of dissent came from – guess who? – a golfer. It was bad enough that a jockey had beaten world number one Lee Westwood and US Open winner Graeme McDowell to the top spot, fumed Ian Poulter, but for darts player Phil 'The Power' Taylor to finish ahead of them as well was an insult too far. 'Get a grip,' he angrily told voters. The *Daily Mail*, though, felt Poulter had missed the cultural significance of the result. 'When gambling and the pub fill the top two places,' the paper told its readers, 'then the BBC have captured perfectly the preoccupations of the sporting male.' But this sort of flippancy was a little unfair on McCoy. He was a superb athlete, who had dominated his sport for 15 years and would go on to dominate it for another five. His true standing as a sportsman was, perhaps, best captured by the *Daily Mirror* on the day of his retirement in April 2015. Under a front-page headline, 'The Greatest', AP was compared to 'Bradman, Maradona and Ali'.[54]

Chapter Notes

45 Damion Sturm, 'Formula One on television', in D. Sturm, S. Wagg and D. Andrews (eds,) *The History and Politics of Motor Racing* (2023), pp.389–399; *Observer*, 15 December 1996; *Mirror*, 21 December 1996; ITV, *Clive James Meets Damon Hill* (1997); Frank Worrall, *Lewis Hamilton: The Biography* (2007), p.75; Rob Steen, *Floodlights and Touchlines: A History of Spectator Sport* (2014), p.257; *Daily Mail*, 13 April 2020; Jackie Stewart, *Jackie Stewart, Winning is Not Enough* (2014), pp.139, 228; Damon Hill, *Watching the Wheels: My Autobiography* (2016), ch.2.

46 *Guardian*, 12 April 2020; *Being Stirling Moss*, dir. Ben Bowie (1998); Robert Edwards, *Stirling Moss: The Authorised Biography* (2001), p.165; Stephen Wagg, '"Who do you think you are? Stirling Moss?" British racing drivers and the politics of celebrity, 1896–1992' in D. Sturm, S. Wagg, D. Andrews (eds.), *The History and Politics of Motor Racing: Lives in the Fast Lane* (2023), p.494; *Daily Mail*, 13 April 2020; *Daily Express*, 25 May 1961.

47 Damian Sturm, 'The star is the car: F1 stardom, driver agency and celebrity culture', in Sturm, Wagg, Andrews (eds.), *The History and Politics of Motor Racing*, p.520; Damian Sturm, 'Formula One on television', in Sturm, Wagg, Andrews (eds.), *The History and Politics of Motor Racing*, p.391; Steen, *Floodlights and Touchlines*, p.257; Stewart, *Winning is Not Enough*, pp.143–146; *Motorsport*, 29 August 2019; *The Jackie Stewart Story: Driven to Win*, dir. Gary Frances (1991); *Times*, 8 October 1973; *Daily Express*, 8 October 1973.

48 Steen, *Floodlights and Touchlines*, p.259; Wagg, 'Who do you think you are?', p.508; Christopher Hilton, *Nigel Mansell: World Champion* (1993), pp.190–191; *Guardian*, 17 August 1992; ITV, *This Is Your Life: Nigel Mansell* (1989); *Observer*, 2 November 1986; *Daily Mail*, 27 October 1986; *Daily Express*, 14 September 1992; *Daily Mail*, 14 September 1992.

49 Damon Hill, *Watching the Wheels: My Autobiography* (2016), p.312; *Daily Mirror*, 15 November 1994, 14 November 1994; *Sun*, 14 November 1994; *Daily Star*, 14 November 1994; *Times*, 20 November 1994; Smith, *Midnight in the Garden*, p.12; Smith and Rider, *BBC Sports Personality of the Year*, p.204; *Sunday Times*, 15 December 1996, 18 December 1994; ITV, *This Is Your Life: Damon Hill* (1999).

50 Ben Carrington, 'Can the Formula One driver speak? Lewis Hamilton, race and the resurrection of the Black athlete', in Sturm, Wagg, Andrews (eds.), *The History and Politics of Motor Racing*, pp.364–366; Frank Worrall, *Lewis Hamilton: The Biography* (2021), p .160; *Independent*, 18 June 2007; Rachel Humphreys, 'How Lewis Hamilton became one of the UK's top sports stars and activists', *Guardian* podcast (2020); Gary Younge, 'Made in Stevenage', *Guardian*, 16 June 2007; BBC, Clive James, 'Black Destiny: On Black Role Models', *A Point of View*, 23 March 2007; *Times*, 17 December, 2014, 15 December 2014; *Guardian*, 10 July 2021, 21 December 2020; *Telegraph*, 17 December 2014.

51 Rider and Smith, *BBC Sports Personality of the Year*, pp.30–32, 54–56; ITV, *This Is Your Life: John Surtees* (1992); *John Surtees: Built to Win*, dir. J. P. Davidson (2021); *Guardian*, 10 March 2017; *Independent*, 10 March 2017.

52 Sturm, 'The star is the car', p.520; *Times*, 15 December 2006; Stewart, *Winning is Not Enough*, p.433; Raymond Williams, *Raymond Williams on Television* (1989), p.34; Wray Vamplew, *Games People Played: A Global History of Sport* (2021), p151; David Broome and Brian Giles, *Twenty-Five Years in Show Jumping* (1981), pp.58, 71; BBC4, *Sport in the 1960s: A TV Revolution*, 23 April 2022; *Hare and Hounds*, 17 April 2020; *Daily Mirror*, 15 December 1960.

53 *Observer*, 6 May 2007; *Daily Express*, 11 December 2019; Channel 5, *Zara and Anne: Like Mother, Like Daughter* (2021); *Daily Mail*, 30 December 2006, 9 December 2006; *Guardian*, 11 December 2006, 11 December 1971; *Times*, 15 December 1971; *Daily Mirror*, 11 December 2006.

54 Vamplew, *Games People Played*, pp.142–143; A P McCoy, *Winner: My Racing Life* (2015), ch.2, ch.6; *The Real McCoy: The Inside Story of Champion Jockey A. P. McCoy*, dir. Rob Sloman (2005); *Daily Mail*, 25 April 2015, 21 December 2010, 16 December 2010, 12 April 2010; BBC2, *Being AP*, dir. Anthony Wonke (2017); *Independent*, 11 April 2010; *Times*, 21 December 2010; *Daily Mirror*, 25 April 2015.

Chapter 6

Red and Yellow and Pink and Green: Cycling

Tommy Simpson (1965) – Chris Hoy (2008) –
Mark Cavendish (2011) –
Bradley Wiggins (2012) –
Geraint Thomas (2018)

I CANNOT remember exactly how old I was when I first attempted to cycle up Mont Ventoux, the Géant of Provence; 13, possibly 14. Emboldened by the young's unshakeable belief in their own physicality, I confidently left my bewildered parents in our Carpentras hotel and set off for the highest point in Provence, a round trip of 80km with over 3,000m of climbing. How hard could it be? By the time I had reached Bédoin, the bustling market town at the foot of Ventoux, I had my answer: very. Heat haze shimmered over the lavender fields as the temperature crept steadily towards 100°F. The tarmac began to melt. Lizards scuttled for shelter. Undaunted, I studiously disregarded the last chance to take on water (bidons being as much a closed book to me as bidets) and set off up the 22km ascent (average gradient 7.5 per cent).

Thankfully, memories of the ensuing torture have faded with time, yet one image remains firmly lodged in my mind. Just a kilometre from the summit, stark against the barren limestone moonscape that tops the mountain, was a simple granite memorial. The inscription reminded passers-by that it was at this spot on 13 July 1967 that 'Tom Simpson, Olympic medallist, world champion, Ambassador of British sport' had died while competing in the Tour de France. It was a name that at the time meant nothing to me but, even to my uninitiated eye, the mass of votive offerings in the form of water bottles and racing caps that lay scattered around proclaimed the location a site of significant sporting weight.

In fact, as I was later to learn, Tom Simpson could lay claim to a string of firsts in British sporting history. The first cyclist from Britain to wear the yellow jersey, to be crowned world champion and, in 1965, to win SPOTY. Indeed, only one other cyclist had even been nominated for SPOTY before 1965 – Reg Harris in 1954 – and it would be over 40 years before the sport would again claim top spot, with Chris Hoy in 2008. Although the supremely talented Nicole Cooke, multi-world and Olympic medallist as well as tour winner, was nominated two years before Hoy, she did not even manage to make it on to the stage with the other nominees. Instead, she was relegated to sit with the also-rans in the main auditorium and forced to endure an excruciatingly patronising interview with Adrian Chiles – 'Do you fall off your bike a lot?' Tellingly, Chiles did not ask Jenson Button, another of that year's contenders, if he ever forgot to switch his indicators off or occasionally filled up his Honda RA106 with diesel instead of petrol.

Tom Simpson was an unlikely choice for SPOTY in 1965. Indeed, even Simpson himself seemed somewhat taken aback when the announcement was made, claiming he was so surprised that he had not got a speech prepared (although, from listening to other winners over the years, it is hard to believe that fine-tuning an acceptance address has ever been high in the SPOTY nominee's list of priorities). Born in the mining village of Haswell, County Durham, Simpson's modest upbringing reflected the unfashionable nature of British cycling in the decades following the Second World War. For most of the British public, cycling, if ever thought of at all, was associated with touring groups escaping grim Victorian mill towns by slogging uphill through rainswept northern fells. Specialist cycling magazines did little to counter this drab image. Their pages were full of uninspiring articles with titles seemingly drawn from a back catalogue of Enid Blyton short stories: 'A Day on Clare Island'; 'An Adventure for Two Lads'.

The sport's dreary reputation was perhaps best summed up by J. B. Priestley in his interwar travelogue, *English Journey*. Passing a group of cyclists on the outskirts of Bradford, he could not help wondering 'exactly what pleasure they were getting from the surrounding country, as they never seemed to lift their heads from the handlebars but went grimly on like racing cyclists'. There was some competitive cycling in Britain in this period but, in stark contrast to the glitz and glamour of the Continental scene, the dowdy amateurism and inflexible volunteerism of British racing ensured that the sport remained largely unbothered by press intrusion. Even as late as 1989, cycling failed to appear in a list of the nation's top 20 (twenty!) most popular sports to watch on television.[55]

That Simpson was able to transcend the stultifying parochialism and innate conservatism of his chosen sport was testament to both his precocious talent and winning personality. Having, by the age of 21, won medals at the Olympic Games in Melbourne in 1956, and the Empire Games in Cardiff in 1958, as well as twice being crowned a national track champion, he was left with little option but to pursue further glories on the ruthless European professional circuit. Despite the step up in competition, the successes kept on coming. In 1961 he won the Tour of Flanders, and in the process became the first Briton in 80 years to win a major classic. Over the following three years he finished on the podium in numerous one-day and stage races, won two more classics, Bordeaux-Paris and Milan-San Remo, and secured sixth place in the 1962 Tour de France.

Yet Simpson's growing reputation was not simply the product of his race results, impressive though these were. It was also down to his approach to racing. Best typified by his audacious break for glory with more than 25 miles remaining of the 1960 Paris-Roubaix one-day classic (caught just three miles from the line, he eventually finished an exhausted ninth), Simpson was an all-or-nothing rider. The raw aggression of his tactics, the suffering and sacrifice he was prepared to display made him a favourite of fans at home and abroad. To the French, Tom Simpson was a throwback to the swashbuckling Tommies of 1944. *L'Équipe*, France's leading sporting daily, trod this well-worn path of wartime nostalgia when it greeted Simpson's heroics on the road to Roubaix in 1960 with the headline, 'The Landing (*Débarquement*) of a Tommy'. For the British public, Simpson epitomised British exceptionalism. He was, as *The Mirror* dubbed him, the 'mad Englishman' who was prepared to fearlessly take on foreigners at their own game. And, to make things better, he could even beat them.

Simpson enthusiastically embraced his media image. He was fully aware that personality made his talent much more marketable. His photogenic good looks, wry sense of humour and store of self-deprecating soundbites ensured that the press pack always had usable copy. How did he celebrate his 1962 yellow jersey? Why, with a pot of tea and some bread and jam at bedtime of course. Dubbed 'Major Tom' by foreign journalists, Simpson was cast as the epitome of the bowler-hatted, umbrella-carrying Little Englander. Although, as the son of a Durham miner, who lived in Belgium and spoke Flemish, French and Italian fluently, this upper-class inward-looking caricature could not have been further from the truth, he was more than happy to play along with the conceit. In endless photo spreads, Simpson, *The Observer* journalist and former Olympic gold medallist Chris Brasher noted, was happy to pose as 'an impeccable Englishman in a Prince of Wales suit'.

Yet Simpson's appeal was not simply as a comedic nod to a patrician England of an imagined yesteryear. Rather like the fictional John Steed, the dapper, aristocratic secret agent in the hugely popular BBC series *The Avengers*, Simpson's Major Tom alter ego was rooted as much in the present as the past. Just like Steed, Simpson was portrayed as a fixture of modern swinging Britain. He drove an Aston Martin; he had soirées with Petula Clark; he was – how could he not be? – a friend of Sacha Distel. And Simpson's life story seemed to fit perfectly with the *zeitgeist* of Britain in the early 1960s. Reforged in the white heat of Labour prime minister Harold Wilson's scientific revolution, this was a nation where the shackles of the old class system were being unceremoniously broken. On the country's cinema screens, the antiheroes of the British New Wave were providing the public with new role models. Joe Lampton in *Room at the Top*, Arthur Seaton in *Saturday Night and Sunday Morning*, Billy Fisher in *Billy Liar* and Frank Machin in *This Sporting Life* were all shown railing against the constraints and pettiness of class-bound Britain. And what better embodied this narrative of a newly assertive, socially mobile working class than the story of a miner's son who now wore a bowler hat, carried a furled umbrella and mixed with the Continental jet set?[56]

By the mid-1960s, Simpson's career was a sufficiently appealing combination of success and showmanship to pique the interest of the otherwise cycle-averse British press. In particular, his dramatic victory in the 1965 Road World Championship in San Sebastian, Spain, in which he outwitted and outsprinted the former winner of the Vuelta a España,Rudi Altig, raised his public profile. Yellow jerseys and classics wins might have meant little to the uninitiated British sports fan, but world champion was a term everyone could understand. And should there just happen to be any lingering doubt about the magnitude of Simpson's achievement, *The Mirror* was there to dispel it. 'Five Years of sweat, toil and disappointment had finally paid off,' it insisted in a back-page leader, blithely consigning to the sporting dustbin three classics wins, a yellow jersey, and numerous victories on the professional circuit. Simpson's triumph was, the paper went on to clarify for its more parochial readers, 'like a French cricket team winning a Test match'. The media interest in Simpson continued unabated in the weeks following his victory in San Sebastian. He was interviewed for the BBC's flagship sports programme *Grandstand*; a rather more sensationalist interview was serialised in the *Sunday People* throughout September and October; the BBC aired a half-hour documentary, *The World of Tom Simpson*, reviewing his life and career; and finally, at the end of the year, he received that ultimate proof of celebrity, an invitation to be gently grilled by Roy Plomley on *Desert Island Discs*.

Throughout this media onslaught, Simpson's impish charm and beguiling openness remained undiminished. Although, just possibly, his openness could have done with a bit of diminishing. In both the *Sunday People* spread and the BBC documentary, he happily discussed cycling's drug culture and his own use of what he quaintly termed 'tonics'. In one particularly telling scene in the BBC documentary, which hindsight has rendered all the more disturbing, Simpson is seen airily waving towards a bedside table stacked with ampoules and medicine bottles, while telling the offscreen interviewer, 'I can't tell you what it all does because it's too complicated for me. I believe what the doctor tells me because it's never done me any harm.' For the current fan of cycling, for whom the Festina affair and the industrial-scale cheating of Lance Armstrong and the US Postal team have punctured the vision of sport as a Corinthian ideal, this, of course, rings alarm bells. But, for less cynical audiences of 60 years ago, such candidness and innocence merely enhanced Simpson's appeal. It was hardly surprising then that, on the back of this wave of media acclamation and public affection, Tom Simpson became the first cyclist to be proclaimed Sports Personality of the Year.

But there is, of course, a darker side to Simpson's story. Professional cycling was, and still is, a brutal sport. Racing cyclists have to learn how to suffer. If you are to win, or even complete, one of the three-week-long Grand Tours, then you must be prepared to push yourself to, and even beyond, your limits. This was particularly true of the sport in the 1960s, when race organisers remained firmly wedded to the pre-war tradition of constructing superhuman challenges. The longest one-day race in the UCI calendar in 2022 was Milan-San Remo at 293km. In 1963, that rather dubious honour went to the Bordeaux-Paris classic, which came in at a soul-destroying 556km. Starting off in the middle of the night, Simpson, the first Briton to win the event in over 60 years, took nearly 16 hours to complete the course.

Stage races were no less daunting. The tragic 1967 Tour de France, at just shy of 3,000 miles, was virtually half as long again as the 2022 version. In order to tackle such extreme distances, it was hardly surprising that competitors felt the need to fall back on a whole array of artificial stimulants. Although the use of drugs had been made illegal in 1965, the professional circuit remained awash with 'tonics'. For riders, desperate to attract the attention of sponsors, racing clean was a luxury only the amateur could afford. As Rudi Altig, runner-up to Simpson in 1965, bluntly put it, 'I am not a sportsman, I am a professional.' And, for all his media-friendly flippancy, Tom Simpson was as professional as they came.[57]

By 1967 a series of disappointing results meant the pressure was building on Simpson. With his Peugeot contract up for renewal, a good showing in the Tour de France was critical if he was to retain his position as one of the sport's top-paid riders. Yet his recent history with the race had not been a happy one. He had been forced to retire with a kidney infection in 1965, and the following year had crashed out after a freak collision with one of the support cars. Ill fortune again dogged him in the early stages of the 1967 tour, when food poisoning saw him lose time to the race favourites as they crossed the Alps. Although he managed to move up to seventh overall after stage 12, he was determined to take advantage of the ascent of Mont Ventoux the following day to make further inroads into the general classification. And, driven professional that he was, he was keen to use all the means at his disposal to maximise his performance.

The drug of choice for professional cyclists in the 1960s was Tonedron, a form of methamphetamine. It was this drug that the journalist Jean Bobet, a former winner of Paris-Nice, saw Simpson take on a blisteringly hot morning in Marseilles at the départ of the 13th stage. By the time the peloton reached the foothills of Ventoux, Tom was already in trouble. Suffering in temperatures touching 100°F, he begged Colin Lewis, one of his domestiques, for a drink. What Lewis then offered would make a modern sports nutritionist weep. Reaching into the back pocket of his sweat-soaked jersey, he fished out a bottle of Coke and, of all things, a half bottle of brandy. The combination of alcohol, amphetamine and intense heat was to prove fatal. A kilometre from the summit, Simpson fell from his bike. Helped back on by his support team, the iron will and indomitable spirit that had driven him to so many victories now drove him to his death. Shrugging off his team mechanic's plea to retire, Simpson summoned from the depths of his soul enough strength to weave another couple of hundred metres up the road before collapsing into the arms of concerned spectators. He never recovered consciousness, and was pronounced dead at a hospital in nearby Avignon later that evening.[58]

Simpson's tragic death dealt a heavy blow to British cycling. Once rumours began to circulate that Tonedron tablets had been found in the back pocket of his racing jersey, the backlash was swift and pitiless. The British cycling authorities, wedded to a culture of gentlemanly amateurism, quickly seized the high moral ground and roundly condemned drug users as nothing more than cheats. The hugely influential *Cycling* magazine was even more vitriolic in its condemnation and called for Simpson to be stripped of all his titles. Of course, such sanctimonious grandstanding did justice neither to the (albeit flawed) sporting genius of Tom Simpson nor to the complex issues surrounding performance-enhancing drug use. The expectations of the media and the public, along with the demands of sponsors and race organisers, all contributed to a toxic culture where drug-taking became the norm rather than the exception. Simpson himself was well aware of this. 'I don't want to have to take drugs,' he had told Brasher in his *Observer* interview, 'but if I don't win a big event soon, I shall have to start taking them.'

Nuance, however, is rarely a feature of back-page editorials or sporting debates. As far as the British public was concerned, Simpson and drug abuse were now irrevocably conjoined. Professional cycling's reputation was fatally tarnished. Media interest, which had been centred on the winning (in more ways than one) persona of Major Tom, fell away sharply. Although coverage of professional races did revive in the 1980s – Channel 4, with its remit to cover minority interests, showed edited highlights of the Kellogg's city centre races from the early 80s and, from 1986, aired the Tour de France with the inestimable Phil Liggett occupying the commentary seat – it was not until the new century that public engagement with the sport once more reached such a level that cyclists would again trouble the SPOTY vote counters.

The crowning of Tom Simpson as Sport Personality of the Year in 1965, however, should not simply be viewed as an aberration, as a brief moment in the sun for one of British sport's poor cousins. Instead, a thread can be clearly discerned that connects the apparent innocence and guilelessness of Major Tom with the laser-focused professionalism of the Olympians and Tour de France jersey winners 40 years later. For Simpson not only acted as pathfinder for ambitious British cyclists seeking fame abroad, but he also served as a role model for the cycling stars of the new millennium. Mark Cavendish, world road race champion and SPOTY winner in 2011, vividly recalls in his memoirs being inspired by a pep talk given by senior endurance coach Rod Ellingworth on the first evening of an elite training camp at the Celtic Manor Hotel in Newport in 2009. In a climactic final flourish, Ellingworth unveiled bold plans for what he dubbed 'Project Rainbow Jersey' by producing Tom Simpson's world champion's top from 1965.

And, in 2021, as the Tour once again tackled the Géant of Provence, Bradley Wiggins, the first British winner of the yellow jersey, highlighted for Eurosport viewers the debt he and his peers owed to Simpson. 'Tommy Simpson started it for all us lot,' he insisted from his precarious commentary position on the back of one of the press pack motorbikes. 'The great Chris Froome, Geraint Thomas, Simon Yates, they are all riding today because of that man, and we must all pay homage and respect to Tommy Simpson because if it wasn't for the likes of Tommy Simpson, who rode for nothing, nothing more than bread and water, we wouldn't get the chance to do this today.' Wiggins's grasp of professional cycling's past financial arrangements may have been a little wide of the mark, but his understanding of Tom Simpson's legacy was, without question, spot on.

Although British cycling did meet with some success in the decades following Simpson's death – most notably Robert Millar winning the King of the Mountains polka-dot jersey at the Tour de France in 1984, and Chris Boardman's series of Tour prologue victories (and hence yellow jerseys) in the 1990s – the sport remained off the radar of most armchair fans. By the turn of the 21st century, the world of professional cycling was mired in a seemingly endless round of drug scandals, and the cloud of Tom Simpson's death continued to hang heavily in Britain. Even among hardcore cycling enthusiasts, disillusionment appeared endemic. A light-hearted poll by *Cycling Weekly,* which placed Chris Boardman just ahead of Tom Simpson as the best British cyclist of all time, resulted in an ill-tempered debate rumbling on for months in the magazine's letters column. 'Why not Tom?' one Boardman supporter rhetorically fumed. 'Well, we know the answer, don't we?' But just in case there was someone, somewhere, who somehow did not, another angry reader took it upon himself to put them straight: 'Simpson died as he had lived, with amphetamine coursing through his veins and a selection of pills in his racing jersey pocket.' 'Boardman,' he therefore concluded, 'deserved the accolade as the top British rider if for no other reason than he was, by general consensus, the cleanest rider in the peloton.' Such were the depths cycling had plumbed that playing fair was now seen as the exception rather than the rule.

If the rehabilitation of British cycling in the new millennium required a hero in which talent and integrity went hand in hand, then the authorities at the National Cycling Centre in Manchester needed to look no further than Chris Hoy. In stark contrast to the Grand Tour favourites of the day, riders such as Ivan Basso, Jan Ullrich, Marco Pantani and Floyd Landis, who were all branded drug cheats, Hoy presented as the embodiment of the Olympic ideal. With the self-effacing charm of the gifted amateur and the strapping physique of the all-rounder – he had rowed for Scotland as a junior and played 1st XV rugby for the prestigious George Watson's College (home of the Hastings brothers no less) – Hoy was a PR consultant's dream. The removal of his specialism, the 1km time trial, from the Olympic programme in 2005 only heightened his appeal. Forced to transition to the technically much more challenging sprint, Hoy, despite already being an Olympic gold medallist, could now be dubbed the plucky underdog as he looked to become the first British man to win cycling's blue riband event.

Yet Hoy had, in fact, graduated to the senior ranks at what was undoubtedly the most propitious time ever for an ambitious British rider. A disastrous performance by the Olympic squad at the Atlanta Games in 1996 had prompted some parliamentary soul-searching. The spotlight, in particular, had fallen on cycling, with Labour's Jon Trickett insisting that Chris Boardman's bronze medal in the track individual time trial was hardly an adequate return for the Sport Council's investment of £½m per year. Such criticism triggered an immediate response. Peter Keen, a sports science lecturer at Chichester University who had coached Boardman to gold at Barcelona in 1992, was brought in as British Cycling's first elite performance director.

With Keen's appointment, the days of the traditional soigneur with a kitbag full of secret tonics and homemade lotions were numbered. Instead, in came teams of performance managers, exercise psychologists, data analysts and sports nutritionists. Buoyed by New Labour's commitment to elite sport and funded by a generous grant from the National Lottery, a World-Class Performance Programme was set up at British Cycling's headquarters in Manchester. To ensure there would be no repeat of the Atlanta debacle, the approach was to be rigorously scientific, with the focus falling on the track, where not only more medals were available, but the racing environment was more readily controllable. Keen's initiative met with almost immediate success. On the opening day of the Sydney Olympics in 2000, Jason Queally won gold in the 1km time trial in a new record time of one minute 1.609 seconds. For Brian Cook, the chairman of British Cycling, Queally's victory was the watershed moment he had long dreamed of. 'It took just 61.609 seconds,' he later claimed, 'for perceptions of the Manchester velodrome to change from white elephant to gold medal factory.' And, inevitably, money followed success. By the time of Hoy's treble gold medal bid in 2008, British Cycling was in receipt of £24.7m and could afford to send 70 ancillary staff to support its team of just 14 athletes.

As a member of the best-funded cycle team at the Games, Chris Hoy's multiple victories in Beijing may not, then, have been totally unexpected, but that does not mean they were any less remarkable. In the space of just five days, he had to negotiate 18 races in three separate disciplines. As he crossed the line to defeat his team-mate, Jason Kenny, 2-0 in the final of the sprint on 19 August 2008, Hoy became the first Briton since Henry Taylor, 100 years earlier, to win three gold medals at the same Games.[99] Back in Britain the tabloids went into overdrive. Puns abounded. Having carried off 'the biggest bullion haul since the Brink's-Mat robbery', Hoy was dubbed 'His Royal Hoyness – the new King of Scotland' by *The Mirror*'s Mike Walters. For *The Star*, he was 'The Hoy Wonder', while the *Mail* went for the (slightly) more cerebral 'Hoycules'. Even *The Times* joined in the fun, noting our triple gold medallist had proven himself to be 'The Real McHoy'. *The Sun*, clearly disconcerted by a broadsheet muscling in on what it saw as tabloid territory, imperiously reasserted its primacy as champion of the pun. Hoy's proper nickname was, of course, 'The Wheel McHoy'.

Unsurprisingly, in a shortlist dominated by Beijing gold medallists, Hoy quickly became the bookies' favourite for SPOTY.[100] Although Lewis Hamilton was briefly installed as the front runner in November, after a dramatic finish in the final lap of the final race to the F1 season saw him pip Felipe

---

99 Taylor, who won his three swimming golds in the 400m freestyle, 1,500m freestyle and 4x200m freestyle relay, did not enjoy quite the same level of support as Hoy. The son of a coal miner, he worked in a cotton mill in Oldham and trained alone (unsurprisingly!) in the Hollinwood Canal during his lunchbreaks. And, of course, no SPOTY or knighthood for Taylor. He had to settle for the posthumous award of a blue plaque on the side of Chadderton baths.

100 The other Beijing champions nominated were Rebecca Adlington (swimming, 400m freestyle and 800m freestyle), Bradley Wiggins (cycling, individual and team pursuit), Nicole Cooke (cycling, road race), Rebecca Romero (cycling, individual pursuit), Ben Ainslie (sailing, Finn class) and Christine Ohuruogu (athletics, 400m).

Massa to the championship by one point, he had to settle for the runner-up spot for a second consecutive year. In fact, the award ceremony at Liverpool's Echo Arena was a triumph, not just for Hoy, but for British cycling generally. As well as the main award, the Olympic squad was voted Team of the Year, ahead of Champions League and Premier League winners Manchester United, while Dave Brailsford, who had taken over from Keen as performance director in 2003, completed a cycling double over the Red Devils by getting the nod for Coach of the Year ahead of Sir Alex Ferguson. In a fitting finale to what was a breakout season for British cycling, it was announced in the New Year Honours List that Hoy would become the first cyclist to be knighted.[101]

Yet, despite all the public acclaim and sporting accolades, cycling – or more specifically track cycling – still struggled to be taken seriously. Appearance frequently trumped talent in the media coverage. Hoy's thighs, in particular, received more than their fair share of attention. They could 'crack walnuts', spluttered Bob McKenzie of *The Express*, while Giles Smith, in *The Times*, mused that, at Beijing, Hoy had 'earned gold medals at the rate of 1.5 per thigh'. There may be no doubting the supreme physicality on display in the velodrome but, for some commentators, there was also something faintly ridiculous about honed athletes, clad in garish Lycra bodysuits, pedalling furiously in circles. As well as track cycling, what other equivalent spheres of human endeavour did the nation excel at wondered *The Observer*, eventually settling for 'hat-

101 On the same day Hoy was knighted, his mother was awarded an MBE for 43 years' service as an NHS nurse. It was never made clear whether Mrs Hoy agreed with a BBC reporter's suggestion that 'he got his gong for sport, but you got yours for actually doing something useful'.

making, pet parading, giant vegetable growing and pole-dancing'. The *Daily Mail*'s take on what went on inside the velodrome was not much kinder. 'The ultimate sitting-down sport,' it snickered.[59]

Although the track squad continued to meet with success after 2008, winning seven gold medals at London in 2012, British Cycling's supremo Dave Brailsford decided to shift the focus towards the roads. In the immediate aftermath of Beijing, it was announced that Sky would plough £24m into a British Grand Tour team over the next five years.[102] The aim was to have a British winner of the Tour de France by 2015. This was an enormously ambitious target for a country that had never troubled the general classification podium, and in which there was no real professional road-racing heritage.

Indeed, Britain's first experience of the Tour had not been a happy one. In 1974, Plymouth council was persuaded that spending £40,000 to bring the world's greatest cycle race to a five-mile stretch of the newly opened A38 Plympton bypass would be money well spent. How wrong it was. Deemed by Barry Hoban, one of only two British riders competing, to be the most boring stage he had ever ridden, the day certainly did not capture the imagination of the local populace. Although a crowd of 80,000 was anticipated, less than a quarter of that turned up. And of those, most seemed to have quickly decided that sitting on the grass verges of a dual carriageway for four hours on a sweltering Saturday in June, watching a group of cyclists (world class or not) sweep by 20 times, was not an afternoon well spent.

102 Sky was, of course, first and foremost a commercial team and only nominally British. Although initially based in Manchester, relatively few riders were, in fact, British, and the team was bankrolled by American money.

'By the seventh or eighth lap,' *The Times* correspondent wryly noted, 'boredom set in and trade in the beer tents picked up.' For the hardy few who stuck it out to the bitter end, even the prize ceremony, at the exotic Marsh Mills Roundabout, was a baffling experience. The unknown winner, Dutchman Henk Poppe, was presented with a bouquet of artichokes courtesy of a collective of Breton farmers who had sponsored the opening stages, while female 'podium hosts' pelted those in attendance with handfuls of vegetables. Perhaps the one saving grace for Plymouth council was that, at the last minute, the BBC had decided to pull out of airing the event live.

Although *The Times* was sure that the whole sorry spectacle on the Plympton bypass had 'killed the race in Britain once and possibly for all', such pessimism proved to be misplaced. Twenty years later, to mark the opening of the Channel Tunnel, two stages were held on the south coast of England, and, in 2007, rapturous crowds in London turned out to watch the Grand Départ, only the second time the honour of hosting the opening stage had gone to a city outside of Continental Europe.[103] Much of the credit for raising the race's profile in Britain has to go to (galling though it may be) Lance 'Le Boss' Armstrong. Winning seven consecutive Tours between 1999 and 2005, Armstrong's extraordinary (albeit drug-enhanced) talent, in conjunction with the sort of inspirational cancer-conquering backstory usually reserved for Hollywood tearjerkers, turned the sport into a global rather than European phenomenon. His 2000 autobiography, *It's Not About the Bike*, shot to the top of the international bestseller

103 The first had been in Dublin in 1998.

lists, and, in 2003, he became just the second cyclist to be named BBC Overseas Sports Personality of the Year.[104]

Armstrong's popularity persuaded British television executives that the sport, or at least the Grand Tours, warranted greater attention. ITV4, launched shortly after the last of Le Boss's seven Tour victories, started to show live coverage of the Tour de France, while, for what Steve Jelbert in *The Guardian* called 'a truly bewildering experience', the committed, if sedentary, domestic cycling fan could spend all day in the company of British Eurosport. Fronted by David Harman and taciturn former pro Sean Kelly ('a man who once answered a radio interviewer with a nod of his head'), Eurosport's wall-to-wall coverage was an inexplicably mesmerising fusion of pulsating sports drama and soothing travel guide. As the sports journalist Martin Kelner rightly noted, the Tour on Eurosport could draw in an eclectic mix of punters: 'Brits, foreigners, cycling enthusiasts, casual viewers who like looking at pretty pictures of rural France and, I suppose, the odd passing pharmacist interested in the latest developments.'

Dave Brailsford was just the man to exploit cycling's new high public profile. With a background in marketing, he was quick to rebrand British cycling as a forward-looking and commercially attractive enterprise. Most famously, he drew on the Japanese business philosophy of Kaizen to introduce a new phrase to the wider public discourse: the aggregation of marginal gains. At

104 The first was Jacques Anquetil in 1963. Of course, after his admission that he was a drug cheat, Armstrong's award of Overseas SPOTY was scrubbed from the records. Although one imagines that this indignity probably seemed small beer compared to the loss of his seven Tour titles.

its heart, as Brailsford himself was first to admit, the concept was hardly earthshattering. 'The whole principle,' he explained to the BBC's Matt Slater, 'came from the idea that if you broke down everything you could think of that goes into riding a bike, and then improved it by 1 per cent, you will get a significant increase when you put them all together.' Simple. What was truly groundbreaking, though, was the scientific rigour and single-minded intensity with which the approach was applied. No aspect that might affect performance was left untouched. Tinkering with kit, bikes and conditioning was a given, but pillows, duvets and mattresses were also carted from hotel to hotel to ensure athletes got the best night's sleep possible. As Geraint Thomas recalled, even his choice of breakfast juice came under close scrutiny: 'It was not just cherry juice, because of its high levels of antioxidants, but juice only from Montmorency cherries, because they were found to be slightly superior to any others.'[60]

Despite the hype of marginal gains, the millions of pounds of sponsorship and the state-of-the-art team bus (dubbed the Death Star), Team Sky's opening season on the professional circuit in 2010 was hugely disappointing. Their highest finisher in the Tour de France was Thomas Lofkvist in 17th, while the much-trumpeted Bradley Wiggins trailed in an exhausted 24th. Yet, as is well known, this was no more than a temporary setback, and the team quickly went on to achieve astonishing success. Between 2012 and 2018, British riders, in the black-and-blue livery of Team Sky, won the Tour de France six times.[105] Indeed, British

105 The winners were, in order, Bradley Wiggins (2012), Chris Froome (2013 and 2015–2017) and Geraint Thomas (2018).

dominance of professional cycling extended beyond Sky. In 2011, Mark Cavendish, competing in the colours of HTC-Highroad, became the first British rider to win the green points jersey at the Tour de France, while Simon Yates, as part of the Orica team, won the best young rider classification at the 2017 Tour and was overall winner of the Vuelta a España the following year.

With the exception of Froome, who was Kenyan born, this new wave of all-conquering British riders was the product of the post-Atlanta lottery-funded National Cycling Centre in Manchester. Wiggins was the first athlete to be signed up to Peter Keen's World-Class Performance Programme in 1998. Cavendish, Thomas and Yates were all graduates of British Cycling's academy. Monitored to within an inch of their lives, honed by the latest advances in sports science, these were athletes whose supreme dominance on the roads pointed towards a new era of big-budget professionalism. Yet ties with a less glamorous past were not completely broken. In Cavendish, Wiggins and Thomas, whose exploits in the Tour de France would help them to the SPOTY crowns in 2011, 2012 and 2018 respectively, the shadow of Tommy Simpson could still be discerned. Like Simpson, all three were presented as ordinary lads from humble backgrounds who cycled for the love of it. The *Daily Mail* summoned the memory of Raleigh Choppers, grey school shorts and scabbed knees to herald Mark Cavendish's triumph in the points competition of the 2011 Tour. His achievement was, it insisted, 'not bad for a lad who a few years ago was racing his mates to the nearest lamppost in Ramsey, the Isle of Man'. The following year, as a victorious Bradley Wiggins, champagne glass in hand, cruised his way into Paris, readers of *The Telegraph* were told to remember that 'kids from Kilburn don't win the Tour de France', while reports of Geraint Thomas's triumph, in 2018, invariably recalled the unassuming young boy who had serendipitously stumbled on Maindy Flyers Cycling Club when going for a swim at his local leisure centre.

And again, just like Simpson, cycling's three new heroes were good box office. Relaxed in front of the cameras, they could always be relied on to provide entertaining soundbites. What better way to prick the pomposity of the Tour de France's bloated victory ceremony on the Champs-Élysées than Wiggins's deadpan 'okay, we're just going to draw the raffle now'? Or Thomas's forgetful ramble through his team-mates' names followed by a weary mic drop? And the quick-witted but ever-emotional Mark Cavendish was a TV producer's dream. In a single interview, noted Ned Boulting, the face of ITV's Tour coverage, the watching public could find themselves confronted by the full range of Cav's personality traits: 'the bullishness, the brutishness, the short shrift, the self-effacing charm, the humility, the respect, the humour'.

Although Brailsford's plan had been to lead this talented new squad to Tour de France victory by 2015, in fact British success first came in green not yellow. Mark Cavendish had long been a household name on the Continent.[106] Professional since 2005, his list of career achievements by 2010 was a match for anyone's: Commonwealth Games champion, double World Championship gold medallist, Milan-San Remo classic winner, and 15 stage wins plus twice runner-up in the points classification at the Tour

106 In 2009 he was voted International Flandrien of the Year, the Belgium equivalent of our Overseas Sports Personality of the Year.

de France. But, for a British public with only a passing knowledge of professional cycling, 2011 was Cavendish's breakout year. At the end of July, as he sped up the Champs-Élysées to his third consecutive victory in the final stage of the Tour de France, and his 20th stage win in total, he became the first Briton to be awarded the green jersey as victor in the points classification. Two months later, in Copenhagen, he joined Tommy Simpson as Britain's only other men's road world champion. You did not need to be steeped in the folklore of Continental cycling to appreciate the sight of the Manx Missile exploding out of the chaos of a bunch sprint.[107]

Here was a Briton showing the Europeans how it was done, in their own backyard. The *Daily Mirror* could hardly contain itself. Proving that a nostalgic romp through the prejudices of the Second World War was not the sole preserve of football journalism, the paper greeted Cavendish's dominance in Paris by declaring, 'With the possible exception of the Wehrmacht, no other foreign power has ever rolled along the Champs-Élysées as if they owned the place.' Writing in *The Guardian*, the former pro, David Millar, was no less gushing although, thankfully, much less Teutophobic. 'The British public should,' he held, 'now worship Cav on a par with the likes of Beckham.' This was maybe expecting a bit much, but when Cavendish was duly voted Sports Personality of the Year at the BBC's gleaming new headquarters in Salford Quays, most people probably did agree with *The*

107 French journalists' nickname for Cavendish, 'the Mozart of the 11-tooth sprocket', pointed (possibly) towards a much more sophisticated range of cultural reference points and (almost certainly) a much closer acquaintance with the intricacies of bicycle gearing ratios than the British press pool possessed.

Guardian's chief sportswriter, Barney Ronay, that he was a 'fitting winner'. With his spiky eloquence and staunch nonconformism, Cav was both sportsman and 'personality'. He was not, as Ronay rather unkindly put it, 'Nigel Mansell on a bike'.[61]

With Mark Cavendish joining Sky for the 2012 season, Dave Brailsford was confident that his plan for a British winner of the Tour de France could now be fulfilled three years ahead of schedule. And Bradley Wiggins duly obliged, beating teammate Chris Froome by over three minutes to become the first British winner of a Grand Tour.[108] Although Wiggins wore the yellow jersey in 2012 for the longest continuous run since five-times Tour winner Bernard Hinault in 1985, his ultimate triumph was not the uneventful procession this might suggest. At the previous year's Vuelta a España, he had been dropped by Froome in the final mountain stages, and this had led to some debate about who should head up Sky's push for yellow the following year. Wiggins's claim to pole position was not helped by beginning 2012 slightly out of condition. He rode the opening few races of the new season, head coach Shane Sutton quaintly recalled, 'as if he couldn't pull the foreskin off a rice-pudding'. The matter eventually appeared settled when Wiggins was given the nod as team leader in June, but Sky management's simultaneous promise to support Froome's 'ambitions in the Tour de France' somewhat muddied the waters. A personal disconnect between the two – Froome's opinion was 'they didn't bring the best out in each other' – meant tensions

108 In fact, Froome now has this honour, having been promoted to first place in the 2011 Vuelta a España after the original winner, Juan Jose Cobo, was retrospectively disqualified following a positive drug test in 2019.

continued to bubble ominously below the surface in the lead-up to the Grand Départ.

Matters finally came to the boil on stage 11, as the Tour entered the Alps. With just 4km of a brutal day in the high mountains left, all seemed normal. Froome, the super-domestique, was relentlessly reeling in the last few general classification (GC) contenders ahead on the road, as he paced race leader Wiggins to another day in yellow, when all hell broke loose. 'He's attacking him! He's attacking him!' a disbelieving Phil 'The Voice' Liggett yelped as Froome accelerated away from his now floundering team captain. With the gap widening, Froome pressed his hand to his radio earpiece to receive a message from Sky's director sportif, Sean Yates, who was watching the drama unfold from the team support car. What was being said? Luckily, 'The Voice' was there to enlighten the viewing millions: 'It's either go faster, or slow down.' It was evidently the latter, as Froome eased off, enabling Wiggins to latch on for the remainder of the climb. Inevitably, any suggestion of team disharmony was quickly played down in the post-race press conference, but in his subsequent autobiography Yates suggested that a despondent Wiggins had been close to quitting.

Wiggins's new superstar status was further cemented, just ten days after the Tour, when he won Olympic gold in the men's road time trial in front of packed crowds at Hampton Court Palace. Despite a stellar shortlist for SPOTY, which included Andy Murray, the nation's first tennis Grand Slam winner for 76 years, and Jessica Ennis and Mo Farah, two of the Olympic gold medallists from 'Super Saturday', the bookies now had Wiggins installed as odds-on favourite for the award. Like Tommy Simpson nearly half a century earlier, his cause was given an additional boost by the airing of a candid documentary a few weeks before the BBC ceremony. In *Bradley Wiggins: A Year in Yellow*, Wiggo, as he was affectionately called throughout, tried hard to live up to the image of stroppy rebel. Who was his role model in the sport? 'Robert Millar. He was difficult to deal with. He was his own man really. He didn't give a fuck about anyone else.' But such braggadocio was consistently undermined by the testimony of those closest to him. As a cyclist he may be 'a bit of a twat', wife Cath candidly admitted, but as a husband 'he is brilliant – he's proper good, patient, kind'. Even gruff, seen-it-all Shane Sutton was prompted to concede, 'I love him like a son,' albeit a son he occasionally needed to 'give a belt round the earhole every now and then'. Wiggo may be prickly and private, *The Guardian* reviewer concluded, but he is also endearingly warm and vulnerable, and as such has 'proven himself to be a very modern kind of hero'.

The public certainly seemed to agree. On the night of the SPOTY awards at ExCel London, Wiggins comfortably topped the telephone poll. Posing for photographers, dressed in a natty velvet suit and sporting a Paul Weller-inspired haircut, he looked every inch the rock-star celebrity. And, if the following morning's papers were anything to go by, he celebrated like one as well. 'Bradley Swiggins!' screamed *The Star*'s front page, as it reported on a 'six hour bender' at Whisky Mist in Mayfair and an early morning breakfast at McDonald's. It was difficult to disagree with the *Daily Mirror*'s claim that here was 'the true people's champion'. Fittingly, the year was rounded off with a knighthood in the New Year Honours List. And even more fittingly the award was greeted with a typical slice of Wiggins irreverence: 'A knighthood is something you can't buy … well you can buy it if you know the right people.'[62]

Sky's success continued into the following years as Chris Froome graduated from super-domestique to multiple Tour winner, only to be usurped, in turn, by his own super-domestique during his attempt to secure a fifth yellow jersey in 2018. Having won the Giro d'Italia just six weeks earlier, with an audacious solo breakaway on the penultimate mountain stage, Froome arrived for the 2018 Tour Grand Départ in the Vendée as Sky's designated team leader.[109] However, Geraint Thomas, who had served as Froome's first lieutenant in the three previous Tours, was in equally spectacular form. Victory in the Criterion du Dauphiné, in early June, had revealed Thomas was racing better than ever. Reluctant to once again sacrifice his own ambitions for those of another, he was given the go-ahead by Dave Brailsford to ride for himself in the opening week of the Tour. The final decision on who would lead Sky's GC challenge would then be made as the race entered its decisive third week.

A crash by Froome ('Calamity Chris') in the final kilometres of the opening stage, which left him nearly a minute behind Thomas, did nothing to dampen media speculation surrounding Team Sky's captaincy. Consecutive victories for Thomas on La Rosière and the iconic Alpe d'Huez, just over a week later, put him in yellow, one minute 39 seconds ahead of second-placed Froome. 'Can we just go to Paris now?' joked the Welshman as he faced repeated questions about team tactics for the remainder of

---

109 At the start of the 2018 Tour de France, Froome was only the third rider ever to hold all three Grand Tour titles at the same time. The other two were Eddy Merckx and Bernard Hinault.

the race. They might as well have. The rider, who had a habit of cracking or crashing in the final stages of Grand Tours, remained rock solid this time, and crossed the line in Paris with an extended lead over Tom Dumoulin in second and Froome in third. Cast as the story of a loyal servant who had finally got to have his day in the sun, it came as no surprise to anyone when it was announced that Thomas had pipped Lewis Hamilton (runner-up for a third time) and Golden Boot winner Harry Kane to the SPOTY title.

The fifth cyclist to be crowned Sports Personality of the Year, and the third in just six years, Thomas's victory should have been a moment of celebration for British Cycling. But the following day's press coverage did not make easy reading for the mandarins at the Manchester velodrome. Thomas was undoubtedly a worthy winner, Alyson Rudd in *The Times* conceded, but his success 'underlined the nuances involved in the public's perception of cycling'. In particular, it begged the question why Froome, 'despite his outstanding record', had never finished higher than sixth in SPOTY. The answer, at least for Rudd, was obvious: Froome's reputation had 'suffered from the controversy over therapeutic use exemption (TUE)' – the right to use a prohibited drug for a specific medical condition. *The Mirror* was even more brutal. Thomas was the public's favourite simply because he 'was not asthmatic, he had never applied for a therapeutic exemption and had never missed or failed a drugs test'.[110]

Team Sky and British Cycling had been increasingly embroiled in drugs scandals since the triumphs of 2012. In October that year,

110 *The Mirror* was making a not-so-veiled reference to Wiggins's and Froome's therapeutic use exemption applications for asthma and Mark Cavendish's missed drugs test in 2011.

Dr Geert Leinders was sacked by Sky when allegations surfaced that he had been involved in systematic doping with his previous employer, the Dutch team Rabobank. The following September, the promising British rider Jonathan Tiernan-Locke, who had only recently signed with Sky, was suspended after discrepancies in his biological passport came to light.[111] Although Brailsford insisted that, in both cases, the alleged offences pre-dated any involvement with Sky, a shadow was, nonetheless, cast over the team's much-vaunted policy of zero tolerance towards ex-dopers.

That shadow became much darker, in 2016, with the release by a Russian-based cyber espionage group, Fancy Bear, of hacked World Anti-Doping Agency documents. Among the leaked medical records was evidence that Wiggins had received therapeutic use exemptions for the banned drug triamcinolone in the lead-up to his Tour victory. Despite being within the rules, the revelation was particularly damaging for a team whose reputation had been built on 'riding clean'. Any questioning of Sky's integrity had always been fiercely rebuffed, not least by Wiggins himself. 'They're just fucking wankers,' he had told journalists in 2012, when asked his opinion of critics on social media who had claimed he and his team-mates were no different from Lance Armstrong's drug-addled US Postal squad. Instead of writing 'shit under a pseudonym on Twitter', a clearly rattled Wiggins had suggested, they should 'get off their arses and apply themselves and work hard at something. Cunts!'

---

111 Leinders was banned for life in January 2015 for 'possessing, trafficking and administering performance-enhancing substances', while Tiernan-Locke was handed a two-year ban in July 2014 for violations of the UCI's biological passport.

But such unflinching denials now rang hollow in the light of the Fancy Bear leaks. 'Clean' was clearly a mutable concept. Shane Sutton may have been right that Sky was '100% a clean team' by the precise parameters of the UCI definition, but it was less certain that the public would see it that way. To many, the use of a potent performance-enhancing drug like triamcinolone on the eve of a critical race did more than, as Wiggins was later to insist, 'level the playing-field'. Such a powerful drug, Professor Brian Lipworth of the Scottish Centre for Respiratory Research told *The Guardian*, should only be used in acute asthmatic emergencies. The idea that it would be regularly prescribed as a treatment for asthma was, a bemused Lipworth felt, 'utterly bonkers'. Perhaps it was left to former pro David Millar to best sum up just how ineffectual the TUE system was. 'It's open to abuse,' he told a parliamentary committee on drugs in sport in 2018. 'Some of the medical conditions used to justify a TUE can be difficult to validate; and an unscrupulous rider and doctor could exaggerate or simply make up symptoms that would merit an exemption or prescription.' As someone who had experienced both the high of a stage win in a Grand Tour as well as the low of arrest by the French police for doping, his assessment was hard to dismiss.[63]

If the controversy surrounding Sky's use of TUEs had ended with the Fancy Bear leaks, the whole affair might have blown over in a few weeks. But a subsequent investigation by UK Anti-Doping (UKAD) and an exposé in the *Daily Mail* served to deepen the crisis. In particular, the focus increasingly centred on the contents of a mysterious jiffy bag that Sky's support team had, in June 2011, gone to great lengths to transport from British Cycling's headquarters in Manchester to the race squad in the

French Alps. Unsurprisingly, UKAD investigators were keen to find out what was in the bag. Possibly equally unsurprising was the inability of anyone at British Cycling or Sky to recall the bag's contents. Phil Burt, a physiotherapist with British Cycling, definitely remembered packing the bag but could not quite bring to mind what it was he had packed, while Simon Cope, British women's road coach, admitted cheerfully transporting the sealed bag through customs without thinking to ask what it might contain. It was all a terrible puzzle. The Sky team doctor who had initiated the order seemed to have the answer. It was fluimucil, a simple decongestant, Dr Richard Freeman helpfully informed the investigation. Unfortunately, the hard evidence to back up this claim was missing. Freeman's laptop, on which he kept all his medical records, had (to his great disappointment) been stolen when he was on holiday in Greece, and (again to his enormous regret) he had not been able to upload any of the materials to Sky's shared Dropbox because he was 'quite IT inept'.

Why Sky would go to so much trouble to deliver a drug that was freely available over the counter near their base in Savoie, no one was ever able to adequately explain. The accusation was, of course, that the jiffy bag contained triamcinolone for which, at that time, no TUE was in place. Although unable to settle the jiffy bag question once and for all, a Digital, Culture, Media and Sport Select Committee on Combatting Drugs in Sport, which reported in February 2018, was in no doubt that 'an ethical line' had been crossed.[112] Team Sky, it damningly concluded, had

112 As Kenny Pryde noted in *The Medal Factory*, there is a certain irony that in 1996, after Atlanta, parliamentary focus was on why British cyclists won so little, whereas 20 years later the spotlight was on why they won so much.

administered triamcinolone 'other than for medical use', and had 'bent the rules to boost [Wiggins's] Tour de France hopes'.

Sky's reputation took a further knock in February 2019 when Richard Freeman was hauled before the General Medical Council (GMC) charged with a series of historic doping-related offences, the most serious of which was that he had placed an order for banned testosterone patches in 2011. Although openly admitting to ordering the patches, Freeman denied they had been procured to boost athlete performance. Rather, he was helping his friend and colleague, Shane Sutton, deal with his erectile dysfunction. Sutton's response to this besmirching of his manliness suggested testosterone deficiency was the least of his problems. Furiously slamming his fist on the table in front of him, he threatened to bring his wife to court to vouch for his virility, before storming out of the tribunal. As *The Sun* neatly put it, Jiffygate had descended into Stiffygate.

Happily for all concerned, the GMC felt the prosecution's evidence was so overwhelming that it need not trouble Mrs Sutton for the finer details of her conjugal obligations, and Freeman was struck off the medical register in March 2021. It made for a sorry end to the Sky story. As with Tom Simpson in 1967, the spectre of doping had once again diminished the achievements of British cycling. Sky's decade of success on the Continental professional circuit, and its two SPOTY winners, had unquestionably acted as a cultural catalyst for the remarkable growth of cycling as a domestic leisure pursuit. Yet its association with the sport had also left a pernicious legacy. Sky's blurring of ethical boundaries had reminded the public that the Grand Tour cyclist, as Simpson's great rival Rudi Altig had noted half a century earlier, was a professional rather than a sportsman.[64]

Chapter Notes

55 Jeremy Whittle, *Ventoux: Sacrifice and Suffering on the Giant of Provence* (2017), p.203; BBC, *Death on the Mountain: The Story of Tom Simpson*, dir. Alastair Thompson (2010); William Fotheringham, *Put Me Back on My Bike: In Search of Tom Simpson* (2007), p.101; Holt, *Sport and the British*, p.197.

56 Fotheringham, *Put Me Back on My Bike*, pp.108–109; 141–144; *Daily Mirror*, 30 June 1960; *Observer*, 25 July 1965.

57 *Daily Mirror*, 7 September 1965; BBC, *The World of Tom Simpson* (1965); *Sunday People*, 3 October 1965, 26 September 1954, 19 September 1965; Chris Sidwells, *Cycling Weekly*, 30 December 2015.

58 Fotheringham, *Put Me Back on My Bike*, pp.151–152, 164–165; BBC, *Death on the Mountain*; Whittle, *Ventoux*, pp.37–39, 97–98; Neil Carter, *Cycling and the British: A Modern History* (2020), pp.233–240; Mark Cavendish, *At Speed* (2014), pp.171–175; Eurosport, *Tour de France Stage 11*, 7 July 2021.

59 Chris Hoy, *Chris Hoy: The Autobiography of Britain's Most Successful Ever Olympian* (2009), pp.13–24, 252–262; Carter, *Cycling and the British*, ch.10; *Guardian*, 11 December 2016; *Daily Mirror*, 20 August 2008; *Times*, 1 December 2008; *Daily Mail*, 29 June 2012; *Daily Record*, 18 October 2008; *Daily Express*, 21 August 2008; *Daily Mail*, 21 August 2008.

60 Carter, *Cycling and the British*, pp.250–254; *Plymouth Herald*, 29 June 2022; *Times*, 19 July 2019, 1 July 1974; *Guardian* 6 July 2007, 18 June 2007; Kenny Pryde, *The Medal Factory: British Cycling and the Cost of Gold* (2020), pp.39–40; Geraint Thomas, *The World of Cycling According to G* (2015), p.307.

61 Cavendish, *At Speed*, pp.171–172; *Daily Telegraph*, 22 July 2012; *Daily Mail* 25 July 2011; Ned Boulting, *How I Won the Yellow Jumper: Dispatches from the Tour de France* (2011), p.150; *Daily Mirror*, 25 July 2011; *Guardian*, 22 December 2011, 25 July 2011.

62 Sky Atlantic, *Bradley Wiggins: A Year in Yellow* (2012), dir. John Dower; Chris Froome, *The Climb* (2014), pp.264–265, 296–308; Bradley Wiggins, *My Time* (2012), pp.212–215; *Guardian*, 31

December 2012, 21 November 2012; *Daily Star*, 17 December 2012; *Daily Mirror*, 17 December 2012.

63 Geraint Thomas, *The Tour According to G: My Journey to the Yellow Jersey* (2018), p.176; *Times*, 17 December 2018; *Daily Mirror*, 17 December 2018; Pryde, *The Medal Factory*; pp.235–261; *Financial Times*, 13 July 2012; *Daily Telegraph*, 21 September 2016; HofC, DCMS Committee Report, *Combatting Doping in Sport*, 27 February 2018.

64 *Daily Mail*, 12 October 2016; DCMS Committee Report, *Combatting Doping in Sport*; *Sun*, 12 November 2019; *Guardian*, 16 January 2023, 13 November 2019; *Daily Telegraph*, 19 March 2021; Fotheringham, *Put Me Back on My Bike*, p.166.

Chapter 7

Mano a Mano: Tennis, Boxing, Snooker

I. Tennis

Ann Jones (1969) – Virginia Wade (1977) – Greg Rusedski (1997) – Andy Murray (2013, 2015, 2016) – Emma Raducanu (2021)

IF CYCLING was a sport peopled by win-at-all-costs professionals high on performance-enhancing drugs, then tennis, in the immediate aftermath of the Second World War, was the polar opposite. In leafy suburbs across the Home Counties, the middle classes met up to play gentle games of mixed doubles, fuelled by nothing stronger than Robinsons Barley Water and bowls of strawberries. This was the habitat of Betjeman's Joan Hunter Dunn. A world of private clubs, where the rich and leisured, 'Furnish'd and burnish'd by Aldershot sun', went to relax with their peers and enjoy some convivial recreation.

But by the late 1960s, the pretence that the country's top players belonged in this idealised amateur Arcadia was no longer sustainable. Not only was the embryonic professional tour gaining ground, but, for the elite club player, an elastic reading by tournament directors of what constituted expenses meant that even those who were nominally competing for fun could, if they wished, make a living out of playing. Such growing commercialisation was seen by the sport's governing body, the Lawn Tennis Association (LTA), as a threat to both the game's social status and, more importantly, its own authority. Aware, however, that it was impossible to put the financial genie back in the bottle, the LTA did what all dictatorial bodies faced by an existential crisis do, and adopted the line of least resistance. In December 1967, tennis was declared an 'open' sport.

Central to the LTA's decision to embrace or at least tolerate professionalism was a desire to protect Wimbledon's status as the world's premier tournament. Wimbledon fortnight was British tennis' cash cow, not least because it was as much a televisual event as it was a sporting one. First covered by the BBC in 1937, by the 1960s it had become a lynchpin of the television calendar. As the sports historians Richard Holt and Tony Mason have noted, for many the coverage of Wimbledon 'was the sporting climax of the year, curtains drawn against the evening sun, Mum and the family peering at a black and white TV, passing the salad cream and the Kraft cheese slices'.

And, reflecting the gender balance of those who actually played tennis, the television audience for Wimbledon, unlike most sporting events, was made up of more women than men. It was, then, not so surprising that the first two tennis players to win the SPOTY trophy were not only Wimbledon champions but also female. But Ann Jones and Virginia Wade had little else in common. Jones was a typical product of suburban middle England. Brought up in King's Heath, a stolidly respectable suburb of Birmingham, she married at 24 and seemed happy to leave her promising sporting career behind as she settled into a life of quiet domesticity. It was, she later recalled, only because of the confidence instilled by her much older husband that she was persuaded, two years later, to give tennis another try.

By contrast, Wade's upbringing was markedly less conventional. After an early childhood in South Africa, where her father was the archdeacon of Durban, her teenage years were passed in the splendour of a rambling 14th-century mansion in Kent, complete with cook, gardener and tennis court. To her academic parents, sport was a social activity not a career choice, and so, on leaving school, their fiercely independent daughter was encouraged to combine her passion for tennis with a maths and physics degree at Sussex University. Ted Tinling, the fashion designer and a confidant of both players, felt that the difference in the two rivals' backgrounds was reflected in their on-court demeanour. While Jones was 'conventionally British' with a 'quiet and determined' approach to the game, Wade radiated 'star quality', although this was offset by her 'psychologically more fragile' temperament. Always self-aware, Wade largely agreed with Tinling. Ann's 'game was like a cake without the icing', she reflected, 'mine had too much icing and no cake'.

Both Jones and Wade turned professional just as the Open Era was evolving. A two-year contract guaranteeing £21,000 was enough for Jones to take the plunge in March 1968. Wade, though, took a bit more persuading. In April 1968 she turned down the £300 prize money for winning the British hardcourt championships in Bournemouth, the first-ever open tournament, as she was not yet prepared to sacrifice her amateur status. Her 'sense of freedom was offended', she later explained, by the idea of becoming 'a puppet to a professional promoter' and by the 'constant talk of money'. It was a commendable stance, but one that probably came easier if you had a 70-room family pile in Kent to fall back on. Eventually, though, any squeamishness about playing for cash was overcome as the victories mounted and the prize pots increased. By September 1968 a beaming Wade was happily accepting the $6,000 cheque for winning the US Open.

As their careers progressed, both players enjoyed remarkable success. In total, Jones won over 100 singles titles and Wade over 50. But both seemed destined to miss out on the one title they most wanted. Jones had turned 30, and was in her 14th Wimbledon before she finally got her hands on the singles trophy. For Wade, the wait was even longer. Victory came at her 15th attempt, when she was just one week short of her 32nd birthday.

Despite beating the great Billie Jean King in the final, the press response to Jones's triumph in 1969 was relatively muted. The *Sunday Times* was one of the few papers to lead with the story, and its headline, 'The Loser Who Turned Up Trumps', was hardly flattering. But the achievement was enough for the British public to vote Jones in as Sports Personality of the Year, ahead of the Open winner, Tony Jacklin, and Manchester United's flawed genius, George Best. For Jones, SPOTY and Wimbledon were the awards she 'valued as much as anything else', and she happily went into semi-retirement to start a family.[113]

---

113 Much to organisers' annoyance, Jones did not even defend her Wimbledon title in 1970. She did, of course, return to Centre Court on many occasions as a commentator for the BBC.

By the time Virginia Wade won Wimbledon eight years later, public interest in the on-court drama at the All England Club was much more intense. In part, this had to do with a confluence of anniversaries. The championship was celebrating its centenary, which, to the organisers' delight, happened to coincide with the Queen's Silver Jubilee. For the first time in 15 years Elizabeth II would be in the royal box for the ladies singles final. But Wimbledon's appeal in the late 70s also came from its reassuring immutability. For many the tournament offered an escape, albeit a temporary one, from the depressing reality of a nation on the brink of collapse. The quaint traditions and well-mannered crowds of SW19 served as the perfect antidote to the scourge of inflation, the violence of the Grunwick picket lines, the depravity of the Yorkshire Ripper and the nihilism of the Sex Pistols. And, even better, it looked like there might be a British winner.

Having defeated the reigning champion and world No. 1, Chris Evert, in the semi-final, Wade was odds-on favourite for the title. Standing in her way was the Dutch player Betty Stove. The *Daily Mail* was sure Stove would offer little resistance. She may look as if she had 'begun life wired to the lightning conductor in some Transylvanian castle', the paper unkindly observed, but 'still big, brave Betty will be no match for our Virginia'. Given such confidence, the final inevitably proved to be a nerve-racking affair. After Wade went down 6-4 in the first set, the *Daily Mirror*'s sports editor, exhausting his supply of Dutch stereotypes, felt certain that 'a couple of million mums about the country must have been in the mood to hurl the Edam in the dustbin, throw the Delft at the TV, and send the kids out to dig up and trample on the tulips'. Luckily, Stove crumbled in the next two sets, saving *Mirror* readers from further references to clogs, dykes and windmills.

The *Mail*'s tennis correspondent was astonished by the pandemonium that engulfed Centre Court as Wade clinched victory. 'The normally restrained crowd,' he breathlessly reported, 'stood and roared and sang, "For She's a Jolly Good Fellow",' while 'cameramen heaved and jostled like a mob of pickets.' Even, he added for good measure, the Queen ('not a tennis enthusiast') was 'moved to excited applause'. Pictures of the new champion with the winner's silver salver adorned the front pages of every newspaper. The £13,500 prize money pushed Wade's annual earnings into six figures, and made her second only to F1 champion James Hunt as Britain's highest-earning sports star. Such was the public clamour surrounding her triumph that rounding off the year with the SPOTY trophy, ahead of gruff Yorkshireman Geoffrey Boycott, was something of a formality.[65]

Although Wade was the last Briton to win Wimbledon in the 20th century, she was not the last tennis player to lift the SPOTY trophy before the advent of the new millennium. This fact is all the more remarkable when the parlous state of British tennis in the 1980s and 1990s is considered. The game, in these decades, seemed caught in a downward spiral. Poor results eroded public interest, which further undermined any prospects of success. As the century drew to a close, the nation's hopes centred on just one player: Tim Henman. Yet, paradoxically, Henman encapsulated all that was wrong with British tennis. He was too middle class, too suburban, too Home Counties and, fine player though he was, too prone to losing. Maybe the only solution was to bypass the LTA and import a winner.

Born in Montreal to a British mother, 21-year-old Greg Rusedski, lured by the promise of greater financial support, opted to switch allegiance to Britain in May 1995. He was not welcomed with open arms. As he strode on to No. 3 court for his debut as a British player at Wimbledon, he was greeted, the *Daily Telegraph* acidly noted, 'with the sort of rippling applause that attends the showing of a reasonably large marrow at a horticultural show'. No matter how many Union Jack bandanas Rusedski wore, the British press insisted on viewing him as a foreign interloper. *The Independent*'s claim that there was 'the whiff of moose and the Mounties about him' was one of the kinder comments. To *The Times*, he was simply 'a grinning Canadian chancer'. The problem, the *Independent on Sunday* astutely noted, was that Rusedski's insistence on 'practising towards a sort of perfection seems rather ungentlemanly'. Fortunately, practice didn't make perfect. Losses at Queen's and then Wimbledon quickly persuaded the public that the new Canadian import was, in fact, a perfect fit for British tennis.

Yet, despite these early defeats, and a disappointing record in Grand Slams, Rusedski's form returned in 1997.[114] A quarter-final at Wimbledon was followed by runner-up spot in the US Open. Although his four-set defeat by Pat Rafter at Flushing Meadows was pushed down the news agenda by coverage of Princess Diana's funeral, the achievement of becoming just the second Briton to reach a Grand Slam final in over 60 years still registered sufficiently for the British public to vote him in as the

114 Before 1997, Rusedski had played three times in the US Open, and each time he had gone out in the first round.

Sports Personality of the Year.[115] And, as proof that he was now fully accepted by his adopted nation, second place in SPOTY went to his quintessentially English rival, Tim Henman.

In fact, Henman was distinctly unimpressed to find himself no longer the country's favourite tennis player. 'Seeing Greg rather than me rise from his chair to receive award after award,' he told one interviewer after the BBC ceremony at the Queen Elzabeth II Conference Centre in London, had reminded him just how much 'coming second was a position I have never enjoyed'. It was fortunate, then, that his subsequent failure to reach a Grand Slam final forever shielded him from the disappointment of the runner-up spot. But Henman was not alone in expressing dissatisfaction with Rusedski's SPOTY win. 'There is something typically British,' thought Jim White of *The Guardian*, 'about bestowing our premier sporting gong on a man whose greatest achievement is to lose a Grand Slam final.' The *Sunday Times*' television correspondent, A. A. Gill, agreed. The SPOTY result, he reflected, merely 'underlined the hopeless whistling in the wind of British sport'. But perhaps the most damning verdict, on not only Rusedski's sports personality award but his career as a whole, came from Stuart Barnes of *The Times*. 'Poor old Greg,' lamented Barnes, 'so very nearly brilliant, so very nearly British.'[66]

One man who was both undeniably brilliant and undeniably British was tennis' next incumbent as SPOTY winner. Yet Andy Murray still struggled, at least for his first few years as a professional, to garner popular support. The problem boiled down

115 The other Grand Slam finalist since Fred Perry's triumphs was John Lloyd. Lloyd lost to Vitas Gerulaitis in the 1977 Australian Open.

to not being Tim. Moody and unpredictable on court, sullen and taciturn off it, Murray presented as the anti-Henman. 'A grumpy teenager,' *The Guardian*'s tennis correspondent pointed out after one particularly egregious bout of in-match swearing early on in Andy's career, 'is not, nor ever will be, a thing of beauty.' Fans of the game, by and large, felt the same way. Used to Henman's restrained urbanity, Murray's explosive ruthlessness alienated the Pimm's and strawberries brigade who made up the bulk of tennis crowds.

Matters were hardly helped when, asked who he would be supporting in the 2006 World Cup now his native Scotland had failed to qualify, Murray replied, 'Anyone but England.' It was a throwaway line, but the tabloids were disinclined to treat it as such. 'Anti-English jibe by ace Scot,' the *Daily Star* screamed. It did not take long for the meme 'Anyone But Murray' to go viral. Unsurprisingly, the incident did little to improve the young Scot's relations with the press, and from then on his media obligations were fulfilled with all the enthusiasm of a man en route to the gallows. As one commentator noted, Murray's expression during post-match interviews tended to confirm P. G. Wodehouse's aphorism: 'It is never difficult to distinguish between a ray of sunshine and a Scotsman with a grievance.'

It took six years for matters to improve, and predictably it was a devastating loss rather than a thrilling victory that proved to be the turning point. 'I'm going to try this and it's not going to be easy,' an overwrought Murray said as he took the microphone to address the crowd after losing to Roger Federer, three sets to one, in the 2012 Wimbledon final. He was right, it was not, and the tears flowed. The press lapped it up. 'It was a moving, humbling experience,' thought the *Daily Mirror*'s Tony Parsons, to be given a chance of 'seeing, for the very first time, the full man'. Jan Moir of the *Daily Mail* was taken by just how 'sweet and vulnerable' Murray had looked. 'You could practically hear the hearts melting all over the country,' she claimed. Victory in the Olympic singles final just four weeks later, this time getting his revenge on Federer, further buttressed Murray's newfound popularity. Even the usually hypercritical Matthew Syed of *The Times* urged his readers 'to stop fretting about the Scot's voice, his hair, his tantrums and his relationship with his mother, and to embrace him without inhibition'. It was good of Syed to overlook such a long list of shortcomings.

As Wimbledon came round again the following year, Murray was still riding the wave of positive publicity. On the eve of the championships, a sympathetic BBC documentary, fronted by Sue Barker, had revealed the British favourite to be not only leading a reassuringly normal life of quiet domesticity with girlfriend Kim Sears, but also coping valiantly with the emotional fallout of being a Dunblane shooting survivor.[116] All that was now needed for the tag of national treasure to be officially conferred was a Wimbledon win. But standing in his way in the 2013 final was Novak Djokovic, a six-time Grand Slam winner. The press cautioned that the country should 'expect the worst and prepare for the worst', as it was more than likely it would 'witness the worst'. As Murray squandered three match points in a row in the

---

116 On 13 March 1996, Thomas Hamilton broke into the gymnasium at Dunblane Primary School and shot dead 16 children and their schoolteacher. Andy, then eight, and his brother, Jamie, two years older, were both in the school at the time. In fact, Andy's class was on its way to the gym when the shooting started.

fourth set, the warning seemed all too prescient. On sofas around the country, 17.3 million people could barely bring themselves to watch. In the stands, Judy Murray's 'heart was pounding so hard in her chest' that she thought she 'might not see the end of the match'. She was not the only one with health worries. Even Andy admitted to being concerned he 'might not be able to finish the job' when his hand started 'shaking uncontrollably' as he prepared to serve his fourth match point. Four strokes later, though, it was all over and 77 years of waiting had finally come to an end.

Predictably, the newspapers instantly forgot they had ever been critical of the new champion. Pictures of Murray with the trophy graced every front page. The *Daily Express* produced a 'Magical Murray Special 12-page Souvenir', while the *Daily Mail* called for an immediate knighthood. But it was the *Daily Mirror* that best captured the mood of the nation with the banner headline 'At Last!' The bookies immediately installed Andy as 28/1 on to win SPOTY, and he more than lived up to such short odds, securing over 55 per cent of the vote, the biggest winning margin in the history of the programme. Apologising for sounding 'incredibly boring' despite being 'very excited and happy', a grinning Murray accepted the trophy via satellite link from his training base in Miami. 'Not bad for a man with no personality,' his Adidas sponsors mischievously tweeted.

But Murray wasn't finished with SPOTY. A fabulous Davis Cup run in 2015, culminating in a 3-1 defeat of Belgium in the final, gave Britain, and by default Murray, who had won all eight of his singles and three of his doubles matches in the course of the tournament, victory for the first time in 79 years. It was unlikely, thought one commentator, 'that in the entire 115-year history of the event, victory owed so much to one player'. The triumph also gave Murray the chance to finally put to bed any lingering questions about his national loyalty. He was, he made clear, both British and Scottish: 'I play Davis Cup for Britain – but I love being Scottish.'

Now a bona fide national hero who had put Britain on the sporting map, a second SPOTY win was a formality. In fact, at the glitzy ceremony at the Odyssey Arena in Belfast, Murray won two awards, securing the Team of the Year as well as the individual title. Insisting that the honour was so unexpected that he had not prepared a speech, he ad-libbed a joke about being duller than a weekend in Worthing, which, he thought, was 'a bit harsh ... on Worthing'.[117] It was a genuinely funny moment. SPOTY was fast becoming the Andy Murray show.

The following year was Murray's most successful yet. Victories at Wimbledon, the Olympics and the ATP Finals gave him a year-end No. 1 ranking. It was an impressive-enough record for nearly a quarter of a million people to make him the BBC's Sports Personality of the Year for a third time. That number, though, did not include his wife. She had voted for the 58-year-old showjumper Nick Skelton. 'Not a smart move,' Murray told the SPOTY audience, 'with Christmas coming up.' Although a frustratingly persistent hip injury means further Grand Slam titles and a fourth SPOTY trophy look unlikely, his achievements to 2016 are more than enough for *The Observer* to justifiably suggest

117 A subsequent admission by Murray that he had never actually been to Worthing prompted the town's mayor, Sean McDonald, to invite him on a tour of the seaside resort's attractions. 'He might even want to have a look at our two tennis courts,' thought McDonald.

that Murray is not only 'the greatest British tennis player in 80 years but also one of the country's finest athletes of all time'.[67]

As Murray's hip injury took its toll, it was hard to see where the country's next Grand Slam winner was going to come from. For the majority of pundits, the most likely candidate appeared to be Johanna Konta, who regularly reached the later stages of major tournaments. Certainly few, even those closely connected with tennis, would have singled out Emma Raducanu, an 18-year-old pupil at Newstead Wood Grammar School. Although she had enjoyed a successful career as a junior, reaching her first Futures event final in Sunderland in February 2020, there was no indication that she was less than two years away from becoming the first British winner of the US Open in over half a century.[118]

Raducanu's big breakthrough came at Wimbledon in 2021. Against all expectations, she reached the last 16 before 'breathing difficulties', brought on by a combination of excitement and tension, forced her to withdraw when a set down against the Australian Ajla Tomljanović. She would have to 'toughen up' if she ever hoped to win a major tournament, stormed the king of faux outrage, Piers Morgan. But, for once, the self-styled straight-talking voice of the people was out of touch. Much closer to the mark was the editor of the *Daily Express*, who hailed the 18-year-old as 'a national treasure who sparkles even in the wake of disappointment'. Certainly, Raducanu was now the darling of the public. She suddenly found herself catapulted into the

118 Futures events are effectively the lowest rung of the professional tennis ladder, providing an opportunity for neophyte pros to gain valuable tournament experience (and some prize money). Virginia Wade was the last British winner of the US Open in 1968.

front ranks of sporting celebrity. When she had been offered up for interview on the eve of Wimbledon, there had only been one taker; less than two weeks later and she was being fought over by every tabloid sports editor, broadsheet feature writer and magazine fashion columnist.

But, astonishing though her Wimbledon run had been, still no one, least of all her own team, was prepared for what was about to happen in the US Open. With three rounds of qualifying to negotiate, simply making the main draw was the initial yardstick of success. And the possibility of a last-16 spot was considered so remote that flights home were booked for the middle Saturday of the tournament. But, of course, an astonishing nine-match run, without dropping a set, saw her become the first qualifier ever to reach a Grand Slam final in the Open Era. Surely 'the impossible, practically unspeakable dream couldn't be about to come true?' asked Bryan Graham of *The Guardian*. It could. Watched by a domestic audience of ten million, Raducanu maintained her perfect record, beating Canadian teenager Leylah Fernandez 6-4, 6-3. It was an incredible achievement. Perhaps the best indicator of just how far the new US champion had come in such a short space of time was the sum written on her winner's cheque. Four months before the triumph over Fernandez, Raducanu had won £75 for reaching the semi-finals of a British tour event in Chingford.[119] She was now taking home a cool £1.8m.

119 Actually, her net winnings were £50 if you deduct the £25 she had to pay to enter.

Inevitably, the final made the front pages of all the newspapers. And, even more inevitably, virtually all the headlines plumped for 'Fairytale of New York' or 'Queen of Queens'. Even in a year that had seen British Olympians win gold and the English men's football team reach a major final for the first time since 1966, this was the sporting story to trump all others. SPOTY voters agreed, and Raducanu became the first woman to win the BBC trophy since Zara Phillips in 2006. Although the unglamorous setting of an Abu Dhabi hotel room, from which the self-isolating people's favourite was compelled to accept her award, was a stark reminder of the pandemic that had devastated everyday life, the unadulterated joy evident in her acceptance speech was just the tonic the nation needed as it emerged from the tribulations of Covid lockdowns.[68]

* * *

II. Boxing

Henry Cooper (1967, 1970) – Barry McGuigan (1985) – Lennox Lewis (1999) – Joe Calzaghe (2007)

ANDY MURRAY is an ardent boxing fan. On the eve of his critical Davis Cup Final match against David Goffin in 2015, he stayed up most of the night watching Tyson Fury defeat Wladimir Klitschko to win the world heavyweight title. His passion for the fight game, he told one interviewer, stems from his belief that tennis is 'like boxing in the sense that you go into the ring and it's just you against the other person. One guy tries to pound the other guy out of the ring. It's beautiful because it's basic.' It was an interesting parallel, but one boxers appeared much more reluctant to make. Maybe, for those in the thick of it, the unalloyed violence of a professional fight seemed rather more distant from the refined elegance of a set of tennis at the All England Club.

Perhaps a better comparison, at least as far as SPOTY is concerned, is that to win the BBC trophy a boxer needs a world title in the same way a tennis player requires a Grand Slam. Yet, as with all good rules, it is the exception that proves it. Henry Cooper, the first boxer to win SPOTY, may have had a great left hook ('Enry's 'Ammer), but he was never really a serious contender for a world belt. The main problem was that Cooper, in the parlance of the sport, was a bleeder. This was never more apparent than in his one shot at a world title, against the great Muhammad Ali at Arsenal's Highbury Stadium in 1966.

Although Ali was odds-on to win the fight, memories of their one previous meeting, three years earlier at Wembley, gave British fans some cause for hope. Then, a young Ali had been caught in the final seconds of the fourth round by 'Enry's 'Ammer ('he hit me so hard it hurt my relatives in Africa'), and had only been saved by the bell and some dubious corner work by his experienced trainer, Angelo Dundee.[120] But the issue that lost Cooper the fight in 1963 came back to haunt him in 1966. In short, the British contender's eyes cut easily. The damage was so bad in the

---

120 It has been suggested that Dundee used smelling salts to revive Ali, and aggravated a small tear in one of his gloves to extend the length of the break. The evidence for both claims is, at best, inconclusive.

Highbury bout that not only was the referee forced to stop the contest in the sixth round, but the cut required immediate surgical treatment. 'Man,' an incredulous Ali remarked after the fight, 'I could hear him bleeding.'[121]

This is not to suggest that Cooper was not a skilled fighter. Although his professional record of 40 wins from 55 fights may have been relatively modest, he, nonetheless, held the British heavyweight title for a record 12 years. But the real root of his popularity was his personality. Born into poverty in South East London, the future British champion, one obituarist noted, 'grew up modestly and stayed that way'. In a sport that was rapidly becoming a byword for braggadocio and sleaze, Cooper remained the embodiment of the noble art from the Marquess of Queensberry's days. He approached the sport with a beguilingly old-fashioned simplicity. The Old Kent Road gym he trained at was unchanged since Jack Broughton codified boxing's rules in the 18th century. His early morning five-mile training runs were completed in army boots. The only innovation his manager, Jim Wicks, introduced to his routine was to replace the traditional boxing pick-me-up of eggs and sherry with a still-Dickensian-sounding concoction of port and Guinness.

And the honesty in training was matched by a purity in outlook. Unsullied by the rumours of match-fixing and petty criminality that enveloped the sport, Cooper was always gracious in defeat and modest in victory. Even his rivals recognised that he was somehow

121 A tendency to cut badly had plagued Cooper for much of his career. When he defeated Brian London to win his first British and Empire title in 1959, the *Daily Telegraph* thought 'both fighters looked as if they had been fighting with meat axes'.

a man apart. 'I reckon even my friends will be rooting for Henry,' Billy Walker quipped before a British title fight in 1967.

Cooper's victory over Walker in that 1967 fight not only helped him win a Lonsdale belt outright for a record third time but also secured him his first SPOTY title. He was awarded the SPOTY crown again three years later, when he regained his British and European heavyweight crowns at the ripe old age of 36. But, just how much his sports personality honours were recognition of his general qualities as a sportsman, rather than his specific skills as a boxer, can be gleaned from the Sportswriters' Sportsman of the Year awards for 1970. Tony Jacklin, who had come second to Cooper in SPOTY, topped the sportswriters' poll, while Cooper only came 34th. Clearly, to the professional expert, Cooper just fell short of genius, but to the lay public he was the model of a sporting hero.

The year after his second SPOTY win, Cooper's career ended in disappointment. Facing the much younger and much heavier Joe Bugner, the two-time SPOTY champion and three-time Lonsdale belt winner lost his British and European crowns. Most observers felt that referee Harry Gibbs had called the fight wrongly. Certainly, the outraged crowd at the Empire Pool, Wembley was unimpressed by the verdict, and chose to show its displeasure by showering the ring with half-finished cans of beer and assorted debris. Predictably, Cooper helped to calm the situation by accepting the decision with dignity. 'The last thing I wanted,' he wryly explained afterwards, 'was for a fight to break out.' In many ways, this last bout captured Cooper perfectly. 'He was,' the boxing commentator John Rawling fittingly observed, 'a good boxer, but an outstanding man.'[69]

The second boxer to take the SPOTY trophy was also celebrated for more than just his sporting achievements. Fighting at a time when conflict in Northern Ireland was at its height, Barry McGuigan managed to bridge the sectarian divide. Born in Clones in County Monaghan, one of the Republic's three Ulster counties, he adopted a steadfastly neutral stance throughout The Troubles. Catholic by birth, he married a Protestant; an Olympian under the flag of the Republic, he won a bronze medal for Northern Ireland in the Commonwealth Games; fighting professionally as a British citizen, he drew as many nationalists as unionists to his contests at the King's Hall, Belfast.[122] The peace symbol he had woven on to his shorts was not just a gimmick, it was central to his belief system. 'Leave the Fighting to McGuigan' his slogan urged, and although that may have been asking too much, the example he set undoubtedly helped bring some hope to a land so desperately short of it.

But McGuigan was only able to act as a force for good outside the ring because of his talent inside it. Having become the youngest-ever Commonwealth boxing champion in 1978, he turned professional in 1981, and quickly made his mark, securing the European title a little over two years later. By 1985, the Clones Cyclone, as McGuigan was now dubbed, was ready to challenge for a world featherweight belt. The reigning WBA champion, Eusebio Pedroza from Panama, with 19 successful title defences behind him, was considered to be one of the best

122 British Boxing Board of Control regulations stipulated that only British citizens could compete for the British title. McGuigan became a British citizen in the summer of 1982, and British featherweight champion the following year.

pound-for-pound fighters in the world. The contest, set for 8 June at QPR's Loftus Road ground, was, *The Guardian* proclaimed, 'the most anticipated fight in Britain since the Cooper-Ali world title fight'.[123]

As it turned out, such anticipation was not misplaced. The fight was a classic. McGuigan's father ramped up the pre-fight emotion with a heartfelt rendition of 'Danny Boy', before the two best featherweights in the world went toe to toe. McGuigan began with such intensity that it seemed unlikely he would last beyond the first few rounds. But, two minutes into the seventh, just as Harry Carpenter warned the 19 million viewers at home that the Irish favourite 'hasn't found his range', the Clones Cyclone landed a right that poleaxed Pedroza. Incredibly, the Panamanian hung on for a further eight rounds before the final bell went and the crowd surged into the ring to acclaim Britain's new world champion.

In the aftermath of the fight, McGuigan was hailed as the nation's 'greatest world champion since the war'. To underline his cross-sectarian appeal, he received admiring telegrams from Garret FitzGerald, the Irish taoiseach, as well as Douglas Hurd, the secretary of state for Northern Ireland. Even Mrs Thatcher was moved to offer her congratulations. Over 70,000, Catholics and Protestants, Loyalists and Republicans, turned out for the victory parade in Belfast. It was the biggest crowd since VE Day. McGuigan's victory, declared the *Daily Mail*, proved 'it was still possible for nice guys to win'. And to underline the

123 Pedroza had refused to fight in Belfast because he considered the city unsafe. Quite an indictment when it came from someone living under the regime of Panama's General Manuel Noriega.

point, the public voted him in as Sports Personality of the Year ahead of Ashes winner Ian Botham and triple world-record holder Steve Cram.

After all the excitement had died down, the new champion discovered that winning titles motivated him far more than defending them. Although he managed two successful defences, against Bernard Taylor and Danilo Cabrera, he came unstuck when he travelled to Las Vegas to face Steve Cruz in June 1986. Fought in Caesar's Palace car park at 6pm, the temperature was touching 120°F when the bell sounded. As the heat took its toll, McGuigan wilted while Cruz seemed to get stronger. At the end of the tenth round, eyes glazed with exhaustion, the Irishman slumped on to his stool and muttered, 'Say a little prayer for me.' But even divine intervention could not help. Barely able to stand, let alone defend himself, McGuigan went down twice in the last round to punches he would have normally shrugged off without a thought. It was a mark of the man that he was able to summon enough energy to rise from his stool to congratulate the new champion when the result was announced. Maybe, then, nice guys did not always win, but Irish rock legend and activist Bono was, for once, right when pointing out that, in a dark time for Northern Ireland, Barry McGuigan was 'more than a champion, he was a hero'.[70]

It was another 14 years until a boxer again won SPOTY. Although Lennox Lewis was just as devastating inside the ring and personable outside it as McGuigan, he struggled to gain the sort of popularity the Irishman enjoyed. The problem was Lewis, like Greg Rusedski, found it almost impossible to shrug off the accusation that he was Canadian rather than British. This was particularly galling as he had, at least, spent his early childhood in England, before leaving to join his mother in Toronto. Although he chose to return to Britain in 1989 to start his professional career, no amount of Union Jack suits or carefully choreographed pictures at his 'beloved' West Ham United could convince a sceptical British public that he was anything other than a North American import. Even becoming the WBC heavyweight champion in December 1992, the first British boxer to hold a world heavyweight title since Bob Fitzsimmons in 1899, did little to boost his popularity. And the newly crowned champion hardly helped matters when, the following year, he called national treasure Frank 'True Brit' Bruno an Uncle Tom, before beating him to a standstill in the seventh round of their title fight at Cardiff Arms Park.

Once again, it took a defeat to bring the public round. By 1999, having lost and then reclaimed his WBC title in two extraordinary meetings with Oliver McCall, Lewis was ready to face Evander Holyfield for the undisputed heavyweight crown.[124] The fight, at Madison Square Garden in New York on 13 March 1999, was dominated by the British champion from start to finish. As Lewis raised his hand in triumph at the final bell, even Holyfield appeared to concede defeat by offering a congratulatory hug. Although Sky's Ian Drake cautioned viewers that Holyfield was a 'Don King fighter in a Don King promotion in America, and we've seen strange things happen before', anything other than

124 In the first McCall fight, Lewis suffered the indignity of becoming the first reigning world heavyweight champion to be stopped while still on his feet. The rematch was even more bizarre. In the fifth round, a tearful McCall simply refused to fight, and the match was awarded to Lewis on a technical knockout.

a unanimous decision in favour of Lewis seemed inconceivable. Then the MC stepped up. As the scores were read out, Giles Smith of *The Times* noted that 'Lewis's jaw dropped to roughly where it would have been if Holyfield had managed to hit it'. The three judges had somehow contrived to come up with a draw.[125] It was, asserted the *Daily Mail*, 'The greatest boxing fiasco since Henry Cooper versus Joe Bugner in 1971.' It was worse than that, the *Daily Express* insisted: 'It was one of the greatest outrages in the history of sport.' Even Labour MP Tony Banks, displaying the sort of insight only a minister of sport could possess, wondered if 'the result gives rise to the thought that it was more about business than sport'. The one consolation for Lewis was that it transformed his public image. Suddenly, he was one of us: a Briton abroad demeaned by unappreciative foreigners.

The opportunity for revenge arrived eight months later. Although most observers judged the rematch, at the Thomas Mack Center in Pasadena on 13 November, to be a much closer affair than the first encounter, this time a unanimous verdict gave Lewis the undisputed heavyweight title. The following month, victory at the sports personality awards, beating a rehabilitated David Beckham into second place, confirmed that the new world champion had finally been accepted by the British public. Both Lewis and Beckham, though, were overshadowed at the BBC ceremony by the presence in the studio of the newly crowned sports personality of the century, Muhammad Ali. As the credits

---

125 In the aftermath of the result, the focus fell on one judge in particular. Eugenia Williams had been nominated for her role by the International Boxing Federation's president, Bobby Lee, who, at the time, was under Grand Jury investigation for corruption. Williams later claimed her view of the fight had been blocked by photographers.

rolled at the end of the show, viewers were treated to the sight of the millionaire superstars of Manchester United's treble-winning team (and Team of the Year) forming an orderly queue to get the great man's autograph.

In the remaining four years of his boxing career, Lewis proved his calibre as a fighter. After a shock fifth-round knockout at the hands of Hasim Rahman in April 2001, he regained his title in the rematch seven months later. Successful defences against Mike Tyson and Wladimir Klitschko, before retirement in February 2004, meant he was only the third heavyweight in history to beat every opponent they ever met. The other two were Muhammad Ali and Rocky Marciano. It was quite a club to be part of. Yet, as Hugh McIlvanney, that doyen of British sportswriters, rightly observed, he never quite received the acclaim his talent deserved.[71]

Joe 'the Italian Dragon' Calzaghe, the most recent boxer, and only the third Welsh sportsperson, to win SPOTY, also struggled to receive the recognition his ability merited.[126] Having excelled as an amateur, winning three ABA titles in a row at different weights, he won his first professional fight, in October 1993, with a first-round knockout. For his opponents, this was a portent of things to come. Over the next 20 fights, only five of them made it beyond the third round, and only one was still standing when the final bell rang. And he lost.

Yet the press remained distinctly unenthusiastic. The accusation was that the bouts were mismatches. In reality, Calzaghe was simply so good, the speed of his combinations and

---

126 Calzaghe's nickname had its roots in his Italian heritage. His father, Enzo, was born in Sardinia.

the power of his punches of such high quality that there were few boxers in the world who could safely step into the ring with him. Even a spectacular points victory over Chris 'Simply the Best' Eubank, to secure the vacant WBO super middleweight title, received only lukewarm praise. Part of the problem was Calzaghe, unlike the flamboyantly eccentric Eubank, eschewed publicity. 'I don't think it's really in Joe's nature to court attention,' his disappointed manager, Frank Warren, complained after his charge had turned down the chance to become 'the face of M&S Y-fronts'. Quite possibly it wasn't his face the Welshman was worried about. But, in truth, the only concerns Calzaghe really had about his body focused on his hands. From the late 1990s onwards, he was plagued by a series of stubbornly persistent hand injuries. Unable to punch with full force, his title defences became increasingly lacklustre and his public image suffered accordingly.[127]

In 2006, though, 'the Italian Dragon' broke through into the sporting mainstream. On 4 March, at the MEN Arena, Manchester, he beat the pre-fight favourite and highly rated, undefeated IBF world super middleweight champion, Jeff Lacy. Lacy was outclassed from the opening bell, and in the 12th round was knocked to the canvas for the first time in his career. It was, declared the *Sunday Times*, 'one of the greatest displays of superb technique, confidence and fighting intelligence a British boxer has delivered in a major contest'. 'Calzaghe,' the irrepressible boxing pundit Steve Bunce insisted, 'has finally established himself as the

127 Asked by one interviewer, 'Why do you think your hands got so bad'? Calzaghe offered up the suggestion, 'Punching people in the head?' It seemed as good a theory as any.

best boxer of his generation, and one of the very best in British boxing history.' An invitation to appear on the BBC's *Strictly Come Dancing* marked just how established the Welsh boxer now was. The invitation was, naturally, turned down. If a pair of sensible M&S Y-fronts was considered beyond the pale, then a sheer, sequined bodysuit was unlikely to appeal.

On the back of the Lacy fight, Calzaghe was now tipped to win SPOTY. He should, thought Jeff Powell of the *Daily Mail*, top the poll 'by a distance'. The boxer, though, did his cause no favours when, in a radio interview on the eve of the show, he criticised the British public for 'only getting behind losers when it comes to the BBC SPOTY awards'. In fact, Zara Phillips, in first place, and Beth Tweddle, in third, were both winners. But Calzaghe remained unimpressed. 'I was beaten by a gymnast and a bloody horse,' he complained.[128]

The following year, another imperious display, this time against WBC and WBA super middleweight champion Mikkel Kessler, meant Calzaghe was, once again, favourite for the SPOTY title. 'If achievement alone was the deciding factor,' argued the *Daily Mail*'s Des Kelly, 'as opposed to straight out celebrity status, then Calzaghe will win SPOTY.' The good news for supporters of the Welshman was that their idol did appear to have finally broken through to the ranks of tabloid celebrity. In the week leading up to sports personality, he was reported to have received more mentions in the press than anyone else. The fact that Madonna, sporting two black eyes as a result of cosmetic surgery, and Adolf

128 Darren Clarke, in second, was also a winner, just not so much in 2006. He did, however, elicit enormous public sympathy that year by helping Europe to Ryder Cup victory, only six weeks after the death of his wife.

Hitler, somewhat belatedly accused of fathering a love child with Unity Mitford, came in second and third possibly watered down the achievement, but it was still something. In fact, it proved to be enough. Calzaghe's SPOTY victory, a relieved James Lawton of *The Independent* reflected, finally put paid to the idea that 'finishing second, however brilliantly or precociously, can ever be ranked above the supreme goal of proving yourself the best'. And to top off a triumphant night for boxing, Calzaghe's trainer, his father Enzo, won Coach of the Year.

Calzaghe fought just twice more before he retired. Moving up to light-heavyweight, he defeated Bernard 'The Executioner' Hopkins, in April 2008, before seeing off one of boxing's all-time greats, Roy Jones Jnr, seven months later. The victories meant he was able to leave the sport on his own terms, as an undefeated champion with a record of 46 wins and no losses. Yet, despite all the accomplishments, he remained underappreciated. Perhaps, the problem was, unlike Ali for Cooper, Pedroza for McGuigan or Holyfield for Lewis, he had no single opponent who defined his career. Or, perhaps, the problem was he was simply too good.[72]

* * *

III. Snooker

Steve Davis (1988)

RATHER LIKE Calzaghe in boxing, the only snooker player to win SPOTY dominated his sport for nigh on a decade. But, unlike Calzaghe, Steve Davis possessed the business acumen to make the most of his time at the top. He was also fortunate to be at his peak at just the right moment.

Until the late 1960s, snooker was on the far margins of the British sporting world. Considered by most to be no more than a pastime, and a shady one at that, there were, in the immediate post-war years, fewer than ten full-time professional players in the country. But in 1969 the game was discovered by the small screen. Keen to promote colour television and anxious, as ever, to keep costs down, the BBC introduced an unsuspecting public to *Pot Black*. To everyone's surprise, not least executives at Broadcasting House, the programme proved to be enormously popular. As 'an exercise in metronomic nothingness', the historian Dominic Sandbrook noted, the spectacle was the perfect fit for TV.

But, initially, *Pot Black*'s popularity had little impact on the wider game. The 1972 World Championship were still held in the cramped, smoked-filled hall of a British Legion in Selly Park on the outskirts of Birmingham. 'Beer supplies held up,' recalled *The Guardian*'s Clive Everton, 'but the toilet facilities proved sadly inadequate.' Before too long, though, the true potential of snooker as a ratings winner was realised, and by 1980 nearly 15 million were tuning in to watch Cliff 'The Grinder' Thorburn defeat Alex 'Hurricane' Higgins in the world final at Sheffield's Crucible Theatre.

Snooker's growth was helped by a slump in the popularity of football. In contrast to the obscene chants and endemic violence that made standing on the terraces of crumbling soccer stadia a markedly unpleasant day out, watching snooker, be it live or from the comfort of home, was a reassuringly relaxing experience. The gentlemanly behaviour of dinner-suited snooker players, the

Sunday Telegraph contended in language very much of the time, 'made a change from the hysterical poofs of the football field'.

Yet, in these early *Pot Black* days, snooker had its own version of the prima donna footballer. Belfast-born Alex 'Hurricane' Higgins was a supreme talent at the table but a deeply flawed individual away from it. Like his fellow countryman George Best, he may have had only three vices – 'drinking, gambling and women' – but he made the most of them. 'He confirmed his hell-raising bona-fides,' the Canadian novelist and teenage pool-room hustler Mordecai Richler once observed, 'by wrecking hotel rooms, pissing in the nearest available plant pot, punching officials, tussling with opponents, heaving his cue at fans, head-butting a referee, scribbling apologies on toilet paper, indulging in reckless gambling, being banned out of too many bars to count, and, for good measure, getting stabbed in the chest while living with a bimbo in a caravan.' It was quite a charge sheet, and initially such antics helped to provide the game with much-needed publicity. But as the sport became more established, there was less room for Higgins's unpredictability. What was needed, instead, was a new-standard bearer for a more professional era.

Steve Davis was just the man for the job. Dedicated to his sport, he was the antithesis of Higgins. 'Life,' he told one journalist, 'was: wake up, practise, go to bed, repeat.' Such focus quickly paid off. Having turned professional in 1978, just after his 20th birthday, within three years he was world champion. Yet, as he continued to collect titles and dominate the sport, he struggled to gain traction with the fans. To many he came across as a little too good, too distant, too professional – in short, too boring. Once more, a defeat proved to be the turning point. From being 9-0 up against the comically bespectacled Dennis Taylor in the final of the 1985 World Championships, Davis lost on the last black of the last frame. The match was so compelling that over 18 million people, the biggest audience ever for BBC2, were persuaded to stay up after midnight on a Sunday to see its conclusion. 'That must be hard to take?' the BBC's David Vine, a master of the blindingly obvious, suggested to the white-faced, dead-eyed Davis as Taylor held aloft the trophy. 'Yes,' was all the Plumstead Potter could manage in reply. It was another Murray tears moment. Even the most diffident onlooker would have needed a hard heart not to have been affected by such vulnerability.

Davis's public image was given a further boost when the satirical ITV puppet show, *Spitting Image*, awarded him the nickname 'interesting'. With help from sports impresario Barry Hearn, the boring tag was monetised. Heinz baked beans were 'really interesting', Crosse & Blackwell's beef stroganoff was one of its 'most interesting recipes', while Irish Life pensions were 'predictable'. By the late 80s, Davis was by far the best-paid snooker player in the world, making in excess of £½m a year in endorsements alone.

In 1988 his dominance at the table was confirmed when he became the first player to win snooker's 'triple crown' – the World Championship, the UK Championship and the Invitational Masters. After two runner-up spots and a third place, the achievement finally put him on the top step of the SPOTY podium. The sports editor of *The Observer* may have been left in 'disbelief' by the result, insisting that Davis and third-placed Sandy Lyle had 'as much charisma as a pair of kippers', but he was fighting against the tide of public opinion. The journalist and former jockey Brough Scott was much closer to the mark. 'The truth is,' he told readers of the *Sunday Times*, 'that the most interesting part of any champion's character is not his lifestyle, his hairstyle or even his post-match quotes. It is winning. By that standard, Steve Davis has personality by the hatful.' He was surely right. The least boring thing about Davis was his ability to win. Paradoxically, though, in one-on-one sports it was frequently the raw emotion of defeat, rather than the fist pump of victory, that first convinced a sceptical public to back serial winners.[73]

Chapter Notes

65 Holt and Mason, *Sport in Britain*, pp.53–55; Kevin Jeffreys, *British Tennis: From the Renshaws to the Murrays* (2019), pp.123–142; Helen Walker, 'Tennis', in Tony Mason (ed.), *Sport in Britain: A Social History* (1989), pp.270–272; Virginia Wade, *Courting Triumph* (1978), pp.74, 102, 150; *Sunday Times*, 6 July 1969; *Daily Mail*, 1 July 1977; *Daily Mirror*, 2 July 1977; *Daily Express*, 2 July 1977.

66 Holt and Mason, *Sport in Britain*, p.141; *Daily Telegraph*, 27 June 1995; Neil Harman, *Dual for the Crown* (1999), pp.50–55; Jack Black, Thomas Fletcher and Robert Blake, 'Success in Britain comes with an awful lot of small print: Greg Rusedski and precarious performance of national identity', *Nation and Nationalism* 26/4 (October 2020), pp.1104–1123; Mark Hodgkinson, *Andy Murray: Wimbledon Champion* (2012), p.141; *Guardian*, 16 December 1997; *Sunday Times*, 21 December 1997; *Times*, 9 April 2007.

67 Robert Lake and Carol Osbourne, 'Andy Murray and the borders of national identity', in Robert Lake (ed.), *Routledge Handbook of Tennis* (2019), p.384; Hodgkinson, *Andy Murray*, pp.235, 265; Robert Lake, *A Social History of Tennis* (2014), p.295; *Daily Star*, 29 June 2006; *Daily Express*, 7 July 1921, 8 July 2013; *Daily Mirror*, 8 July 2013, 9 July 2012; *Daily Mail*, 7 December 2013, 8 July 2013, 9 July 2012; *Times*, 22 December 2015, 21 December 2015, 14 December 2013, 9 July 2012; BBC1, *Andy Murray: The Man Behind the Racquet* (June 2013); Jeffreys, *British Tennis*, p.189; Alan Bairner, 'From old Tom Morris to

Andy Murray: an example of the Scottishness of Scotland's sporting celebrities', *Celebrity Studies* 14/3 (2023), pp.350–365; *Guardian*, 30 November 2015; *Sun*, 18 December 2016; *Observer*, 7 January 2018.

68 Mike Dickson, *Emma Raducanu: When Tennis Comes Home* (2022), pp.73, 95–97; *Daily Star*, 13 September 2021, 7 July 2021; *Daily Express,* 13 September 2021, 7 July 2021; Amazon, *Emma: Living Her Dream* (2022); *Guardian*, 8 September 2021.

69 Hodgkinson, *Andy Murray*, pp.117–118; *Daily Express*, 16 December 2013; *Guardian*, 2 May 2011, 1 May 2011; Robert Edwards, *Henry Cooper: The Authorised Autobiography* (2012), pp.71–87, 214, 243; *Daily Mirror*, 23 May 1966; Henry Cooper, *Henry Cooper: An Autobiography* (1972), p.81; *Sunday Times*, 20 December 1970; *Henry Cooper: Maestro* (1984), dir. Jeff Goddard.

70 Rob Steen, *Floodlights and Touchlines: A History of Spectator Sport* (2015), p.302; Barry McGuigan, *Cyclone: My Story* (2011), pp.90–92, 147; Jim Sheridan, *Leave the Fighting to McGuigan* (1985), p.115; *Guardian*, 6 June 1985; *Times*, 23 June 1986; 10 June 1985; *Daily Mail*, 10 June 1985.

71 Gavin Evans, *Mama's Boy: Lennox Lewis and the Heavyweight Crown* (2004), p.62; *Lennox Lewis: The Untold Story* (2020), dir. Rick Lazes and Seth Koch; Lennox Lewis and Ken Gorman, *Lennox Lewis: Champion* (1993), p.205; Giles Smith, *Midnight in the Garden of Evel Knievel: Sport on Television* (2000), p.303; *Daily Mail*, 15 March 1999; *Daily Express*, 15 March 1999; *Sunday Times*, 23 March 1999; Steve Rider and Marin Smyth, *BBC Sports Personality of the Year* (2003), p.222.

72 *Mr Calzaghe* (2015), dir. Vaughan Sivell; Joe Calzaghe, *No Ordinary Joe: The Autobiography* (2007), p.292; *Sunday Times*, 12 March 2006; *Independent*, 16 December 2007, 11 December 2007, 6 March 2006; *Daily Mail*, 4 December 2006; *Times*, 8 December 2007.

73 BBC2, *Gods of Snooker: Episode 1* (2021), dir. Martin Fuller; Dominic Sandbrook, *Who Dares Wins: Britain 1979–1982* (2019), pp.485–497; Martin Kelner, *Sit Down and Cheer: A History of Sport on TV* (2013), pp.120–124; Alwyn Turner, *Rejoice! Rejoice! Britain in the 1980s* (2010), pp.127–139; Steve Davis, *Interesting: My Autobiography* (2015), p.259; *Observer*, 18 December 1988; *Sunday Times*, 11 December 1988.

Conclusion

Mary Earps (2023)

WHEN JAYNE Torvill and Christopher Dean announced, in December 2023, that the England goalkeeper, Mary Earps, had won SPOTY, the decision seemed an uncontroversial one. Earps's heroics at that summer's World Cup, in which she had not only saved a penalty in the final but also walked away with the Golden Glove award for the tournament's best keeper, had made her the bookies' odds-on favourite to win the BBC trophy. Even Prince William thought her triumph was 'well deserved'. But, predictably, there were some who were less happy. TalkTV's Kevin O'Connor worried that Earps's victory, following as it did on the heels of Mead's and Raducanu's, revealed a competition that had 'descended into an abyss of wokery so only women can win'. 'Lots of men,' he asserted, 'say why do we even bother to turn up.' Perhaps, viewers might well have been thinking, because men had won for 14 consecutive years between 2007 and 2020?

But, at least, O'Connor had a twinkle in his eye when offering up his opinion. Rather less light-hearted was Joey Barton's contribution. 'To win before Ronnie O'Sullivan and Frankie Dettori,' he fumed on Twitter, 'well, that's just madness to me. Both almost genius like in their respective fields. They've lost to a big sack of spuds that plays in goal for a girls' team.' And, for those who found this view too nuanced, he later added, 'I'd score 100 out of 100 penalties against Mary Earps. Any day of the week. Twice on a fucking Sunday. #perspective.'[129]

It was quite a tirade, but not wholly unexpected. Barton had form for expounding misogynistic views. During a nervy appearance on *Question Time* some years earlier, he had suggested that the options available to the public in a forthcoming European election were like a choice between 'four really ugly girls'. But then, although the 'ugly' comment had been roundly condemned, his overall punditry had been widely praised. He had proved, thought Katie Hinds of the *Daily Mirror*, that 'he is a very smart man who appeals to the general public'. Few were suggesting this in 2023. From politicians to fellow professionals, Barton was dismissed as bitter and out of touch. The *Daily Mail* even went so far as to reprint some top trump cards that compared Barton's and Earps's careers. Only in 'red cards', 'beaten up opponents' and 'days in jail', did the former QPR man come out ahead.

Although Earps wisely chose not to become too caught up in the whole imbroglio, it did not stop her worrying, she confided to an interviewer from *Women's Health* magazine, that Barton's misogyny reflected 'what people across the country think'. But her SPOTY award should have provided her with some solace. Admittedly, BBC viewers might not have constituted a perfect cross-section of society, but they were still a better representation

---

129 Catherine Bennett of *The Observer* was certain that Barton would also be able to 'punch Earps unconscious much more quickly than the other way round, any day of the week'. That, Bennett caustically added, was 'yet another talent for which men like him get no credit'.

of popular opinion than football's so-called 'philosopher king'. And not only had sports personality voters opted for women as champions in the last three years, but they had also, since the new millennium, increasingly supported female sports stars generally. In the first 46 years of the show, less than 17 per cent of those who had stood on the SPOTY podium were female; since 2000 the percentage has risen to nearly one third. There is, of course, more that needs to be done, but at least progress is being made. And as the profile of women's sport continues to grow, SPOTY will be there to celebrate the fact. The show may unfailingly enflame the Twittersphere and the tabloid talk shows, but that is only because it is such a good reflection of our nation's sporting passions.[74]

Chapter Notes

74 *Observer*, 28 January 2024; *Guardian*, 30 May 2014; *Daily Mirror*, 30 May 2014; *Daily Mail*, 20 December 2023; *Independent*, 23 January 2012; *Women's Health*, March 2024.

Acknowledgements

I'M ENORMOUSLY grateful to everyone at Pitch Publishing, especially Jane Camillin, for commissioning the book and guiding it from proposal to completion. Huge thanks are also due to Duncan Olner, Andrea Dunn, Ivan Butler and Graham Hales for all their help in preparing the text. Many long suffering friends and relatives, too numerous and modest to name, provided invaluable support by pointing out errors, offering constructive criticism or simply feigning passing interest. I, of course, take full (if grudging) responsibility for any remaining mistakes.

All the photographs inside the book are reproduced courtesy of Getty Images with the exception of the pictures of Jim Laker, Anita Lonsbrough, Mary Rand, Damon Hill and Kelly Holmes which were supplied by Alamy.

Further Reading

NEARLY ALL the winners of SPOTY have published autobiographies, and some of the most celebrated have produced one or more updates. Michael Owen's first memoir, for example, came out when he was only 20; it left a lot of living still to tell us about. I will not list the titles here but they can all be found in the notes that accompany each chapter. There are, of course, libraries full of works on British sport generally, but what follows is a brief survey of those that were particularly helpful in uncovering some of the themes and stories that connected the men and women who have had the privilege of being heralded as the nation's favourite sportsperson. For the wider context of British society in the 70 years since Chris Chataway became the first winner of SPOTY, it is hard to beat the series of histories by Dominic Sandbrook:

Never Had It So Good: A History of Britain from Suez to the Beatles (2005)

White Heat: A History of Britain in the Swinging Sixties (2009)

State of Emergency: The Way We Were: Britain, 1970–1974 (2010)

Seasons in the Sun: The Battle for Britain, 1974–1979 (2012)

Who Dares Wins: Britain, 1979–1982 (2019)

Also Alwyn Turner:

Crisis? What Crisis? Britain in the 1970s (2008)

Rejoice! Rejoice! Britain in the 1980s (2010)

A Classless Society: Britain in the 1990s (2013)

*All in it Together: England in the Early 21*st *Century* (2021)

Both authors have a deliciously light touch and a gift for seamlessly merging the grand narrative of high politics with the telling detail of everyday life.

Broader histories of British sport in this period are also numerous, but among the best are Tony Mason and Richard Holt, *Sport in Britain, 1945–2000* (2000) and Wray Vamplew, *Games People Played: A Global History of Sport* (2021). They cover not only the nation's most popular sporting pastimes, but also some of the more niche pursuits that only infrequently troubled the SPOTY vote counters. Similarly, David Goldblatt's *The Games: A Global History of the Olympics* (2016) provides both a hugely readable history of the Olympic movement in the modern era and a fascinating insight into some of those more niche sporting activities that most of us know very little about but still become expert in for a few weeks every four years. SPOTY is, of course, as much about spectating as it is participating, and two superb studies of sport and the media are Roger Domeneghetti, *From Back Page to the Front Room: Football's Journey through the English*

Media (2014) and Martin Kelner, *Sit Down and Cheer: A History of Sport on TV* (2012).

As far as specific sports go, there were numerous works that proved to be enormously helpful. For cricket, Derek Birley's *A Social History of English Cricket* (1999) remains the go-to text, while Stefan Szymanski and Tim Wigmore's *Crickonomics: The Anatomy of Modern Cricket* (2022) expertly brings the story of the game into the 21st century. Tony Collins, with *A Social History of English Rugby Union* (2009) and *Rugby League in Twentieth Century Britain: A Social and Cultural History* (2006), is the Derek Birley of rugby (both union and league).

There are excellent introductory texts for tennis – Robert Lake, *A Social History of Tennis in Britain* (2014); motor racing – Damion Sturm, Stephen Wagg and David L. Andrews, *The History and Politics of Motor Racing* (2023); and cycling – Neil Carter, *Cycling and the British: A Modern History* (2020). For the latter, an honourable mention should also be given to Kenny Pryde's *The Medal Factory: British Cycling and the Cost of Gold* (2020), which lifts the lid on some of the less savoury aspects of the sport's recent successes. Steven Downes and Duncan Mackay, with *Running Scared: How Athletics Lost its Innocence* (1996), provide the same service for track and field.

To single out just one book on football is a fool's errand – so here goes. David Goldblatt's *The Game of Our Lives: The Meaning and Making of English Football* (2014) is not only a meticulously researched study of the modern game but also an enormously entertaining read. It was, however, published just as the Women's Super League was establishing itself, and so, for a more detailed survey of female football over the past decade, the discerning reader might want to take a look at Suzanne Wrack's *A Woman's Game: The Rise, Fall, and Rise Again of Women's Football* (2023) and Carrie Dunn's *The Pride of the Lionesses: The Changing Face of Women's Football in England* (2019).

Two academic studies, Martin Polley's *Moving the Goalposts: A History of Sport and Society since 1945* (1998) and Adrian Smith and Dilwyn Porter's edited volume, *Amateurs and Professionals in Post-War British Sport* (2000), not only explore the issue of gender in sport further but also tackle questions centring on class and ethnicity.

Finally, it would be remiss of me not to give a shout out to the BBC's own book celebrating 50 years of sports personality. If this current work is only an *amuse-bouche* when it comes to SPOTY facts and figures, then Steve Rider's *BBC Sports Personality of the Year* (2003) should serve as the full gastronomical blowout.